COMING OF AGE IN SHAKESPEARE

Marjorie Garber

COMING OF AGE IN SHAKESPEARE

METHUEN
LONDON & NEW YORK 1981

To G. Evelyn and Margaret Hutchinson

First published in 1981 by
Methuen & Co. Ltd
11 New Fetter Lane, London EC4P 4EE
Published in the USA by
Methuen & Co.
in association with Methuen, Inc.
733 Third Avenue, New York, NY 10017
© 1981 Marjorie Garber
Phototypeset in Linotron 202 Aldus by
Western Printing Services Ltd, Bristol, England
Printed in the United States of America

British Library Cataloguing in Publication Data

Garber, Marjorie B
Coming of age in Shakespeare.
1. Shakespeare, William – Knowledge – Psychology
2. Maturation (Psychology) in literature
I. Title
822.3'3   PR3065   80-41920
ISBN 0-416-30350-1

CONTENTS

❧❧❧

PREFACE

✦⟫⟫ ⟪⟪✦

In one of those curious coincidences that seem to illumine our lives, I found myself on the morning of 15 November 1978, having completed at last a draft of this book, listening to a radio report of the death of Margaret Mead. I was not only saddened but profoundly disturbed. For as long as I have had this project in mind – which is almost as long as I have been talking to students about Shakespeare – I have intended to give it the title it bears, a title frankly borrowed, in great admiration, from Mead's first major anthropological work. I began my lecture that morning – a lecture rather appropriately concerned with the nature of love in *As You Like It* – by announcing the news of Mead's death to the class. When they seemed indifferent I was freshly disturbed. Had they not been listening to me all term? How could they not see – as I tried to explain to them – how much my approach to Shakespeare resembled, and was indebted to, Mead's approach to the nature of primitive societies?

Of course, I expected too much. My students' minds were full of other important matters – the weekend impended, and so did the paper deadline. Many had doubtless not yet read *As You Like It* – perhaps some had never heard of Margaret Mead. Few recognized that the study of Elizabethan culture and language was at all relevant to our own. But it is nonetheless in the spirit of Mead's inquiry into the cultures of other peoples, and in particular the process of maturation, that this book was written – and will, I hope, be read. I should like therefore to quote the final paragraph of her introduction to *Coming of Age in Samoa* as a brief preface to my own argument – substituting only the name of the civilization I propose to explore for that which she has so vividly documented, and noting that similarities, as well as contrasts, are frequently to be found between the practices and beliefs of the two societies.

Because of the particular problem which we set out to answer, this tale of another way of life is mainly concerned with education, with the process by which the baby, arrived cultureless upon the human scene, becomes a full-fledged adult member of his or her society. The strongest light will fall upon the ways in which [Shakespearean] education, in its broadest sense, differs from our own. And from this contrast we may be able to turn, made newly and vividly self-conscious and self-critical, to judge anew and perhaps fashion differently the education we give our children.

ACKNOWLEDGMENTS

This study could not itself have come of age without the generous support of many persons and institutions. A fellowship from the American Council of Learned Societies permitted me to complete the first draft; a grant from the A. Whitney Griswold Fund and a semester of leave from my teaching responsibilities at Yale University were likewise instrumental in preparing this book for publication. The staff and services of the Beineke Rare Book and Manuscript Library and the Sterling Memorial Library, both at Yale, provided valuable assistance, as – at a later date – did the librarian and staff of the Haverford College Library.

Among the many people who gave generously of their encouragement and advice, my special thanks go to Rhoda Garber, whose scrupulous stylistic criticisms proved again and again that reason and love *can* keep company together nowadays, and to Charles Long, whose literary acumen, judgment and patience have contributed much to what may be useful in these pages. Margaret Ferguson, Penelope Laurans and Barbara Packer also offered aid and comfort at crucial times; to all these friends and colleagues I 'stand indebted, over and above, / In love and service'.

I owe as well a continuing debt to my mentors in the field

of Shakespeare and Renaissance literature: Alvin Kernan, Maynard Mack, Louis Martz, Susan Snyder and Derek Traversi. Their examples as great teacher-scholars and their humanistic commitment to literature have been of the highest importance in shaping my own sense of vocation and craft. Finally, I should like to thank those many brilliant and inventive younger scholars who have served as my teaching fellows in Shakespeare courses over the past several years. To them, and to the students whom we taught together, I will always be particularly grateful.

Note: Chapter 2 appeared in a somewhat different form in the *Yale Review*, LXVI, and parts of Chapter 7 were published in *Renaissance Drama*, IX. I am indebted to the original publishers for permission to reprint this material.

References throughout the book are to the *Signet Classic Shakespeare*, general editor Sylvan Barnet (New York: Harcourt Brace Jovanovich, 1972).

1

INTRODUCTION

'THY PASSAGES OF LIFE'

❧❧❧

Jaques' celebrated observations on the seven ages of man in *As You Like It* (II. vii. 138–65) reflect a philosophical and icono-graphic tradition that had its roots in antiquity and was still flourishing in Shakespeare's time. The true number of the ages was in dispute, since learned authorities had espoused a number of figures. Aristotle, for example, divided man's life span into three, Pythagoras, Horace and Ovid four, Marcus Varro five, Avicenna and St Augustine six, and Ptolemy and Hippocrates seven; virtually no number from three to twelve was without its proponents.[1] Seven, the magic number associated not only with the ages but also with the planets, the liberal arts, the virtues and the deadly sins, was a popular choice, and Jaques' seven ages have a certain pedantic quality not unsuited to his temperament. But what is more interesting from our point of view than the number of ages he describes is the way he elects to describe them.

The infant mewls and pukes in his nurse's arms, the boy creeps reluctantly to school, the lover (like Orlando) pens bad poems to his mistress's eyebrow. All these are what we might call typical activities for the ages they characterize, of the same genre as those pictorial representations of boys spinning tops, young men hawking, and old men playing backgammon which were frequently to be seen in frescoes, stained-glass windows, and engravings. The soldier, justice and pantaloon, however, are not really engaged in actions at all; instead they are described in terms of their physical appearance, and especially of their language. The soldier is bearded and 'full of strange oaths' (149), the plump justice speaks in 'wise saws and modern instances' (155), the pantaloon, dwarfed by his clothing, finds his 'big manly voice / Turning again toward childish treble' (160–1). A glance back at the earlier 'ages' will reveal that this characterization in terms of utterance is a constant element throughout the passage: the 'mewling' infant, the 'whining' schoolboy and the 'sighing' lover will speak, and illustrate their stages of life as they do so. Jaques' set piece, in other words, is not only a conventional listing of types and vignettes, but also a unified portrait of human development, taking speech as a common characteristic from childhood to senility. When we look more closely at the tradition of the ages of man, the presence of such a pattern appears increasingly significant.

In many cases the ages were combined with such other sequences as the pilgrimage or voyage of life, the wheel of fortune, or the passage of the months – each a temporal progression accompanied by changes in the fortunes and actions of the central figures. Thus January might depict children playing; June, a wedding; November, illness; and December, death. A painting dated 1533 by Dürer's assistant, Hans Schaufelein – which has been in England since Tudor times, and is now at Chatsworth – shows four figures ranged along the circumference of Fortune's wheel, each representing a different age.[2] A beardless youth sits at the base, and is succeeded halfway up the wheel by an elegant young gentleman with a stylishly trimmed beard, wearing a brimmed hat. At the apex of the wheel sits a man in early middle age, wearing a full beard and a king's crown, and to his right, descending, is a patriarchal figure in flowing robes and beard, who seems to be tumbling toward the bottom of the frame. Similarities in dress, feature and carriage strongly suggest that the painting depicts the same man at four stages – or ages – of his career, with earthly success conjoined with maturity at the height, and the inevitability of loss and change emblematized by the falling figure of the old man and the presence of the wheel itself. Another pictorial example from about the same period, attributed to Baldung Grien, is a painting (presently in Munich) of 'The Three Ages' designed as a diptych to balance 'The Three Graces'.[3] In fact, 'The Three Ages' seems to be almost a parody of the 'Graces', since its three principal figures are similarly linked arm in arm, but instead of three lovely women in the prime of youth we see one young woman, one woman decidedly aged (with drawn face and slightly pendulous breasts) and, in place of the third, a skeleton with a death's head, holding an hourglass and a scythe. Even for the more robust sensibility of the time this pendant to the pleasant aesthetic cliché of the timeless graces might well give one pause; it is a work that might well have appealed to Jaques.

In a less mordant mood, Shakespeare in sonnet 7 also describes three ages, each associated with the position of the sun in the sky (first 'new-appearing', then 'Resembling strong youth in his middle age', and finally 'weary' and 'reeling' 'like feeble age'), with a warning in the couplet that the beloved should get a son while he is in the noon of life – before his own sun sets. In these instances, as in many others, the design is at once typical and teleological; the actions of common life are joined with a version of *memento mori*, and the meaning of the entire sequence depends upon an acknowledgment of the transitory nature of health, wealth, fame, and power.

Sometimes, however, a further degree of unity can be found in the sequence. Just as Jaques uses speech as an index of human development, in the morality play *Mundus et Infans* the constant – and constantly changing – element is the protagonist's name. At birth his mother calls him Daliance, but at the age of six the World renames him Wanton. At fourteen his name is changed to Love–Lust–Liking, and at twenty-one to Manhood. Later in life Folly will call him Shame, and finally Conscience will give him the name of Repentance.[4]

In a rudimentary way, *Mundus et Infans* places its emphasis upon the moment of change, rather than the subsequent perception of differences. In other words, it indicates a series of crises or turning points. Whereas other versions of the 'ages' theme show typical though temporary stages in a general and inexorable cycle, this play stresses the moments of transition for the individual, as his experiences in the world change him virtually into a different person.

Another example from the Tudor period may help to clarify this distinction between *difference* and *change*, and to suggest the relevance of such patterns to our understanding of maturity. As a young man, Sir Thomas More designed a 'fyne paynted clothe' for his father's house which combined elements of the *Trionfi* of Petrarch with a representation of the traditional ages of man. These 'nyne pageauntes', as More describes them – for they have since been lost – included four that traced the progress from youth to age. The first panel showed a boy spinning a top – a common emblem of childhood. The second through fourth panels, however, included not one but two figures or sets of figures, and in each case the subject of the previous panel was depicted being conquered by the next. Thus the picture of the second age showed a young man on horseback, engaged in the traditional activity of hawking – but the boy of the first age lay beneath the horse's feet. The third age proved the adolescent's downfall, for now he was himself trodden beneath the feet of Venus and Cupid, signifying love. In the fourth age, an old man stood upon the recumbent bodies of Venus and Cupid. In each of these tableaux, the presence of the outdated or superseded figure(s) offered a vivid reminder of the struggle intrinsic to passage from one stage of human development to the next.[5]

To this point we have been speaking of literary or pictorial artifacts; More's 'pageauntes' were both, since verses of his own composition accompanied each painted panel. But as we have already seen, interest in the ages of man extended beyond artists and poets to astronomers, philosophers, physicians and mathematicians – in short, to anyone concerned with the study of human nature. In its preoccupation with the planets and the seasons, the scrutiny of man's life-span included such disciplines as astrology and even theology, while the contemplation of the wheel of fortune led scholars to history and political philosophy, and the phenomenon of physical deterioration (so explicitly chronicled by Jaques) to medicine. We should not be unduly surprised, therefore, to find the 'new' social sciences of our time – anthropology, psychology and sociology – engaged in a version of the same intellectual quest: to determine the fundamental patterns of human development, and in the course of doing so concentrate upon critical points for growth and change. The relationship between literature and such humanistic disciplines has always been mutually helpful. It is in the nature of new scientific advances to provide suggestive insights into old problems, and just as the hypotheses of Freud, Darwin and Marx offered provocative directions for the scholar concerned with the history and behavior of earlier periods, so the researches of the last century in the area of human relations may indicate some striking new facts about patterns of development in Shakespeare's plays.

*

It may be useful to take account of the concept of 'rites of passage', a term first applied by Arnold van Gennep to the ceremonies accompanying 'life crises' for the individual.[6] Drawing primarily upon the behavior patterns of semicivilized peoples, but also upon the practices of the ancient Greeks and certain Christian, Jewish and Islamic traditions, van Gennep observed that there were three major phases which distinguished each of these rites: separation (*séparation*), transition (*marge*), and incorporation or reintegration (*agrégation*). For some social events one of these phases might be more important than another, but most frequently the three phases were found in conjunction with one another. Thus marriage, which we think of primarily as a rite of incorporation, was often at the same time a rite of separation, both from a previous family or clan and from the social group of age-mates constituted by unmarried girls (or boys). In the course of this study we will see how this combination of rites and motives will influence such Shakespearean characters as Desdemona, Cordelia and Cressida in their transition from one stage to another. Similarly death and mourning, which we might consider to be self-evidently rites of separation, frequently include rites of incorporation as well: for the deceased, incorporation with those who have died before them, and for the mourners, reintegration into normal society. Here again Shakespearean analogues are not hard to find. The last words of Romeo and Juliet, Antony and Cleopatra, and Lear and Kent all indicate a wish for reunion with a loved one after death. Consider in particular Antony's words on learning the (false) news that Cleopatra is dead: 'I come, my queen. . . . Stay for me. / Where souls do couch on flowers, we'll hand in hand, / And with our sprightly port make the ghosts gaze' (IV. xiv. 50–2). On the other hand, the final speeches of the survivors of tragedy – Horatio, Edgar, Malcolm, Octavius Caesar, Prince Escalus – all stress the need for a return to a more normal mode of life. The life of the society is altered by the tragic deaths, but cannot cease or die with the dead.

In his introductory remarks on classification of rites in *Les Rites de passage* van Gennep explains that

> transitions from group to group and from one social situation to the next are looked on as implicit in the very fact of existence, so that a man's life comes to be made up of a succession of stages with similar ends and beginnings: birth, social puberty, marriage, fatherhood, advancement to a higher class, occupational specialization and death. For every one of these events there are ceremonies whose essential purpose is to enable the individual to pass from one defined position to another which is equally well defined.[7]

If we compare this statement to Jaques' speech, we will notice a similar list of stages (coincidentally in this case also seven), but with the important addition of an explanation for the ceremonies marking each stage. It is not the condition of being in any given stage, but rather the passage from one to the next, that is the crucial (and sometimes traumatic) time for the individual. Thus a key element in van Gennep's schema — and in the writings of those who followed him — is the concept of the *threshold* separating neutral zones from those that are sacred. 'Whoever passes from one to the other', he explains,

> finds himself physically and magico-religiously in a special situation for a certain length of time; he wavers between two worlds. It is this situation which I have designated a transition, and one of the purposes of this book is to demonstrate that this symbolic and spatial area of transition may be found in more or less pronounced form in all the ceremonies which accompany the passage from one social and magico-religious position to another.

The term 'magico-religious' may seem uncomfortably specific to anthropology, but if we pause for a moment to consider Shakespearean worlds like the Forest of Arden, the Athenian wood, Prospero's island or the country of Bohemia, we may well discern in them a separate spatial world in which certain quasi-magical events take place: physical transformations, mysterious sleeps and wakings, apparitions, sounds and sweet airs that give delight and hurt not. Indeed there is no need to confine our concept of such sacred zones to the comedies and romances; the heaths in *Lear* and *Macbeth* and the fertile world of Egypt are equally set apart and equally representative of territorial (and psychological) passage. Northrop Frye calls this kind of place a 'green world'.[8] Alvin Kernan calls it a 'second place';[9] C. L. Barber calls its time zone 'holiday' as distinct from 'every day'.[10] In short, van Gennep's concept of a 'sacred zone' corresponds to some observations literary critics have already made about the plays. Literary and anthropological schemes agree, and lead us to very similar insights about stages in human development.

Recent work in anthropology has applied van Gennep's concept of the threshold to both preliterate and modern societies, and extended it to secular as well as religious ritual. The anthropologist Mary Douglas has written convincingly about 'persons in a marginal state', 'people who are somehow left out of the patterning of society',[11] like unborn children and pubertal initiands in some tribal cultures, or ex-prisoners and mental patients in our own. According to Douglas, such persons are in a condition of 'danger', 'contagion' and 'pollution', and may behave in an antisocial manner. 'Danger lies in transitional states', she writes, 'simply because transition is neither one state nor the next, it is undefinable. The person who must pass from one to another is himself in danger, and emanates danger to others.'[12] Douglas' description of social marginality and its effects is both relevant and instructive when considered in the context of Shakespeare's plays. Figures like Mariana ('neither maid, widow, nor wife' [*Measure* v. i. 177–8]), Edgar disguised as Poor Tom, or Coriolanus banished from Rome – to choose only a few examples – may aptly be characterized as marginal persons, whose outcast conditions threaten both themselves and the social worlds they inhabit.

Equally suggestive for students of Shakespeare is the work of Victor Turner, and particularly Turner's theory of 'liminality',[13] which he defines as 'any condition outside or on the periphery of everyday life'[14] – clearly an idea very close to Douglas' 'marginal state', or indeed to Barber's 'holiday'. Turner, however, is chiefly interested in social organization and in the tensions that underlie social groups, tensions he sees as taking the form of a dialectical movement from structure to anti-structure, or from 'fixed' to 'floating' worlds. He argues for the existence of a three-part model of social development, from 'structure' to 'communitas' to 'societas',[15] that corresponds with remarkable accuracy to the Shakespearean pattern of court–country–court or city–wilderness–city. 'Structure', for Turner, is a highly organized, hierarchical system that involves political, legal and economic differentiation; here we might think of Theseus' Athens, Duke Frederick's court or the Venice of both *Othello* and *The Merchant of Venice.* 'Societas', the third stage, produces a renewed and relatively enlightened structure, much like the reconciliations and marriages that end *As You Like It* or the reunions and unmaskings in the last act of *The Winter's Tale.* But the key and transforming element in Turner's system is 'communitas', the stage of liminality.

'Communitas' is 'an unstructured or rudimentarily structured and relatively undifferentiated *comitatus*, community, or even communion of equal individuals'[16] – a description that seems highly appropriate for such temporary but transforming Shakespearean confraternities as that of Duke Senior and his 'co-mates and brothers in exile' (*AYLI* II. i. 1) – or even of England at war in *Henry V.* In fact, Turner cites Shakespeare on this topic directly, describing Gonzalo's imaginary commonwealth in *The Tempest* as an example of 'ideological communitas' or 'the ideal structureless domain',[17] and noting in particular the factors of social equality and absence of property that seem to be constant in such utopian visions. But he also points out the innate fallacy in Gonzalo's commonwealth, since it omits any necessity for work, and therefore for social organization. Gonzalo's slip in imagining himself 'king' (II. i. 150) of a place that is to have 'no sovereignty' (161) Turner interprets as Shakespeare's self-correcting acknowledgment of the absurdity of such a plan in the real world. 'Communitas', like the commonwealth, is an 'Edenic fantasy', 'a phase, a moment, not a permanent condition'.[18] Yet it is what makes possible the renewal and transformation of human society – whether primitive or modern, experiential or fictive.

For Turner and Douglas, as for van Gennep, the act of crossing the threshold – of becoming a 'marginal person' or a 'liminary' – is both a danger and an opportunity, testing the individual's ability to grow and change. Substantially the same view, as we will see, is presented in Shakespearean drama. Literal thresholds are occasionally mentioned in Shakespeare's works, and references to them there suggest a background in folk custom and superstition. When Richard approaches the gates of York in *3 Henry VI* and finds them barred, he senses a bad omen: 'For many men that stumble at the threshold / Are well foretold that danger lurks within' (iv. vii. 11–12). Virgilia, the wife of Coriolanus, refuses to leave the house while her husband is in danger: 'I'll not over the threshold till my lord return from the wars' (*Cor.* i. iii. 74–5). Here the home becomes a sacred or magical place, assuring protection to its absent master. At the close of *A Midsummer Night's Dream* Puck tells the audience that he is 'sent with broom, before, / To sweep the dust behind the door' (v. i. 388–9). He comes 'before' the married pairs and sweeps their threshold clean, not only of dust, but also of evil spirits. In *The Rape of Lucrece* an anthropomorphized threshold attempts to warn Lucrece of Tarquin's entry: 'The threshold grates the door to have him heard' (306), and 'each unwilling portal yields him way' (309); the next threshold to be crossed will be that of her virginity. (In the same spirit we hear of Chaucer's Wife of Bath, an ancestor of the Nurse in *Romeo and Juliet*, that 'Housbondes at chirche dore she hadde fyve' – the church door again identified as a threshold separating the married and the unmarried.)

But the concept of the threshold may be understood to refer not only to doors, gates and portals, but also rivers to be crossed, mountains to be climbed, the foundations of a house to be laid and consecrated.[19] The traditional custom of carrying the bride over the threshold upon first entering a new house is a popular manifestation of this rite in contemporary culture – as might be, for example, the launching of a ship with a libation of champagne. (We might note that the ship is officially *named*, or christened, in this ceremony.) Thresholds of this kind are omnipresent in Shakespearean drama, in part because city gates, castle walls and battlements are so frequent a part of the plays' dramatic architecture. Romeo leaps a wall into Juliet's garden, Coriolanus bursts alone through the gate of Corioles. Lysander tells Helena that 'through Athens' gates we have devised to steal' (*MND* i. i. 213), and the King of Navarre instructs the Princess of France that she 'may not come . . . within my gates' (*LLL* ii. i. 171) – gates that she herself describes as 'forbidden' (26). Each gate leads to a new place which might fairly be described as a sacred zone, as opposed to the neutral space of the streets of Verona or the city of Athens.

Further, in at least two plays Shakespeare makes the threshold a significant feature of his dramatic design. In *The Comedy of Errors* Adriana mistakes the Syracusan Antipholus and his Dromio for her husband and his slave. She scolds them for their tardiness and 'strange'-ness, and commands that Dromio 'keep the gate' (II. ii. 207), 'play the porter' (212) and 'let none enter' (219). The subsequent arrival of Antipholus of Ephesus leads to more angry discussion of the barred threshold – 'my door is locked' (III. i. 30), 'get thee from the door' (35), 'What patch is made our porter?' (36). The wrong Antipholus and Dromio have been permitted to pass from the neutral zone of the mart into the Phoenix; with justice Dromio of Syracuse observes that 'this is the fairyland' (II. ii. 190), while Antipholus of Ephesus complains, 'There is something in the wind, that we cannot get in' (III. i. 69). *The Comedy of Errors* is throughout concerned with magic, magicians, and privileged localities; the incident of the door translates into a literal event the rites of transition which are in the process of befalling its characters.

But of all Shakespearean thresholds surely none is as vivid, or as dramatically accentuated, as that guarded by the Porter in *Macbeth*. He himself compares it to 'hell gate' (II. iii. 2), and those who pass through (in this case Macduff and Lennox) are indeed entering a kind of hell. Earlier we have heard Lady Macbeth exult 'the raven himself is hoarse / That croaks the fatal entrance of Duncan / Under my battlements' (I. v. 38–40) – another deliberate reference to the threshold – and Macbeth, mulling the murder, reminds himself that 'as his host / [he] should against his murderer shut the door' (I. vii. 14–15). While we are speaking of Macbeth, it is interesting to note that one of the commonest of rites carried out on the threshold in primitive societies is that of purification through washing, a rite of separation from previous surroundings to be followed by a rite of incorporation, like the sharing of a meal.[20] Although they attempt to do so, Macbeth and Lady Macbeth cannot wash their hands, and thus symbolically – as well as psychologically – cannot separate themselves from the murder (II. ii; v. i). In each case the attempt is accompanied by the real or imagined sound of knocking at the gate, a reminder of Duncan's death and thus of his murderers' passage into unhallowed territory.[21] The 'great feast' (III. i. 12) or 'solemn supper' (14) planned to commemorate Macbeth's accession to kingship (another life crisis) is similarly polluted and disrupted as the ghost of Banquo sits in the place of the host, and so Lady Macbeth must instruct her guests to 'stand not upon the order of [their] going' (III. iv. 119). Together the two broken ceremonies – hand washing and feasting – signify a failure of the incorporation of the protagonists into the normal or 'neutral' world. As such these ceremonies are further emblems of the outcast status conferred by the act of murder – an increasing isolation and derangement which no ceremonial lustration can cure.

In many primitive societies and some more advanced ones rites of separation, transition and incorporation (also known as preliminal, liminal – i.e. threshold – and postliminal rites) commemorate the great events of a lifetime: birth, puberty, marriage, pregnancy, childbearing and death. Some rites may be repeated at several stages of the individual's development. For example, *naming* occurs shortly after birth as an act of incorporation into society, but a man's or woman's name is frequently changed, sometimes several times, as he or she matures and enters a different stage of social development. A name change may also indicate some specific achievement (e.g. in hunting or war), or signify a physiological or psychological characteristic. Examples from the Bible, from antiquity, from Arthurian legend and from popular practices of more recent times (like the 'nickname' – etymologically from Middle English *ekename*, an additional name) attest to the presence of related rituals in literate western societies, and as we shall see below (Chapter 3) such a pattern of renaming is significantly present in Shakespeare's plays.

But of all the life crises it is the initiation rite that has attracted the most attention from anthropologists, sociologists and psychoanalysts, as well as literary scholars. Van Gennep observes that initiation rites are rites of separation from the asexual world followed by rites of incorporation into a world of sexuality – and at the same time into a single-sex age group. The young boy is ceremonially separated from his mother and instructed in the mysteries of manhood by male elders of the tribe or clan, and he undergoes this experience in the company of other adolescent males who constitute his new society. Often initiation rites take the form of a ritual death and rebirth: the novice is confined in a dark place or covered with blankets, and no light, not even starlight, is allowed to enter. As Mircea Eliade suggests, 'the novice emerges from his ordeal endowed with a totally different being from that which he possessed before his initiation; he has become *another*'. [22] By common belief the child must die before the adult is born, and this process constitutes *'the end of a mode of being* – the mode of ignorance and of the child's irresponsibility'. [23] Here we might compare St Paul's words to the Corinthians: 'When I was a child, I spake as a child, I understood as a child, I thought as a child: but when I became a man, I put away childish things' (1 Cor. 13 : 11). Paul's designation of language as one mark of a stage in personal maturity ('I spake as a child') may once more remind us of Jaques's seven ages, and it is clear that changes in speech, or even the acquisition of entire new languages, are frequently found in the initiation patterns of semicivilized peoples. More about language as an index of maturity will be found in the pages that follow. For the present, however, it may be sufficient to acknowledge that the initiatory rituals which symbolize the transition between childhood or adolescence and adulthood among more developed societies have certain congruences with the practices of those groups studied by field anthropologists, and that such rituals seem to generate a common series of metaphors: the symbolic death of the child, his incubation in darkness, and his rebirth or resurrection into a newborn state where he must learn to speak again, receive a new name and be incorporated into a new society or social group.

Initiation ceremonies for women are not always wholly distinct from rites of betrothal and marriage, since marriage rites, too, are rites of separation as well as incorporation. The young woman is separated from her parents, family or clan, and incorporated into the family or clan of her husband. In some cases – as with matrilineal tribes – the process is reversed, and the young man becomes a member of his wife's family. Like the novice's separation from the mother, the separation of the bride (or groom) is a necessary step in the passage from one age group to another. Each now becomes joined not only to a spouse, but also to the entire group of married women (or men). As was the case with rites of naming and of language, so with marriage rites we have biblical evidence of the continuity of such practices among the ancient Semites: in the book of Genesis, the Gospels of Matthew and Mark, and St Paul's Epistle to the Ephesians we are instructed that a man shall leave his father and mother, and cleave to his wife (Gen. 2:6; Matt. 19:5; Mark 10:7; Eph. 5:31). The happy euphony of 'leave' and 'cleave' in the King James version may serve as a metaphor for the rhythmic relationship of the two states: once again the initiate must ceremonially depart from childhood in order to assume his new status as an adult.

The concept of a pattern of rites that accompany – and therapeutically assist – the individual's progression from youth to maturity is hardly the exclusive province of the anthropologists. The psychologist Erik Erikson has devoted much of his career to exploring what he was among the first to term the 'identity crisis' in an individual's psychic development. Erikson notes that the word 'crisis' has come to be accepted as 'designating a necessary turning point, a crucial moment, when development must move one way or another, marshalling resources of growth, recovery, and further differentiation'.[24] The so-called 'identity crisis', according to him, normally occurs in adolescence or young adulthood, although – as we shall see – it may upon occasion be displaced or retarded; Erikson advances a very interesting argument about Hamlet as a victim of 'identity confusion', and goes so far as to suggest that 'tragic man' is frequently denied a 'positive identity' because of the conflict between his inner feelings and the world in which he lives. Erikson also offers a schema of his own, a kind of 'eight ages of man', which he calls the 'Epigenesis of Identity' in the life cycle of the individual. The stages he suggests, and which he correlates with man's increasing chronological age, are: I Trust v. Mistrust; II Autonomy v. Shame, Doubt; III Initiative v. Guilt; IV Industry v. Inferiority; V Identity v. Identity Confusion; VI Intimacy v. Isolation; VII Generativity v. Stagnation, and VIII Integrity v. Despair. As a psychologist, Erikson is willing to speak in terms which literary critics may well find uncomfortable. For example, he cites with approval Marie Jahoda's definition of a 'healthy' personality in an adult: 'a healthy personality *actively masters* his environment, shows a certain *unity of personality*, and is able to *perceive* the world and himself *correctly*.[25] But he sees no inconsistency in discussing literary figures side by side with historical and contemporary personalities, and the judgments he offers are well documented and frequently persuasive. Perhaps of the greatest interest to this study is Erikson's insistence upon the connection between identity and self-reflectiveness – what will be described in Chapter 6 as the rite of comparison and distinction: 'in psychological terms', he asserts,

> identity formation employs a process of simultaneous reflection and observation, a process taking place on all levels of mental functioning, by which the individual judges himself in the light of what he perceives to be the way in which others judge him in comparison to themselves and to a typology significant to them; while he judges their way of judging him in the light of how he perceives himself in comparison to them and to types that have become relevant to him. This process is, luckily, and necessarily, for the most part unconscious except where inner conditions and outer circumstances combine to aggravate a painful, or elated, 'identity-consciousness'.

We can see here the essential outline of a theory of human development which is based upon self-knowledge. The stages through which the developing individual will – and must – pass are all predicated upon an apprehension (conscious or unconscious) of his own place in society. If we return for a moment to Jahoda's definition of 'health' – 'to *perceive* the world and himself *correctly*' – we may perhaps suggest that both Jahoda and Erikson would respond hospitably to the idea, fundamental to this study, that a dramatic character is challenged with understanding the play of which he is a part. The failure of Richard III and Macbeth (and, more controversially, of Othello) to do so is part of their tragedy. At the same time it is also emblematic of their failure to attain 'maturity' – or 'identity' – or a 'healthy personality' in the context of a specific, created, dramatic situation.

Like Erikson, Bruno Bettelheim addresses himself to the 'psychological problems of growing up',[26] and does so in part by reference to literary models. Bettelheim defines 'psychological maturity' as 'gaining a secure understanding of what the meaning of one's life may or ought to be'.[27] (Macbeth's 'tomorrow' speech, with its despairing reference to a life 'signifying nothing', provides a close Shakespearean analogue.) Even more directly than Erikson, Bettelheim is concerned with justifying the application of psychological and psychoanalytic theory to a branch of literature – in this case, the fairy tale, a genre traditionally interesting to anthropologists and students of mythology.

His estimation of the life crises facing an individual on the path to maturity is not unlike Erikson's epigenetic cycle; and it may be worthwhile to quote his central argument at some length.

> In order to master the psychological problems of growing up – overcoming narcissistic disappointments, oedipal dilemmas, sibling rivalries; becoming able to relinquish childhood dependencies; gaining a feeling of self-hood and of self-worth, and a sense of moral obligation – a child needs to understand what is going on within his conscious self so that he can also cope with that which goes on in his unconscious. He can achieve this understanding, and with it the ability to cope, not through rational comprehension of the nature and content of his unconscious, but by becoming familiar with it through spinning out daydreams – ruminating, rearranging, and fantasizing about suitable story elements in response to unconscious pressures. By doing this, the child fits unconscious content into conscious fantasies, which then enable him to deal with that content. It is here that fairy tales have unequaled value, because they offer new dimensions to the child's imagination which would be impossible for him to discover as truly on his own. Even more important, the form and structure of fairy tales suggest images to the child by which he can structure his daydreams and with them give better direction to his life.[28]

Fairy tales, in other words, have two key functions: they provide available analogues for ideas latent in the child's imagination, and they offer suggestions, if not solutions, for the working out of his unexpressed fears and hopes. Thus for Bettelheim 'Hansel and Gretel' is an exploration of the child's reluctance to separate himself from his parents and enter the world of action, while 'Snow White' confronts the pubertal problems of the adolescent girl, who for the first time perceives herself as a sexual being in competition with her step-mother (or mother). In this case, once again, the element of comparison is an essential factor in self-definition and self-discovery.

Bettelheim's claims for the fairy tale as a catalyst of the youthful imagination are of particular interest because he boldly bridges the gap between life and art, or fact and fiction, to approach a literary work in psychological terms. This is a kind of criticism about which literary scholars have been extremely nervous, with some justification. It is worth observing, however, that this decorous reluctance is equally true of the social scientists. Eliade confronts the problem directly in his study of initiation rites, when he comes to deal with such literary motifs as the grail quest, the 'waste land', and the descent into Hell. Cautiously, he observes that

> We here touch upon a problem that is beyond the competence of the historian of religion, for it belongs by right to psychology. But I must touch upon it, in order that we may understand what happened to the majority of initiatory patterns when they had lost their ritual reality; they became what, for example, we find them to be in the Arthurian romances – literary motifs. This is as much as to say that they now deliver their spiritual message on a different plane of human experience, by addressing themselves directly to the imagination.

He then goes on to speak directly of fairy tales, asserting that 'it is impossible to deny that the ordeals and adventures of their heroes and heroines are almost always translatable into initiatory terms', and that 'initiatory scenarios – even camouflaged as they are in fairy tales – are the expression of a psychodrama that answers a deep need in the human being'.[29]

It is tempting to linger for a moment upon Eliade's choice of words here. 'Scenario' and 'psychodrama' are words which had not even been coined by Shakespeare's time; the first is an invention of the nineteenth, the second of the twentieth century. But the impulse to see rites of initiation in dramatic terms reflects a basic truth about those rites. They mark a turning point in the life of the individual, and it is of such turning points – crises and peripeties – that drama is made.

Perhaps this is one reason why the vocabulary of the theater is being used increasingly by social scientists in their attempts to understand the function of both religious and secular ritual in human life. Thus Victor Turner speaks of 'social dramas',[30] by which he means those disharmonious developments in society that lead to change; 'social dramas' in turn may be divided into 'acts' and 'scenes', and will ultimately lead to some kind of climax. In a similar spirit Mary Douglas comments that 'there are no items of clothing or of food or of other practical use which we do not seize upon as theatrical props to dramatize the ways we present our roles and the scene we are playing'.[31] But the most influential use of theatrical terminology for the analysis of human behavior has probably been that of the sociologist Erving Goffman. In *The Presentation of Self in Everyday Life* and elsewhere Goffman speaks of social 'settings', of 'performances', of 'cues' and 'props', 'routines' and 'parts', 'staging areas' and 'backstage' communication.[32] His 'dramaturgical approach' to the structure of social encounters in effect interprets every encounter as a staged confrontation, in which the individual (as both 'performer' and 'character') must present himself effectively to his 'audience', whether that audience is made up of one or many members.

A more directly literary approach to the relationship between drama and ritual behavior was taken by a group of cultural anthropologists during the early years of this century. The Frazer–Cornford–Harrison school of myth and ritual criticism theorized that the roots of drama were to be found in the 'mysteries' of ancient and primitive religions, and sought to find analogies between ancient ritual practice and later dramatic works. Jane Ellen Harrison pointed out that descriptions of the Eleusinian mysteries by later Greek authors 'use constantly the vocabulary of the stage',[33] and later suggested that the Don Juan legend originated in 'a fertility ritual'.[34] Likewise Sir James Frazer's concept of the dying and reviving god was applied – with modifications – by Gilbert Murray to the origins of Greek tragedy, by F. M. Cornford to Attic comedy, and by other scholars to such diverse dramatic survivals as the European Mummers' Play and the Punch-and-Judy show.[35] Murray took a further step, suggesting that ritual origins lay behind the sophisticated drama of Shakespeare, in his 1914 lecture, 'Hamlet and Orestes'.

Whatever the merits of the claim for 'origins', the work of the Cambridge school, like the 'dramaturgical approach' of contemporary social scientists, suggests a persuasive series of analogies between ritual behavior and dramatic action. Moreover, in recent years an explicitly anthropological approach to Shakespeare has been employed by such critics as Francis Fergusson, Northrop Frye and C. L. Barber.

There is an important distinction to be made, however, between the kinds of patterns that interest Barber and Frye, and the rites of passage with which this study will be concerned. Frye draws an analogy between the seasonal cycle and the literary genres, discerning, for example, an important parallel between the movement from winter to spring and the comic progress from trouble to joy. Barber examines holiday festivals and entertainments, and suggests a persuasive formula, 'through release to clarification', which underlies not only those festivals but also a number of Shakespearean plays. In anthropological terms, these are known as 'cyclic group rites', or 'rites of intensification',[36] based largely upon changes in the natural round. Seasonal changes, changes of the sun and moon, agricultural activities like sowing, planting and the harvest of the first fruits are occasions for a ceremonial demonstration of the entire populace, whether it be a family, a clan or the citizens of a city or nation. The festival of Lupercalia, which is being celebrated as *Julius Caesar* opens, is one example of such a cyclic rite. During this fertility festival, held annually on the fifteenth day of February, young men ran naked through the city striking those they met with leather thongs. Plutarch tells us that many noblewomen and gentlewomen 'put forth their hands to be stricken . . . persuading themselves that, being with child, they shall have a good delivery, and also, being barren, that it will make them to conceive with child'.[37] It is noteworthy that Caesar, who will later claim to put no credence in omens, nonetheless reminds Antony to strike his wife Calphurnia: 'for our elders say / The barren, touch'd in this holy chase, / Shake off their sterile curse' (*JC* I. ii. 7–9).

Elsewhere in Shakespeare's plays patterns of seasonal change frequently mirror patterns of human development – in *Love's Labor's Lost*, for example, with its concluding songs of winter and spring, or in *The Winter's Tale*. Hamlet is often compared to one of Frazer's 'dying and reviving gods', and the play has been considered in the context of the year-king tradition.[38] Vestiges of a similar mythic pattern appear at the close of *Henry V* and *Richard III*, particularly in the agricultural images used by the soon-to-be-victorious Richmond, who speaks to his troops of 'summer fields and fruitful vines' (*RIII* v. ii. 8) of 'reap[ing] the harvest of perpetual peace' (15), and of 'smiling plenty, and fair prosperous days' (v. v. 34). Richmond's emergence as a harbinger of fertile days – when he will 'unite the White Rose and the Red' (v. v. 19) – reminds the audience of its escape from Richard's perpetual winter of discontent. Likewise at the close of *Macbeth*, Malcolm revives the growth imagery of his murdered father, to speak of things 'which would be planted newly with the time' (v. viii. 65). In all of these instances – and in many others – an underlying pattern of decay and rebirth in nature is clearly discernible, and corresponds to the periodic, cyclic and societal ceremonies known to anthropologists as rites of intensification.

By contrast, rites of passage are individual and non-periodic. The crises which provoke them have to do not with the season, but – in most cases – with some aspect of the family system. Where rites of intensification affect all the members of a group at once, rites of passage affect a single person directly, and others only as a result of their relationship to him. As we have already seen, the symbolic pattern of an initiation ritual, like that of an agricultural festival, is based upon a metaphorical experience of death and rebirth. But the life crisis that provokes that experience occurs not as a result of changes in the external world, but rather as a result of changes in the individual. As he grows to maturity – as he comes of age – the novice is separated from a former identity, and integrated into a new social role. It is this kind of crisis, and this kind of rite, that I have attempted to discover and analyze in the patterns of Shakespeare's plays.

It may be useful here to note that seasonal rites frequently provide metaphors for individual rites, as in a phrase like 'green youth'; conversely terms from the cycle of individual maturation may become associated with the larger patterns of times and seasons – e.g. 'the aged year'. In this context, 'maturity' for Shakespeare means ripeness or readiness, and signifies a moment of transition. We hear, for example, about a revolt which is 'almost mature for the violent breaking out' (*Cor.* IV. iii. 24–5), and of a 'mature time' (*Lr* IV. vi. 277) to put a certain course of action to the test. Hamlet's declaration that 'The readiness is all' (v. ii. 224) and Gloucester's similar acknowledgment that 'Ripeness is all' (*Lr* v. ii. 11) both allude to an acceptance of death, of man's going hence as well as his coming hither. Touchstone's witty parody of Jaques' seven ages speech likewise stresses the element of change: 'And so, from hour to hour, we ripe and ripe, / And then, from hour to hour, we rot and rot' (*AYLI* II. vii. 26–7).

The word 'mature' itself, however, is frequently used in a normative way, to denote a certain stage of human experience. At the beginning of *The Winter's Tale* we are told that Leontes and Polixenes were childhood friends, and that they have maintained their friendship 'since their more mature dignities and royal necessities made separation of their society' (I. i. 27–8). Ulysses describes Troilus as 'The youngest son of Priam, a true knight, / Not yet mature, yet matchless' (*T&C* IV. v. 96–7), and in *Antony and Cleopatra* Caesar criticizes the revelling Antony by comparing him to 'boys who, being mature in knowledge, / Pawn their experience to their present pleasure / And so rebel to judgment' (I. iv. 31–3). In all of these instances maturity denotes a specific level of development, determined by social responsibilities (Leontes and Polixenes), physical and mental readiness, perhaps including initiation in war (Troilus), and self-knowledge (Antony). The value placed on the maturity depends, of course, upon the speaker and context.

Of all the direct references to the maturity of dramatic characters, however, perhaps the most suggestive is the description of Posthumus Leonatus which occurs at the beginning of *Cymbeline*. The speakers are the First and Second Gentlemen, and as is often the case with Shakespearean opening scenes, these minor characters – who will never again appear – offer opinions which may be taken at face value, precisely because there is no filtering personality to interfere with what they say. In other words, they exist only to speak the truth – or at least the truth as the prevailing opinion has it. And what they tell us is that

Posthumus is an exemplary man. 'In's spring [he] became a harvest, lived in court – / Which rare it is to do – most praised, most
loved, / A sample to the youngest, to th' more mature / A glass
that feated them, and to the graver / A child that guided dotards'
(I. i. 46–50). In time we will consider the metaphor of the glass in
some detail and take note of such other human mirrors as
Hotspur and Hamlet. But what is of chief interest here is the
sense that Posthumus is a man for all seasons. To the youngest,
to the more mature and finally to the elderly he supplies a
needed complementarity; he is what we might today call a 'role
model' to children, and a prop and stay to the old. To the 'more
mature', – the adults – he is a reflection of their own virtue. Here
we have a variation on the theme of the ages of man metaphorically applied to a single individual at a unique time of life. Yet
the passage is not without portents of difficulty. To be a harvest
in the spring is to risk a loss of ripeness as well as to violate
seasonal decorum, and in Posthumus' susceptibility to Iachimo's
blandishments we do see something of his vulnerable youth.
There are things about life and love that he has still to learn.

In fact the concept of maturity implicitly includes this expectation of growth and change; a mature person, like a mature
crop, must have progressed from an earlier stage of greenness.
This is no less true in literature than in nature, and from at least
the time of Virgil the phrase 'green youth' has been a common
one, connoting inexperience, and sometimes also simplicity or
gullibility. Thus Polonius calls Ophelia 'a green girl, / Unsifted
in . . . perilous circumstance' (Ham. I. iii. 101–2), although ironically his advice is calculated to keep her unready for adult responsibility. Likewise Cleopatra alludes to her own youth as 'my
salad days / When I was green in judgment' (A&C I. v. 73–4),
and throughout the plays 'green' will carry this double connotation of rawness and promise. At the other end of the continuum
are a number of references to autumnal decline: sonnet 73, for
example, and Macbeth's description of his way of life as 'fall'n
into the sear, the yellow leaf' (v. iii. 23).

In almost every case, the Shakespearean protagonist is challenged to change as his or her circumstances change – to adapt to
the world, and the people, around him. Those who fail to do so,
as we shall see, fail to undergo a rite of passage, and instead of
being incorporated into a new identity or social role, they remain

static, imprisoned by their own natures and banished or rejected from the world of the play. The wicked Don John of *Much Ado about Nothing* is one such character, and Malvolio is another; a third, and particularly striking example, is Juliet's Nurse. When we first meet the Nurse we are delighted by her bawdy language and frank sexuality, especially in contrast to the tedious and stilted conversation of Lady Capulet. Our delight continues, virtually unabated, through Act II scene v, in which Juliet waits impatiently for a message from Romeo. When she returns, inevitably late, the Nurse is elaborately out of breath, and some fifty lines intervene before Juliet can pry from her the happy news that her wedding will take place that very day. A few scenes later, however, when the play has been transformed from comedy to tragedy by the duel, the deaths of Mercutio and Tybalt, and the banishment of Romeo, the same behavior leads to a quite different result. Again the Nurse has been abroad, and again she returns, rambles and replies confusedly. Someone is dead – is it Tybalt or Romeo? Are they both dead? What has the prince decreed? The delay in the delivery of this second message is painful, not amusing. Similarly the Nurse's earthy pragmatism is attractive in the early scenes, much less so when she urges Juliet to commit bigamy and marry Paris. Her failure to change serves as an index or foil, against which we can measure the growth – and the consequent isolation – of Juliet. In much the same way the static nature of Don John points up the changes undergone by Benedick and Claudio, and Malvolio's failure to grow emphasizes, by contrast, the growth toward maturity of Olivia and Orsino. Perhaps the quintessential Shakespearean example of such a contrast between stasis and change is the relationship between Prince Hal and Falstaff. In the tavern world, as in the comic scenes of *Romeo and Juliet*, Falstaff's humor (and humors) are not only appropriate but captivating. With the crossing of the threshold into war, however – and later when Hal crosses a further threshold and becomes king – Falstaff's failure to change is a sign of his unfitness for Hal's new world: 'What, is it a time to jest and dally now?' (*1HIV* v. iii. 57).

Inimitably Shakespearean, characters like these are far removed from mere types, although they are related in some cases to the older dramatic forms of the Vice and the Machiavel, and in others to the comedy of humors. By their very nature, however, such figures are radically limited, and the audience will usually find itself more deeply engaged with those characters who do grow and change in the course of the plays. Not only are they more complex, they are also closer to our own challenges and our own experience – to the questions we pose for ourselves about the problems of life and the answers – satisfactory or not – we provide. In the course of four days (or 'the two hours' traffic of our stage') we see Juliet grow from a submissive daughter for whom marriage is 'an honor that I dream not of' (*R&J* i. iii. 66) to a sexually self-knowledgeable lover who longs for 'love-performing night' (iii. ii. 5). The plays involving Prince Hal are overtly a chronicle of education, and *Hamlet* too is (among many other things) a play about the problems of coming of age. To speak of maturity for Juliet or Hal or Hamlet is hardly to do violence to the fictive nature of the plays which contain them; the 'identity formation' of which Erikson speaks is crucial to both the protagonist and the secondary characters who surround and influence him. The same could be said of the dramatic development of Leontes, or Lear, or Benedick, each in his own generic context, and, to a lesser but still important extent, of the lords in *Love's Labor's Lost*, Kate in *The Taming of the Shrew*, Olivia in *Twelfth Night* – to cite a random few. Macbeth, too, changes, although in the opposite direction, away from conscience and toward monstrous indifference to life. If we are willing to use the vocabulary of psychoanalysis, we could – and I think should – say that he regresses.

All these are fairly obvious instances, in which some visible alteration occurs in the dramatic character. But what of such figures as Cordelia or Desdemona, who seem so attractive when first we meet them, and who retain their attractiveness for us throughout the play? Is a term like 'maturity' (or its invidious opposite, 'immaturity') applicable to them? Many who admire the plays will bridle at the idea of Cordelia as 'immature', or of an Othello who does not act like an adult. Yet if we consider the experience of the play as one of progress toward self-knowledge, a growth and change for its main characters as well as for the audience, we may find a certain usefulness in these terms. No one, presumably, would wish *King Lear* to end after the opening scene, with Cordelia's acquiescence to her father's demand for a verbal expression of love. But her failure to offer such a pledge, her determination to love and be silent, does help to precipitate the tragedy. In one sense at least her silence is a self-regarding act, as inflexible as the imperious father whom she so much resembles. Her own phrase as she leaves the court is a suggestive one: 'with washed eyes / Cordelia leaves you' (I. i. 268–9). She has seen something in that first scene which will change her. When she next appears, much later in the play, she is no longer a gnostic emblem of silent wisdom: she is a woman – and she speaks.

The broken Lear, awakening from sleep, gradually allows himself to believe that Cordelia is his child. When he receives her assurance ('and so I am, I am'), he poses his initial question again, although in a different key: 'I know you do not love me; for your sisters / Have, as I do remember, done me wrong. / You have some cause, they have not' (IV. vii. 73–5). Gone is the arrogance of royalty – but the implicit demand remains: tell me that you love me. And Cordelia's enigmatic reply, 'No cause, no cause' (75), is an answer not only to this second question, but also to the first. There is 'no cause' for her to hate him, despite his actions in the past, because the bonds of love and blood which bind her to him are not susceptible to change by reason of circumstance. This is what she had tried to tell him by her silence, and failed. Here she speaks, and speaks what might at first be taken for a falsehood – for in one sense at least she does have 'cause'. But her action in speaking, and her willingness to speak to the question behind the question, mark a change, if not in her moral rectitude and purity of love, then in her capacity to translate that love into a social act of reintegration. Just as her failure to reply in the first scene led to a separation of father and child, so her spoken answer here leads to an incorporation, a new bond, the formation of a new social unit, however brief and fragile. It is this ability to come to terms with the world around her, its social necessities as well as its moral issues, that I have in mind when I speak of 'maturity'.

Desdemona poses a different problem, for she seems from the first to be gifted with womanhood and self-knowledge. Her choice of a husband over a beloved father, as we will see, is a rite of separation and incorporation at once, an explicit and definitive rite of passage. How then can we say that she needs to grow or change? With her, as with some other Shakespearean figures

NOTES

1 Several of these are cited in *The Forest: or, Collection of Historyes no less profitable, than pleasant and necessary*, Thomas Fortescue (trans.) (London, 1571; rpt. by John Daye, 1576), pp. 37–40, a translation of a French version of an Italian translation of Pedro Mexia's *Silva de varia leccion* (Seville, 1542). Fortescue's examples and others are mentioned by Samuel C. Chew, 'This strange eventful history', a valuable study of the history of the 'ages' theme, in James G. MacManaway, Giles E. Dawson and Edwin E. Willoughby (eds), *Joseph Quincy Adams Memorial Studies* (Washington: The Folger Shakespeare Library, 1948), p. 159.

2 Salomon Reinach, *Répertoire de peintures du moyen age et de la renaissance (1280–1580)* (Paris: Maison Ernest Leroux, 1918), IV, p. 626.

3 Reinach, II, p. 711.

4 Chew, p. 162.

5 The remaining five panels show the successive victories of Death, Fame, Time, Eternity, and finally the Poet, over his immediate predecessor. While this departs from a strict adherence to the 'ages' scheme, it is itself suggestive. Thomas More, *The Works . . . in the English Tonge* (London, 1557), sigs. $^2\P2^v$–4^r. Cited in Chew, pp. 171–2.

6 Arnold van Gennep, *Les Rites de passage* (1908). All citations from van Gennep refer to the English translation, *The Rites of Passage*, Monika B. Vizedom and Gabrielle L. Caffee (trans.) (Chicago: University of Chicago Press, 1960).

7 Van Gennep, p. 3.

8 Northrop Frye, 'The argument of comedy', in D. A. Robertson (ed.), *English Institute Essays 1948* (New York: Columbia University Press, 1949), pp. 58–73.

9 Alvin Kernan, 'Place and plot in Shakespeare', *The Yale Review*, LXVII, 1 (Autumn 1977), 48–56.

10 C. L. Barber, *Shakespeare's Festive Comedy* (Princeton: Princeton University Press, 1959).

11 Mary Douglas, *Purity and Danger: An Analysis of the Concepts of Pollution and Taboo* (London: Routledge & Kegan Paul, 1966), p. 95.

12 Douglas, p. 96.

13 Victor Turner, *The Ritual Process: Structure and Anti-Structure* (Ithaca: Cornell University Press, 1969), pp. 94–6 and passim. See also Turner, 'Variations on a theme of liminality', in *Secular Ritual*, Sally F. Moore and Barbara G. Myerhoff (eds) (Amsterdam: Van Gorcum, Assen, 1977), pp. 36–52.

14 Victor Turner, *Dramas, Fields, and Metaphors* (Ithaca: Cornell University Press, 1974), p. 47.

15 Turner, *The Ritual Process*, especially Chapter 3, 'Liminality and communitas', pp. 94–130.

16 Turner, *The Ritual Process*, p. 96.

17 Turner, *The Ritual Process*, p. 134.

18 Turner, *The Ritual Process*, p. 140.

19 Van Gennep, pp. 22–3.

20 Van Gennep, p. 20.

21 Among primitive societies the ideas of holiness and uncleanliness (in persons and in places) are often not distinct from one another, and even in some advanced societies the two concepts may meet or overlap. See Mary Douglas, *Purity and Danger*.

22 Mircea Eliade, *Rites and Symbols of Initiation: The Mysteries of Death and Rebirth*, Willard R. Trask (trans.), (originally published as *Birth and Rebirth*) (New York: Harper & Brothers, 1958; rpt. Harper & Row, 1975), p. x.

23 Eliade, p. xiii.

24 Erik Erikson, *Identity: Youth and Crisis* (New York: W. W. Norton, 1967) p. 16.

25 Erikson, p. 92; citing Marie Jahoda, 'Toward a social psychology of mental health', in M. J. E. Benn (ed.), *Symposium on the Healthy Personality* (Supplement II: Problems of Infancy and Childhood), Transactions of Fourth Conference, March 1950 (New York: Josiah Macy, Jr, Foundation, 1950). Following extract: pp. 22–3.

26 Bruno Bettelheim, *The Uses of Enchantment: The Meaning and Importance of Fairy Tales* (New York: Alfred A. Knopf, 1976), p. 7.

27 Bettelheim, p. 3.

28 Bettelheim, pp. 6–7.

29 Eliade, p. 126.

30 Victor Turner, *Schism and Continuity in an African Society* (Manchester: Manchester University Press, 1957). See also 'Social dramas and ritual metaphors', in *Dramas, Fields, and Metaphors*, pp. 23–59.

31 Douglas, p. 100.

32 Erving Goffman, *The Presentation of Self in Everyday Life* (Garden City, New York: Anchor Books, 1959). More recently Goffman has returned to this question of the relationship of 'everyday life' to the 'theatrical frame' from a somewhat different perspective. See his *Frame Analysis* (Cambridge, Mass.: Harvard University Press, 1974).

33 Jane Ellen Harrison, *Prolegomena to the Study of Greek Religion*,

3rd edition (Cambridge: Cambridge University Press, 1922; rpt. New York: Meridian Books, 1960), p. 568.

34 Jane Ellen Harrison, *Epilegomena to the Study of Greek Religion* (Cambridge: Cambridge University Press, 1921), p. 26, n. 1.

35 Gilbert Murray, 'Excursus on the ritual forms preserved in Greek tragedy', in J. E. Harrison, *Themis* (Cambridge: Cambridge University Press, 1912), pp. 341ff; F. M. Cornford, *The Origin of Attic Comedy* (Cambridge: Cambridge University Press, 1914); R. J. Tiddy, *The Mummers' Play* (Oxford: Oxford University Press, 1923); P. Toschi, *Le origini del teatro italiano* (Turin, 1955).

36 The term is that of E. D. Chapple and C. S. Coon, in *Principles of Anthropology* (New York: Henry Holt, 1942). Ch. 20, pp. 484–506, discusses rites of passage in detail. See also Edward Norbeck, *Religion in Primitive Society* (New York: Harper & Row, 1961), pp. 138–68.

37 'Life of Julius Caesar', in T. J. B. Spencer (ed.) *Shakespeare's Plutarch: The Lives of Julius Caesar, Brutus, Marcus Antonius and Coriolanus in the Translation of Sir Thomas North* (Middlesex, England, and Baltimore, Maryland: Penguin Books, 1964; rpt. 1968), p. 82.

38 For example, Herbert Weisinger, 'The myth and ritual approach to Shakespearian tragedy', in John B. Vickery (ed.), *Myth and Literature: Contemporary Theory and Practice* (Lincoln: University of Nebraska Press, 1966), pp. 138–68.

39 Norman N. Holland, *Psychoanalysis and Shakespeare* (New York: McGraw-Hill, 1964; rpt. Octagon Books, 1976), p. 253.

2

SEPARATION
AND INDIVIDUATION

'A DIVIDED DUTY'

For reasons which are probably both historical and dramatic,
there are very few children in Shakespeare's plays. Those who do
appear are both pert and malapert, disconcertingly solemn and
prematurely adult: the Princes in the Tower, whose uncle's
exasperation with them may be shared to a degree by the audience; Macduff's and Coriolanus' sons, both pathetically martial
copies of their fathers; Mamillius, whose proposal to tell a 'sad
tale . . . for winter' reveals an intuitive comprehension of the
problems of Sicilia and of his own impending doom. These are
not, by and large, successful dramatic characters; their disquiet-
ing adulthood strikes the audience with its oddness, and we are
relieved when these terrible infants leave the stage. We may feel
it to be no accident that almost all go to their deaths.

More frequently, the condition of childhood is described in
the plays retrospectively – either in passages of nostalgic re-
miniscence, or at moments of dramatic choice, when the identity
of the child as obedient follower of its parent is called into
question. In both of these situations, what is principally at stake
is the child's claim to his or her own individual role, distinct from
that of playfellow or parent. The pattern of sexual maturation in
Shakespeare is one of deliberate separation – a movement away
from group identification either with peers or with a nuclear
family unit, freeing the individual to contract new bonds. And
this pattern of individuation is closely linked to a characteristically Shakespearean concern for fertility and the cycle of nature,

the renewal of life and the procreation of the ancestral lineage achieved, perhaps paradoxically, by a necessary act of separation from that lineage. Those characters in the plays who accept this necessity, regardless of their individual fates, are presented to us as figures of moral strength and of self-knowledge; those who cannot accept it – like Ophelia and Coriolanus – are presented as moral weaklings, incapable of coming to terms with the complex worlds they inhabit, and incapable, too, of successfully replacing the fraternal or filial bond with the more fruitful bond of marriage.

A common Shakespearean paradigm for the condition of childhood is that of twins and twinned experience, in which a pair of friends, usually of the same sex, appear to themselves and to others as identical and interchangeable, undifferentiated in character, feature, or affection. Literal twins appear, of course, in *The Comedy of Errors* and in *Twelfth Night*; in both, the twins are repeatedly taken for one another in situations which threaten their societal, and particularly their marital and procreative, roles. Antipholus of Syracuse is claimed as husband by Adriana, his brother's wife; he has himself fallen in love with her sister, Luciana, who rebuffs his advances, thinking they come from her brother-in-law. This inappropriate, indeed wholly stymieing, situation appears to be insoluble, until Egeon and the Abbess are revealed as the long-separated parents of the pair, and the twins' identities are established. Her sons are restored to the Abbess, who now leaves the chastity of the convent to rejoin her husband, and with this token of restored fertility the Antipholuses are matched with their proper ladies. In *Twelfth Night* Viola finds herself in a situation which is, if possible, even more awkward; disguised as a boy, and dressed in conscious imitation of her brother Sebastian, whom she believes to be drowned, she falls in love with Orsino, in whose service she is employed, and becomes herself the discomfited object of passionate demonstrations from Olivia, to whom Orsino has sent her as emissary of his love. The appearance of the real Sebastian reassorts the pairs, making two fruitful couples where there had been only fruitless error. Individuation, the finding and asserting of identity, is in these plays closely related to sexual maturity and cyclical change; as one grows in self-knowledge, one moves from the confused and mingled identity of twinship, which thwarts fertile pairing, toward productive courtship and marriage. Both of these plays present the familiar Shakespearean theme of losing-oneself-to-find-oneself, but they do so with a novel particularity. The condition of loss or confusion of identity is matched with twinship, and though the love represented by the fraternal bond is not lost, it cedes its primacy to a sexual bond which celebrates human uniqueness.

But literal twins are far from the only instance of childhood twinning in the plays. Frequently, nostalgic recollections of youthful experience utilize the twin image as a sign of inter-changeability and lack of differentiation. Such a situation is clearly indicated by Helena's reproach to Hermia in Act III of *A Midsummer Night's Dream*:

> We, Hermia, like two artificial gods,
> Have with our needles created both one flower,
> Both on one sampler, sitting on one cushion,
> Both warbling of one song, both in one key;
> As if our hands, our sides, voices and minds,
> Had been incorporate. So we grew together,
> Like to a double cherry, seeming parted,
> But yet an union in partition;
> Two lovely berries molded on one stem;
> So, with two seeming bodies, but one heart.
>
> (III. ii. 203–12)

The twinship of these two young women, innocent and explicitly parallel to twin forms in nature, is closely analogous to the relationship between Celia and Rosalind in *As You Like It*, as Celia sets it forth early in the play:

> We still have slept together,
> Rose at an instant, learned, played, eat together;
> And wheresoe'er we went, like Juno's swans,
> Still we went coupled and inseparable.   (I. iii. 72–5)

Nor is this imagistic twinning an exclusively female pattern. Perhaps the best known of Shakespeare's images of twinned pairs is that of the two kings in *The Winter's Tale*. There Polixenes, asked by Hermione to describe his childhood friendship with Leontes, gently but firmly refutes her attempt to differentiate them:

Polixenes   We were, fair queen,
Two lads that thought there was no more behind
But such a day tomorrow as today,
And to be boy eternal.
Hermione   Was not my lord
The verier wag o' th' two?
Polixenes   We were as twinned lambs, that did frisk i' th'
     sun,
And bleat the one at th' other; what we changed
Was innocence for innocence; we knew not
The doctrine of ill-doing, nor dreamed
That any did.   (I. ii. 62–71)

Certain characteristics common to all three of these passages
suggest a kind of imagistic unity of approach to childhood: all
three pairs are described in natural metaphors of fruit or animal
twinning; all imply a springtime landscape commensurate with
the youth and incipient maturation of their subjects; all assert,
with an insistence almost polemical, the innocence of those
described and their undifferentiated nature. If encountered at
this stage, all three speakers imply, Hermia could not be told
from Helena, Celia from Rosalind, or Leontes from Polixenes.

    The tone of each of these verbal descriptions is notably placid,
implicitly or explicitly eternizing: 'we grew together'; 'still we
went coupled and inseparable'; 'to be boy eternal'. But in
Shakespeare's plays any hint of stasis, or resistance to the cyclical
pattern of growth and decay, maturity and mortality, is highly
suspect and leads to disaster, as Ferdinand's exclamation in *The
Tempest*, 'Let me live here ever!' leads to the breaking of the
masque and Prospero's memory of the plot against his life.
The desire to be 'boy eternal' effectively precipitates the split
between Leontes and Polixenes by exposing their lack of self-
knowledge and knowledge of cyclical process. In fact, all
three of these passages, despite or perhaps because of their calm
expectation of timelessness, are framed by the anticipation of
present reversal. Helena's lament is provoked by her belief that
Hermia is in league with Lysander and Demetrius to mock her
unrequited love:

     Is all the counsel that we two have shared,
     The sister's vows, the hours that we have spent,

When we have chid the hasty-footed time
For parting us – O, is all forgot?
All school days friendship, childhood innocence?

*   *   *   *   *

And will you rent our ancient love asunder,
To join with men in scorning your poor friend?
(*MND* III. ii. 198–216)

The advent of sexual love, in the case of Helena and Hermia, has brought about separation and differentiation, each here presented in the image of a fall. The fall and its attendant Christian overtones are even more explicit in Polixenes' speech, where they serve as a prolepsis to the larger dislocation of trust and friendship which forms the central action of the play:

> *Polixenes*   We knew not
> The doctrine of ill-doing, nor dreamed
> That any did; had we pursued that life,
> And our weak spirits ne'er been higher reared
> With stronger blood, we should have answered heaven
> Boldly, 'Not guilty'; the imposition cleared,
> Hereditary ours.
> *Hermione*   By this we gather
> You have tripped since.
> *Polixenes*   O my most sacred lady,
> Temptations have since then been born to's, for
> In those unfledged days was my wife a girl;
> Your precious self had then not crossed the eyes
> Of my young playfellow.   (*WT* I. ii. 69–80)

Once again, the spur to separation, differentiation, and subjection to the process of time has been sexual; the 'stronger blood' to which Polixenes makes reference is the blood of sexual passion, and the fall, trivialized as 'tripped' in Hermione's playful challenge, is identified as the 'temptation' posed by marriageable, i.e. by sexually mature and desirable, women. The twinned state is disrupted by a remembrance of man's sexual nature; he turns away from the unfallen paradisal timelessness of the innocent twinned lambs, and embraces, as he must, the fallen state of mortal man, his passions and his 'blood'.

The inseparable swans of Celia's account, like the double

cherry and the twinned lambs, are an instance of natural pairing in an ideal world, here the mythological realm of Juno, whose chariot they were said to draw. There may be a hint, in the selection of this image, that it too is to be superseded; Juno is the goddess of marriage, and for Celia and Rosalind, as for Hermia and Helena, marriage will replace their 'coupled and inseparable' relation to one another with the more fruitful coupling of sexual love. Celia's idyllic description, like Helena's and Polixenes', is immediately contradicted, in this case by her father, Duke Frederick, who has banished his brother, Duke Senior, from the court, and wishes now to banish his niece, Rosalind.

> *Duke Frederick*   She is too subtile for thee; and her smooth-
>   ness,
>   Her very silence and her patience,
>   Speak to the people, and they pity her.
>   Thou art a fool. She robs thee of thy name,
>   And thou wilt show more bright and seem more virtuous
>   When she is gone.   (*AYLI* I. iii. 76–81)

Where Celia sees a twinship, Duke Frederick perceives the contrast of jewel and foil. His more worldly, yet radically circumscribed, vision can only accommodate a fallen state of competitive theft – 'she robs thee' – as Hermia accuses Helena, and Leontes Polixenes, of sexual theft. As Celia departs with Rosalind for the Forest of Arden, pursuing, as she thinks, the paradisal state of twinned loyalty, she finds herself, as does Rosalind, entering a world of sexual maturity. 'Banished' like Adam and Eve, they 'fall' like Adam and Eve into sexual awareness, and replace their twinned but limited union as sisters with the more inclusive prospect of marriage to two brothers. The choice of a pair of brothers, though inherited from Lodge's *Rosalynde*, also has the effect of transforming an impossible pattern into a possible one; as we have seen, much the same educative reversal takes place in *The Comedy of Errors*, where two brothers marry two sisters, and in *Twelfth Night*, where Olivia's impossible love for Viola–Cesario is shifted to Viola's twin brother Sebastian in the nick of time.

The Celia–Rosalind situation, however, remains relatively dormant as a metaphor. Duke Frederick's dark hints about Rosalind's attractions are not borne out in the plot, and there is no competition between Celia and Rosalind for the love of either brother. The Duke's suspicions do bear fruit, however, in another and later play, in which we are once again confronted with a pair of young women twinned by circumstance. This pair, found in *Pericles*, are Marina and Philoten, and their situation is described by Gower:

> Our Cleon hath
> One daughter, and a full grown wench,
> Even ripe for marriage rite. This maid
> Hight Philoten; and it is said
> For certain in our story, she
> Would ever with Marina be.
> Be't when she weaved the sleided silk
> With fingers long, small, white as milk;
> Or when she would with sharp needle wound
> The cambric, which she made more sound
> By hurting it; or when to th' lute
> She sung, and made the night-bird mute,
> That still records with moan; or when
> She would with rich and constant pen
> Vail to her mistress Dian; still
> This Philoten contends in skill
> With absolute Marina: so
> With dove of Paphos might the crow
> Vie feathers white. Marina gets
> All praises, which are paid as debts,
> And not as given. This so darks
> In Philoten all graceful marks
> That Cleon's wife, with envy rare,
> A present murderer does prepare
> For good Marina, that her daughter
> Might stand peerless by this slaughter.
>
> (IV. Prol. 15–40)

The creative activities of singing and sewing link these twinned young women to Hermia and Helena, though in this case a distinction in skill is clearly indicated; Cleon's wife reasons, as does Duke Frederick, that Philoten 'will show more bright and seem more virtuous' when Marina is gone. Significantly, Philoten – whom we never see – is characterized by Gower as 'a full grown wench, / Even ripe for marriage'. The attempt on Marina's life is precipitated, not by generalized rivalry, but by a mother's sexual jealousy on behalf of her daughter: 'She did distain my child, and stood between / Her and her fortunes' (IV. iii. 31–2). For fourteen years Marina has lived safely in Tharsus; it is only when maturity and the prospect of marriage come upon her that her life is threatened, and she is seen to be individuated from Philoten.

We might here take note of an interesting variant of this twinning pattern, in which the specter of an offstage 'twin' or 'sister' offers a strong contrast to the onstage protagonist and acts as an index of her progress. Thus when Lady Capulet broaches the question of Juliet's marriage to Paris by alluding to her 'pretty age', the Nurse reminds her that she can 'tell her age into an hour', because Juliet was 'of an age' with the Nurse's own daughter, Susan. But 'Susan is with God', dead in childhood, and although Juliet will also die young, her experiences with love, sex, pain and loss are enough for a lifetime of adulthood. Susan is almost forgotten as the play unfolds, but her alternative fate is instructive in our observation of Juliet's growth to maturity.

Likewise we hear in *Love's Labor's Lost* that Katherine, one of the ladies who attends the Princess of France, had a sister who died of love; Cupid made her 'melancholy, sad, and heavy; / And so she died; (v. ii. 14–15). But 'Had she been light, like you,' says Katherine to her friend Rosaline, 'Of such a merry, nimble, stirring spirit, / She might ha' been a grandam ere she died. / And so may you, for a light heart lives long' (15–18). The play does not last long enough to fulfill this prediction, but by its close we have seen the ladies all learn much about the nature of love, combining an appropriately melancholy sadness at the death of the King of France with the promise of future marriages to the lords of Navarre.

Viola–Cesario invents a similar sister, who never told her love and pined away like Patience on a monument, smiling at grief. Her purpose in this invention is, most directly, to educate the obtuse Orsino about the strength of a woman's love. At the same time, however, the 'sister' displaces Viola's own hidden and hopeless passion for Orsino himself; her tale is simultaneously a fiction and a truth. Yet Viola herself is not the type to pine away, and having expressed her feelings in this oblique and emblematic way, she resolutely goes on with the unwelcome task of wooing Olivia – with unexpected but gratifying results. Once again the absent sister serves as a useful reminder of what might have been and a sign of Viola's (and the French ladies') ability to grow, learn and change.

The state of sexual maturity is thus presented by Shakespeare as one of individuation and differentiation. The fraternal or sororal bond is necessarily a limited one, which must yield priority to a marital and sexual bond, as the timelessness of the twinned-lamb and double-cherry images must yield to an acceptance of time and change, and a consequent stress upon fructification and the natural round. A refusal to acknowledge the limits of fraternity or twinship is tantamount to a blindness to self; to be boy eternal is not only impossible, but also undesirable, and it is in coming to terms with the necessity of their 'stronger blood' that Hermia will win her Lysander, and Marina her Lysimachus.

Moreover, the example of Hermia serves, in fact, a double purpose, for in her choice of Lysander Hermia directly disobeys her father Egeus, who has insisted that she marry Demetrius. And it is here that we encounter the second half of the fraternal–filial pattern. Just as it is a sign of self-knowledge and of an acceptance of maturity to cease to be a twinned lamb and become a king and father, so it is also such a sign to turn away from one's duty to a parent and toward one's duty to a spouse. Theseus must learn this before his own marriage day, and ironically so, since he tells us that his own courtship was accomplished not by parental consent but with his sword; yet the choice he ordains for Hermia, marriage to Demetrius or the life of 'a barren sister . . . chanting faint hymns to the cold fruitless moon', is clearly unacceptable both in terms of comedy and in terms of larger patterns of fertility and renewal. Hermia's defiance of both these father figures, Egeus and the Duke, is a freeing action which liberates all the play's lovers, and leads them into the Athenian wood, with all its sexual passions, temptations and confusions. Avoiding the Scylla of the nunnery, Hermia sails dangerously close to the Charybdis of Titania's lust for the ass-headed Bottom, but emerges safely, and somewhat more self-knowledgeably, into the orderly harbor of marriage.

A less fortunate but even more educative journey is undertaken by Juliet, who, like Hermia, finds herself faced with the choice between a father and a lover. Juliet expresses the nature of her dilemma early in the play, in lines which are so often quoted out of context that their true import is in danger of being obscured: 'Deny thy father and refuse thy name; / Or, if thou wilt not, be but sworn my love, / And I'll no longer be a Capulet' (II. ii. 34–6). This election of identity is forced upon her by circumstance, but there is no doubt of her resolution; she knows the nature of her allegiance, as is clear from her impassioned response to the news of Tybalt's death and its aftermath:

> Tybalt's death
> Was woe enough, if it had ended there;
> Or, if sour woe delights in fellowship
> And needly will be ranked with other griefs,
> Why followed not, when she said 'Tybalt's dead,'
> Thy father, or thy mother, nay, or both,
> Which modern lamentation might have moved?
> But with a rearward following Tybalt's death,
> 'Romeo is banishèd' – to speak that word
> Is father, mother, Tybalt, Romeo, Juliet,
> All slain, all dead.   (R&J III. ii. 114–24)

Manifestly Juliet is neither hardhearted nor of an unloving disposition, yet she prefers the death of both her parents to the banishment of her lover. Moreover, it is she, and not Romeo, who is most outspoken about the sexual nature of their bond – she who, waiting in the orchard for Romeo to come to her bed, calls upon the horses of the sun in a frank reversal of Ovid's *lente currite, noctis equi*:[1] 'Gallop apace, you fiery-footed steeds, / Toward Phoebus' lodging! . . . Spread thy close curtain, love-performing night. . . . O, I have bought the mansion of a love, / But not possessed it' (III. ii. 1–27). Juliet's choice is a measure of her maturity and self-knowledge. Awakening in her tomb to find the body of Romeo beside her, she cannot accept the Friar's offer to 'dispose' of her 'among a sisterhood of holy nuns', any more than Hermia can accept the fate of a 'barren sister' threatened by Theseus. As always in Shakespeare, the alternative of a celibate life in a nunnery is presented as a wrong path, an infertile solution which denies the fundamental nature of humanity; even the abbesses of *The Comedy of Errors* and

Pericles are only temporary inhabitants of the cloister, both mothers who regain by play's end their lost husbands and children – and Angelo in *Measure for Measure* learns the hard way that he is not really 'a man whose blood / Is very snow-broth' (I. iv. 57–8). Juliet's choices, of life with Romeo rather than with father or mother, death with Romeo rather than the convent without him, provide a paradigm of the Shakespearean pattern of achieved womanhood, as it will be manifested in the major tragedies and the romances.

We may see in Portia, as well, an anticipation of this pattern and a full expression of it. In a play constantly concerned with various kinds of fathers and their relationships to their children – Portia's father and his legacy of the casket choice; Shylock and Jessica; old Gobbo and Launcelot; God the Father and His legacy of mercy through His Son – Portia learns with ease and resolution the lesson of necessary filial separation. Subjected to her father's will, she at first laments her condition to Nerissa: 'I may neither choose who I would not refuse nor refuse who I dislike, so is the will of a living daughter curbed by the will of a dead father' (I. ii. 22–4). Yet her father's will is finally one of free will, which leaves her sufficient to stand, though free to fall, and the choice of the three caskets is presented in contrast to the absolute tyranny of Shylock over Jessica, in which daughter and ducats are indifferently interchangeable. The legacy left Portia is one of liberation, not of bondage. When Bassanio chooses the right casket, she significantly gives herself to him in a solemn and ceremonious speech culminating in her bestowal of a ring, a deliberate reversal of the traditional marriage ceremony in which the ring is given by the husband, worn by the wife. And Jessica, too, partakes of this freeing pattern. A more orthodox figure of rebellion against repressive fatherhood, she flees with Lorenzo as Hermia attempts to flee with Lysander, and in the Belmont world she is moved to assert confidently, 'I shall be saved by my husband' – an allusion to 1 Corinthians 7 : 14:'For the unbelieving husband is sanctified by the wife, and the un-believing wife is sanctified by the husband.' Salvation and self-knowledge are once again manifestly linked to the rejection of a father's repressive control, and the willed choice of a husband.

A briefer but equally striking version of this choice occurs at the beginning of *All's Well That Ends Well*, when Helena is torn between the appearance of public grief for her father, and the reality of private grief about Bertram. Lafew and the Countess of Rousillon have spoken feelingly of the untimely death of Helena's father, whose talents as a physician are sorely missed in the court of the afflicted King of France. When she is left onstage alone, however, Helena confesses immediately that her thoughts are elsewhere:

> I think not on my father,
> And these great tears grace his remembrance more
> Than those I shed for him. What was he like?
> I have forgot him; my imagination
> Carries no favor in't but Bertram's.   (1. i. 82–6)

Significantly, both Bertram and Helena have recently been bereaved of their fathers; equally significantly, Helena starts in unhappy fear when the countess offers to be a 'mother' to her, explicitly declaring that she does not want Bertram as her brother. She wants him, of course, as a husband. But the problem of incest nonetheless pervades this troubling play, and the much-reviled Bertram may perhaps be forgiven something of his churlishness in the light of what we have been saying about stages of maturation.[2] Helena's tears, we are told by the countess, are 'the best brine a maiden can season her praise in' (1. i. 49–50). Bertram, she tells us a few lines later, is an 'unseasoned courtier' (72). Helena's ready acknowledgment of the choice of husband over father places her at a different stage of development from Bertram, who is evidently weary of the exclusively female companionship (and apparent domination) of his mother and Helena. The first line of the play is the Countess' disturbingly ambiguous remark that 'In delivering my son from me I bury a second husband.' At once a newborn child and his mother's (forbidden) husband, Bertram chooses instead the hegemony of the king (described by Lafew as Bertram's new 'father') and the fellowship of other lords in the wars. This period of what is frequently called 'male-bonding' is an essential transition for Bertram from the child–parent relationship to a place in adult society. His treatment of Diana, whom (despite her name) he tries to seduce, is almost as shoddy as his treatment of Helena, but All's Well will not, I think, finally permit us to see all the blame on his side. The play offers, instead, a complex and sophisticated network of personal relationships, in which Helena's crucial declaration that she has forgotten her father for Bertram must be partnered by Bertram's discovery that the metaphorical 'sister', however low-born, is not a sister at all, but a responsive sexual partner (who found him 'wondrous kind' in bed – v. iii. 310) and the mother of his child. From the opening line's unwelcome suggestion that he is still an infant to be 'delivered', the play has developed to a point where Bertram himself is to assume the desirable roles of father and husband.

In another of the dark comedies, *Measure for Measure*, we once again encounter the problems of twinning and individuation combined with the motif of dependence on a father – but in this case the problem is not so happily resolved. Isabella refers to Juliet as her 'cousin', explaining that she uses the term 'Adoptedly, as schoolmaids change their names / By vain, though apt, affection' (i. iv. 47–8). The childhood relationship of the two girls thus seems to have followed the pattern of Hermia and Helena, or Celia and Rosalind. But where both members of those twinned pairs proceeded eagerly toward marriage, Isabella and Juliet have followed paths that are diametrically opposed. As the play opens we hear that Juliet is pregnant by Isabella's brother, Claudio, while Isabella herself is about to enter a nunnery. When Angelo demands that she sleep with him as ransom for her brother's life, Isabella not only declares ringingly that 'More than our brother is our chastity' (ii. iv. 184) – she also hastens to Claudio's cell to ascertain that he is prepared to die. And when he, with more bravado than truth, asserts that he is ready, she discovers in him not only a brother but also a father. 'There spake my brother, there my father's grave / Did utter forth a voice' (iii. i. 85–6). Claudio does not yet know of the proposed bargain, but Isabella has deftly manipulated circumstances so that her father – though dead – appears to support her determination to remain a virgin. She clings to the submissive role of a child, turning away from adult responsibility and sexuality in a single gesture. Her later remark in the same scene, 'Is't not a kind of incest, to take life / From thine own sister's shame?' (138–9), may also be psychologically revealing: her 'cousin' has slept with her beloved brother and is carrying his child.[3] Isabella's fanatical chastity seems here not unrelated to taboo, as well as to a regressive return to domination by the father. The play's problematic ending – will she or won't she marry the duke? – is rendered even more disturbing if the duke is conceived of as a man of Isabella's father's generation. Since Lucio calls him an 'old fantastical Duke of dark corners', and the duke alludes to either 'nineteen' (I. ii. 171) or 'fourteen' (I. iii. 21) years of rule, this conjecture seems quite possible. If we are to judge by the tenets and practice of the other plays, however, even a December–May marriage would be preferable, in Shakespearean terms, to a life forever spent in the nunnery – which is not to say that the audience can, or must, assume that such a marriage will take place. The ending remains both disturbingly and fruitfully ambiguous: a striking example of the complex problems of sexual growth and choice.

It is the mature tragedies, however, which most vividly display the importance of this kind of filial choice. Desdemona, summoned to the Venetian council chamber in the middle of the night, replies composedly to her father's question:

> *Brabantio* Do you perceive in all this noble company
>   Where most you owe obedience?
> *Desdemona*   My noble father,
>   I do perceive here a divided duty.
>   To you am I bound for life and education;
>   My life and education both do learn me
>   How to respect you. You are the lord of duty,
>   I am hitherto your daughter. But here's my husband,
>   And so much duty as my mother showed
>   To you, preferring you before her father,
>   So much I challenge that I may profess
>   Due to the Moor my lord.   (*Oth.* I. iii. 177–87)

The argument could not be more clearly put. Loyalty to father must give way to loyalty to husband. At stake for the society is lineal succession, the fertile round; for the individual, what is at stake is achieved maturity, the fruits of life and education. Desdemona, like Juliet, expresses her commitment in terms which are frankly and unmistakably sexual, in her plea in the same scene to accompany Othello to Cyprus:

> That I love the Moor to live with him,
> My downright violence, and storm of fortunes,

May trumpet to the world. My heart's subdued
Even to the very quality of my lord. . . .
So that, dear lords, if I be left behind,
A moth of peace, and he go to the war,
The rites for why I love him are bereft me,
And I a heavy interim shall support
By his dear absence. Let me go with him.
                                        (*Oth.* I. iii. 243–54)

When she arrives at Cyprus, Desdemona is greeted by Othello as 'my fair warrior'; Portia had likewise assumed, in costume rather than in metaphor, the guise of a man. Yet these are not, surely, evidences of androgyny – no figures are more fulfilled in their femininity than these Shakespearean heroines – but rather confirmatory signs of the mature entry of these women into the world of active passions and state affairs, a world which can only be entered by casting aside the passive modesty of an obedient Ophelia.

Desdemona's recognition of 'a divided duty' is echoed, of course, by Cordelia, in the most famous of all Shakespearean scenes of choice. Demanded by her father, as Desdemona was by hers, to declare the extent of her love and allegiance, she replies in similarly resolute terms:

Why have my sisters husbands, if they say
They love you all? Haply, when I shall wed,
That lord whose hand must take my plight shall carry
Half my love with him, half my care and duty.
Sure I shall never marry like my sisters,
To love my father all.   (*Lr* I. i. 99–104)

Goneril and Regan, so quick and glib in their own assurances of filial devotion, are exposed in the course of the play to be 'tigers, not daughters' – and this is Goneril's husband's phrase. They are incapable of love, prey to sexual passion without moral scruple or concern, mutually destructive and wholly lacking in self-knowledge. Theirs is the alternative path of Shakespearean offspring; for, as we shall see, the child who clings to its parent, rejecting, whether in passivity, guile or psychological dependence, the claims of marital love, appears repeatedly in the plays as a figure of consummate self-ignorance, unwilling or unable to come to terms with the demands of mature adulthood.

A pivotal example of this condition can be found in the behavior of Cressida, who begins, apparently, as a lover in the Juliet–Desdemona pattern, denying her father's claim upon her:

> *Pandarus* Thou must to thy father and be gone from
> Troilus. . . .
> *Cressida* I will not, uncle. I have forgot my father;
> I know no touch of consanguinity –
> No kin, no love, no blood, no soul so near me
> As the sweet Troilus. O you gods divine,
> Make Cressid's name the very crown of falsehood
> If ever she leave Troilus!   (*T&C* iv. ii. 92–102)

Yet her resolve is rhetorical, not real. The next scene presents her as already resigned to separation, the exchange of tokens with Troilus here almost a travesty of Portia's solemn ring-giving, and only a few hundred lines later Cressida is in full flirtation with the assembled Greek generals. Ulysses' withering epithet for such women, '*daughters* of the game' (iv. v. 63), suggests the crucial division between childhood and wifehood which lies at the root of her dilemma. Diomedes, who will become her lover in a key far removed from the Petrarchan idealism of Troilus, has the final word in this encounter, and it is a telltale one:

> *Diomedes* Lady, a word. I'll bring you to your father.
> [*Exeunt Diomedes and Cressida*]   (*T&C* iv. v. 53)

Here we have the spectacle of a return to the parent, the filial choice inverted. Cressida is not a wicked woman, like Goneril, but she is a weak one, not cast in the same heroic mold as Desdemona, or Portia, or Juliet. We may pity her, we may feel that in a sense she has no choice – but the reversal of the pattern of necessary filial separation here becomes its own metaphor, an emblem of Cressida's moral insufficiency.

In this Cressida is, oddly, very like Ophelia, whom she does not otherwise resemble. Cressida is worldly wise, sexually appetitive if not mature enough to comprehend the fuller complexity of marital love; Ophelia, of course, is her polar opposite. Yet Ophelia, too, is confronted with an opportunity to temper, if not to avert, tragedy through moral choice; and Ophelia, too, cannot choose. From the first moment that we see her, we are made aware of her passivity and filial subjection with regard to Hamlet's courtship:

> *Polonius*   I must tell you
> You do not understand yourself so clearly
> As it behooves my daughter and your honor. . . .
>   You speak like a green girl,
> Unsifted in such perilous circumstance.
> Do you believe his tenders, as you call them?
> *Ophelia*   I do not know, my lord, what I should think.
> *Polonius*   Marry, I will teach you.   (*Ham.* I. iii. 95–105)

This is the same first-act challenge Brabantio made to Desdemona, and Lear made to Cordelia. But Ophelia turns away from mature love, turns back to her father and away from life. Hamlet's agonized and punning cry, 'Get thee to a nunnery', exposes a brutal truth about Ophelia's capacity for growth and for sexual love.[4]

As with the pattern of twinship, this choice between parent and lover is largely but not exclusively female. Ophelia's submission to her father, and the consequent tragedy which overtakes her, find a close counterpart in the tragedy of Coriolanus, whose excessive affection for and dependence on his mother Volumnia prove his downfall. It is no accident that the one insult Coriolanus cannot bear is Aufidius' taunt of 'boy'. It torments him because of its truth, and the more he protests – 'Alone I did it [took Corioli]. "Boy?" ' (v. vi. 114) – the more he brings on his own tragic death, suicidally taking refuge for his pride in a claim of martial heroism, when the wilier Aufidius attacks his manhood. He is a 'boy' in his uncritical submission to Volumnia; his tragic condition is such that he is either her submissive son or a mechanical man who 'moves like an engine' and has 'no . . . kin'. His failure to break the filial bond is indissolubly linked to his fate, and is, as with Cressida, an emblem of it.[5]

Coriolanus, Ophelia and Cressida are still children in their limited capacity for moral understanding and choice – weak, rather than wicked. Goneril and Regan are more malevolent and purposeful nay-sayers, whose choice of their father, though plainly cosmetic and fictive, is a sign of their moral corruption.

Akin to them in this, and in her treatment of her husband as 'the baby of a girl', is Lady Macbeth. Goneril twits Albany for his resistance to bloodshed and his allegiance to the king: 'Marry, your manhood mew.' She equates maturity with murder, masculinity with bloodthirstiness. Lady Macbeth holds the same view: 'When you durst do it [the murder of Duncan], then you were a man' (I. vii. 49); she has persuaded Macbeth to her purpose in part through a challenge to his manhood. The men–children he exhorts her to 'bring forth' and the imaginary infants she declares her willingness to destroy are replaced for her by the man–child Macbeth.[6] Her relationship to him is not one of support and respect, nor one of sexual passion; instead of declarations of desire we have from her impassioned speeches about the slaughtering of children. Her affection for her husband is constantly tinged with contempt, and it is, unsurprisingly, for her father that she reserves the final commitment of love.

There is only one mention of the bond between father and daughter in the play, but it is strategically placed and, in light of the other examples we have considered, persuasive. It occurs at the moment when Lady Macbeth has returned from Duncan's chamber, having drugged his guards with drink, and is alarmed by an outcry:

> Lady Macbeth   Alack, I am afraid they have awaked
>   And 'tis not done! Th' attempt and not the deed
>   Confounds us. Hark! I laid their daggers ready;
>   He could not miss 'em. Had he not resembled
>   My father as he slept, I had done 't.   (Mac. II. ii. 9–13)

Not a twinge of moral doubt, but Duncan's resemblance to her father, has alone prevented her from committing the murder herself. The contrast between this bond of allegiance and her attitude toward Macbeth is vivid; from this point Lady Macbeth will move inexorably toward guilt and remorse – and, like Ophelia and Coriolanus, toward self-destruction.

Shakespeare's romances, of course, are full of situations in which filial choice and moral strength are paralleled: Florizel's defiance of Polixenes, Imogen's marriage to Posthumus above the protests of Cymbeline and his queen, Miranda's resolute and immediate choice of Ferdinand. In a way, though, it is *Pericles* in which the issue is most arrestingly posed, perhaps because the incidents of filial choice in *Pericles* are relatively schematic and clear-cut, exemplary rather than dramatic. The opening act of the play depends to a great extent upon a contrast between two father–daughter pairs: the incestuous Antiochus and his unnamed daughter, and the virtuous Simonides and Thaisa. Both women are approached by Pericles for their hands in marriage. Antiochus' corrupt relationship with his daughter is, of course, the secret hidden behind the riddle Pericles first deciphers to win her. Interestingly, Antiochus assumes a pose of generosity, pretending to invite suitors and to desire their success, while secretly he is unwilling to give up his daughter–mistress and fearful lest their relationship be publicly known. By contrast, Simonides affects a pretense of sternness toward Thaisa's suitors – 'Thou hast bewitched my daughter,' he charges Pericles, in echo of Brabantio and anticipation of Prospero – but his parental firmness conceals a genuine pleasure at her maturity and happiness. Thaisa, like Juliet and Desdemona before her, is forthright in her claim of love:

> *Pericles*   Resolve your angry father if my tongue
>   Did e'er solicit, or my hand subscribe
>   To any syllable that made love to you.
> *Thaisa*   Why, sir, say if you had,
>   Who takes offense at that would make me glad?
>   (*Per.* ii. v. 66–70)

And Simonides is unambiguous in his joy once he has tested the faith of the lovers: 'It pleaseth me so well,' he tells them, 'that I will see you wed; / And then, with what haste you can, get you to bed' (ii. v. 90–1). His acceptance of the sexual aspect of marriage is a key acknowledgment, here, of the necessity for sexual choice and the insurance of fertility, as aspects of order in a Shakespearean society.

The ways in which this order is attained in Shakespeare's plays are as various for individual characters as they are for kingdoms and nations. The central pattern of transition from childhood to adulthood, however, seems to encompass a series of related choices and confrontations, each of which serves to differentiate one character from another and to prepare him for his place in a world conscious of its own constant need for renewal. Twin confronts twin, bosom friend confronts bosom friend, daughter confronts father, son confronts mother – for each the choice is finally that of submission or independence, passive acquiescence or hard-won self-knowledge. The sundering of one bond is the necessary prelude to the forging of another, and readiness for a mature relationship with husband or lover is tied inextricably to self-definition. Twinship and kinship are replaced by selfhood.

It is useful to remember that in Shakespeare's time 'self' meant not only the individual, or that individual's consciousness of his own identity, but also, in an adjectival form, 'same' or 'identical'. Thus Regan claims that she is made of the 'self metal' as her sister, and the Duchess of Gloucester reminds John of Gaunt that her husband was fashioned in the 'self mold' as he was – that is, by the same parents. But by the close of many Shakespearean plays principal characters have been asked to decipher the riddle that so perplexed the onlookers in 'The Phoenix and the Turtle': 'that the self was not the same'. One individual may resemble another, or be born of the same flesh, but no two are identical, and no natal bond can retain primacy over the new bonds of sexual love and marriage. It is this process of individuation and differentiation that prepares the protagonist for his next rite of passage: entry into the full and complex world of adulthood.

We may none of us wish for the fate of a Juliet or a Desdemona, but who among us does not admire them? We may all sympathize with Polixenes, and with Coriolanus, indeed even with Leontes – but who among us can find instruction in their willingness to be 'boy eternal'? All of this Shakespeare knew, and made it a recurrent and fundamental part of his plays – for with St Paul he knew that there was a time to seize, at whatever cost, upon knowledge of self:

> When I was a child, I spake as a child, I understood as a child, I thought as a child: but when I became a man, I put away childish things. For now we see through a glass, darkly; but then face to face: now I know in part; but then shall I know even as also I am known.   (1 Cor. 13:11–12)

NOTES

1 Harry Levin, 'Form and formality in *Romeo and Juliet'*, *Shakespeare Quarterly*, XI (1960), 3–11.

2 Otto Rank, in an early work, *Das Inzest-Motiv in Dichtung und Sage* (1912), 2nd edition (Leipzig: Frank Deuticke, 1926), p. 394n, comments on a slightly different aspect of the incest-motive in *All's Well*. Norman N. Holland, in *Psychoanalysis and Shakespeare* (New York: McGraw-Hill, 1964; rpt. Octagon Books, 1976), p. 154, summarizes Rank as follows:

> The noble Bertram taking to wife the woman he himself has dishonored corresponds to the son whose own birth proves that his mother was dishonored (i.e., had relations with his father). The woman in the dark is taboo, her forbidden quality represented by the dark and the subterfuge; like tabooed women in general, she stands ultimately for the mother.

3 Rank notes an incest-motive in *Measure* as well. In Holland's summary (p. 230),

> Angelo is slipped a maiden he himself dishonored in lieu of the sister, Isabella, who is ostensibly devoted to her brother. Rank says this is a rearrangement of an incest situation: the girl in the dark is the 'dark', tabooed mother, whom the son has himself dishonored, his own birth proving the fact that she has had intercourse with a man. The incest taboo is transferred to the brother–sister relation and expressed in terms of Isabella's chastity.

Rank does not, however, comment on Isabella's odd identification of father and brother, or her desire (presumably also in some ways incestuous) to cleave to the father's imagined precepts and retain her virginity.

4 The literature on *Hamlet* and incest is voluminous, and would be difficult to recapitulate or summarize here. The reader is referred to Norman Holland's excellent and extensive treatment of writings on that play in *Psychoanalysis and Shakespeare*, especially pp. 59–63, 88–95 and 163–206.

5 Plutarch's 'Life of Martius Coriolanus' is explicit on this subject, and Shakespeare's play is faithful to its spirit. 'Touching Martius,' writes Plutarch,

> the only thing that made him to love honour was the joy he saw his mother did take of him. For he thought nothing made him so happy and honourable as that his mother might hear everybody

praise and commend him; that she might always see him return with a crown upon his head; and that she might still embrace him with tears running down her cheeks for joy. . . . Martius thinking all due to his mother that had been also due to his father had he lived, did not only content himself to rejoice and honour her, but *at her desire took a wife* also, by whom he had two children; *and yet never left his mother's house therefore.* [Emphasis added] ['Life of Martius Coriolanus', in T. J. B. Spencer (ed.) *Shakespeare's Plutarch: The Lives of Julius Caesar, Brutus, Marcus Antonius and Coriolanus in the Translation of Sir Thomas North* (Middlesex, England, and Baltimore, Maryland: Penguin Books, 1964), p. 300.]

Not surprisingly, Coriolanus' personality has been of great interest to psychoanalytic critics. Some particularly provocative studies on this subject are Otto Rank, *Inzest-Motiv*, Ch. 6; Charles K. Hofling, 'An interpretation of Shakespeare's Coriolanus', *American Imago*, xiv (1957), 407–35; Rufus Putney, 'Coriolanus and his mother', *Psychoanalytic Quarterly*, xxxi (1962), 364–81; and David B. Barron, '*Coriolanus*: Portrait of the artist as infant', *American Imago*, xix (1962), 171–93. See also I. R. Browning, 'Coriolanus – boy of tears', *Essays in Criticism*, 5 (1955), 18–31.

6 On the image of the babe in *Macbeth*, see Cleanth Brooks, 'The naked babe and the cloak of manliness', in *The Well Wrought Urn* (New York: Harcourt, Brace & World, 1947), pp. 22–49.

3
NOMINATION AND ELECTION
'AN ADOPTED NAME OF PRIVILEGE'

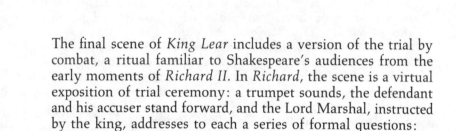

The final scene of *King Lear* includes a version of the trial by combat, a ritual familiar to Shakespeare's audiences from the early moments of *Richard II*. In *Richard*, the scene is a virtual exposition of trial ceremony: a trumpet sounds, the defendant and his accuser stand forward, and the Lord Marshal, instructed by the king, addresses to each a series of formal questions:

> What is thy name? And wherefore com'st thou hither
> Before King Richard in his royal lists?
> Against whom comest thou? And what's thy quarrel?
> Speak like a true knight, so defend thee heaven.
> (RII I. iii. 31–4)

Mowbray and Bolingbroke identify themselves by name and degree, and the combat may begin. But in *Lear*, when Edgar appears at the third trumpet to challenge his brother Edmund, this customary pattern is violated. Albany stands for the king, and at his instigation a herald proclaims the ritual questions:

> What are you?
> Your name, your quality, and why you answer
> This present summons? (Lr v. iii. 120–2)

Our expectation is that the disputants will fulfill the form, and answer the questions; the ensuing combat would seem to depend upon their acquiescence to the ceremony. But our expectation is frustrated, and frustrated in a startling fashion: the disguised Edgar, denying the ritual request, declares instead his intention to retain his disguise. 'Know,' he says, 'my name is lost; / By treason's tooth bare-gnawn and canker-bit' (122–3). Disowned by his father, cheated and betrayed by his brother, Edgar has lost his name by necessity, and throughout the play he chooses to keep it concealed by policy. No longer accepted by his lineal relations, he becomes by turns Poor Tom, and the countryman who leads Gloucester to 'Dover cliff', and the second countryman who finds him after his 'fall' – and ultimately the anonymous masked challenger of the trial by combat. Only when Edmund lies dying at his feet does he reclaim his lost name and lineage: 'My name is Edgar, and thy father's son' (171).

Significantly, this repossession of both name and family comes at a time when Edgar recovers his stolen birthright: both Gloucesters are dead, and he stands at the head of his line. What is even more significant, however, is the dramatic chronology which makes this revelation possible. For Edgar has reclaimed his name before this, in the poignant confrontation with Gloucester in which, he says, 'I revealed myself unto him . . . and from first to last / Told him our pilgrimage' (v. iii. 194–8). It is in fact this self-naming which leads directly to Gloucester's death: 'His flawed heart . . . too weak the conflict to support . . . Burst smilingly' (198–201). But although the reunion between parent and child precedes the trial by combat in historical time, it is described after it in the dramatic action; moreover, the incident takes place offstage, and is retold by the son, rather than presented directly to the audience. This dislocation places dramatic emphasis, not upon the filial recognition scene, but on the son's reclamation of his name. For a playwright so consistently interested in the motif of the family reunion, this is a surprising departure, which underscores the importance of Edgar's action. The transition from 'Know, my name is lost,' to 'My name is Edgar, and thy father's son,' marks a crucial development in the tragedy, and constitutes nothing less than a rite of passage.

In view of the ritual origins of drama, it is perhaps not surprising to encounter in Shakespeare a dramatic pattern based upon names and naming which corresponds to some well-known aspects of primitive religious practice. Among ancient Greek and Semitic tribes, and for a number of primitive tribes today, the name was thought of as part of the extended self of the individual, and therefore as vulnerable: to know another's true name was, in some sense, to have power over him. Hence there developed a practice of dual naming; in which a publicly used personal name, often a sur- or nickname, was substituted for the secret or sacred name of the individual. In some Australian tribes, as Frazer points out,[1] the secret name was known only to fully initiated members of the group – that is, to those who had come of age. Likewise in ancient Egypt two names were bestowed upon the child; the 'good' or 'little' name was in public use, while the other, the 'true' or 'great' name, was kept concealed. The names of kings, priests, and other sacred persons were guarded with especial care in such societies, since to hold power over them would be particularly desirable. To give the child the name of a living person became an ambiguously valued action – it might either sap the vitality of the original bearer, or, alternatively, revitalize him and guarantee him extended life. Often the names of the dead were taboo, and could not be mentioned; the inference is that to do so would be to evoke the ghost. For the same reason, those who held the same name as a dead person might choose another, lest the ghost think he was called when his namesake was addressed. The word 'name' in Hebrew and other Semitic societies is in fact a virtual synonym for 'posterity', and to bless or curse the name is thus to affect the entire family and future of its bearer.

Now, some equivalences between these patterns and certain details in Shakespeare's plays will be immediately apparent – as for example the dramatic tension produced by the fact that Hamlet bears the same name as his father, or the resonance of Richard II's poignant cry, 'Arm, arm, my name.' Of special interest to the reader of Shakespeare, however, is the explicit congruence suggested between the rite of initiation and the gaining or learning of a name (or a new name). Eliade notes that the initiation rite itself represents a symbolic death and resurrection, and describes the practice of certain African tribes who severely beat the novice, 'which is said to "kill" his old name so that he may be given another.'[2]

We need not, of course, restrict our search for such rituals to the practice of primitive tribes or non-western cultures. In Genesis, Jacob wrestles with an angel, and is given a new name: 'Thy name shall be called no more Jacob, but Israel: for as a prince has thou power with God and with men, and hast prevailed' (32 : 28). At the time of the covenant, God likewise renames Abram: 'Neither shall thy name any more be called Abram, but thy name shall be Abraham; for a father of many nations have I made thee' (Gen. 17 : 5). Moses, cast into the Nile as a nameless infant, is given a name which signifies both his identity and his destiny: Pharaoh's daughter 'called him Moses: and she said, Because I drew him out of the water' (Exod. 2 : 10). When Saul accepts Christ, he is known as Paul, and Simon known as Peter; in the Vulgate the significance of the name is clear: 'Tu es Petrus, et super hanc petram aedificabo ecclesiam meam' (Matt. 16 : 18). 'Christ' itself is a cognomen or epithet meaning 'the anointed one', which is frequently substituted for or added to the given name of Jesus. The book of Revelation explicitly describes a ritual of renaming: 'To him that over- cometh will I give to eat of the hidden manna, and will give him a white stone, and in the stone a new name written, which no man knoweth saving he that receiveth it' (2 : 17), and it is also in Revelation that we hear of one who sat on a white horse, and was called Faithful and True; 'and he had a name written, that no man knew, but he himself' (19 : 11–12).

The Arthurian legends, which probably represent the period of English literature most overtly concerned with initiation rituals, place a similar stress upon the acquisition or revelation of the name. In Malory, Arthur finds his true name and title only after he succeeds in drawing a sword from a stone; the sword bears an inscription which identifies its owner as 'rightwise king born of all England'.[3] Galahad is knighted by his father, Lancelot, but will not tell his name; the name is revealed for the first time by the graven letters on the Siege Perilous, which describe him as 'Galahad, the haut prince'.[4] He then performs the confirmatory ritual of drawing another sword from a stone, this one engraved to 'the best knight in the world',[5] and acquires the shield of Joseph of Arimathea, reserved for 'Galahad, the good knight',[6] 'the worthiest knight of the world'.[7] In a similar way Gareth, the younger brother of Gawain, comes incognito to Arthur's court, where he is mockingly called Beaumains ('Fair- hands') until he proves himself a knight and discloses his true identity.

Classical literature offers the example of Oedipus, perhaps the most suggestive of all legendary searches for the name. Oedipus begins his adventures confident of who and what he is: the son of Polybus of Corinth. By the close of Sophocles' play, he has learned not only the significance of his given name, 'Swollen-foot', but also his real identity and the identity of the murderer he seeks; tragically, the two are the same. The new Sphinx riddle posed for Oedipus is the same as that posed for Shakespeare's tragic heroes: 'who am I?' – and the form taken by that riddle *is* the name, as Bernard Knox suggests:

> οἶδα the knowledge of the tyrannos, πούς the swollen foot of Laius' son – in the hero's name the basic equation is already symbolically present, the equation which Oedipus will finally solve.[8]

Oedipus the son of Polybus and Merope is also Oedipus the son of Laius and Jocasta; Oedipus the son of Jocasta is also Oedipus, Jocasta's husband. When Jocasta finally learns the truth, she addresses him in despair: 'Unfortunate. This is the only name I can call you.'[9] He is no longer either husband or son. As the meaning of his name is revealed, the name itself is at once lost and agonizingly regained.

In these cases, the loss or abdication of the name need not imply the bearer's ignorance: the true name must be earned through a ritual of initiation, and once the rite of passage is successfully undergone, the other initiates – e.g. the Knights of the Round Table, the Apostles – are permitted to share the once concealed or forbidden knowledge. As was the case with Edgar, the true name includes both a personal name (Joseph, Galahad, Arthur) and a surname or cognomen, which may be generic (Israel), titular ('the best knight in the world') or both ('king born of all England'). In Shakespeare's plays, this surname is often called an 'addition'. The hero of *Cymbeline* is named 'Posthumus' because his parents predeceased him, but his other name, 'Leonatus', was given to his father as a 'sur-addition' because of his bravery in war (i. i. 28–33). As this suggests, Shakespearean additions, like their ritual counterparts, must be earned; they may prove dangerous and even fatal if the rite which qualifies the bearer has not been completed, or is somehow reversed or undone. Thus the proud surname of 'Coriolanus' proves Caius Marcius' death warrant when he uses it in Corioles, and once Lear resolves, 'Only we shall retain / The name, and all th' addition to a king' (I. i. 135–6), he is ultimately deprived not only of title but also of name: 'Does any here know me? This is not Lear' (I. iv. 227).

The most clear-cut example of the dangerous addition is probably that of Macbeth, where the tantalizing sequence of 'Glamis', 'Cawdor', and 'King hereafter' leads ineluctably to murder and self-destruction. Ross has greeted Macbeth with the title 'Thane of Cawdor', unconsciously echoing the trifold 'hail' of the witches: 'In which addition, hail, most worthy thane!' (I. iii. 106). But Macbeth's subsequent actions, in killing the king and seizing his title, are not emblems of achieved maturity, but rather the opposite: 'brave Macbeth – well he deserves that name' (I. ii. 16) is transformed first into 'the baby of a girl' (III. iv. 106), and then into the monster of the final scenes, who is neither man nor child, and whose name has lost its personal qualities to become itself a 'title', the synonym for tyrant:

> *Young Siward* What is thy name?
> *Macbeth* Thou'lt be afraid to hear
> it.
> *Young Siward* No; though thou call'st thyself a hotter name
> Than any is in hell.
> *Macbeth* My name's Macbeth.
> *Young Siward* The devil himself could not pronounce a title
> More hateful to mine ear. (v. vii. 5–9)

As was the case with Jacob and with Oedipus, man's name here becomes his fate. It is a pattern we will see repeated frequently, with varying permutations, throughout Shakespeare's tragedies and histories.[10]

One assumption which lies behind the quest for a name is that of a natural reciprocity between the name and the thing – a concept that is often expressed in the tag phrase *nomen–omen*.[11] The name is thought to embody the qualities of its bearer, and becomes a sort of talisman. In Shakespeare this kind of name magic usually represents a lost ideal, an earlier and simpler world in which one-to-one correspondences between names and things existed, and in which, therefore, the name did not have to be sought or earned. John of Gaunt, who represents just such a world in *Richard II*, puns on his name – rather in the manner of Donne's final hymns – as he lies on his deathbed:

O, how that name befits my composition!
Old Gaunt indeed, and gaunt in being old!
Within me grief hath kept a tedious fast;
And who abstains from meat that is not gaunt?
For sleeping England long time have I watched:
Watching breeds leanness, leanness is all gaunt.
The pleasure that some fathers feed upon
Is my strict fast – I mean my children's looks –
And therein fasting hast thou made me gaunt;
Gaunt am I for the grave, gaunt as a grave
Whose hollow womb inherits naught but bones.
                                            (II. i. 73–83)

Richard's impatient response ('Can sick men play so nicely with
their names?' – 84) characteristically misses the point, and
Gaunt's explanation stresses the necessary link between the
personal and familial aspects of the name: 'Since thou dost seek
to kill my name in me [by banishing his son Bolingbroke, and
thereby ending his line] I mock my name, great king, to flatter
thee' (86–7). But the play on 'Gaunt' also suggests an inherent
appropriateness between the name and its bearer – an appropriateness which is about to die in England, as Gaunt is dying,
and as the name of England itself has lost its power. Indeed,
Gaunt's great 'this England' speech, which immediately
precedes the puns on his own name, sets up precisely the same
pattern of correspondences. 'This royal throne of kings, this
scept'red isle . . .' (II. i. 40ff) – in all there are eleven lines of verse
and thirteen appositive metaphors before the name of 'England'
is introduced, yet the speech, which is a single sentence of
twenty lines, is perfectly clear, because its metaphors are persuasive. The equation between 'this other Eden, demi-paradise' (42)
and 'this England' (50) is – or was – so exact that the listener
assumes the subject. But now, argues Gaunt, the proper name
for England is not 'Eden' but 'tenement or pelting farm' (60); the
easy equivalence between name and thing has been lost, and
with it the power which that name wields. The lesson here for
Richard lies in the third, unspoken, equivalence, also assumed
by an earlier and simpler world: the equivalence between the
names of 'Richard' and 'king'.
    A similar pattern of *nomen–omen* appears in *Coriolanus*, a

play much concerned with the losing and finding of names. Here
the reference is to one Censorinus, an ancestor of Caius Marcius,
'And nobly naméd so, twice being censor' (II. iii. 246). The detail
is taken from Plutarch,[12] and the comment made by one of the
hostile tribunes in persuading the citizens to revoke their support for Coriolanus. His implication is clear, and is underscored
by the succeeding dialogue: once there was a time when magistrates, and indeed magistrates of this noble family, were fit for
their posts – so fit that their names and posts were identical. But
this is no longer the case; despite his honorable lineage, Caius
Marcius, surnamed Coriolanus, is unfit to be consul.

Of all Shakespearean *nomen–omen* instances, however, none
is more striking than the episode of Cinna the poet in *Julius
Caesar*. (The Roman plays, with their natural interest in the
cognomen, seem to take 'name' as a thematic element with some
consistency.) On his way to Caesar's funeral, Cinna is halted by
a gang of plebians who challenge his loyalty and ask his name.
Unluckily, he bears the name of one of the conspirators, and the
plebians, taking the name for the thing, fall upon him and beat
him:

> *Cinna*   I am Cinna the poet! I am Cinna the poet!
> *Fourth Plebian*   Tear him for his bad verses! Tear him for his
>   bad verses!
> *Cinna*   I am not Cinna the conspirator.
> *Fourth Plebian*   It is no matter, his name's Cinna; pluck but
>   his name out of his heart, and turn him going.
>   (III. iii. 31–7)

The scene is a vivid emblem of the confusion which has fallen
upon Rome after the murder of its ruler. When times are bad for
anyone, the poet suggests, they are particularly bad for poets.
Behind the wry Shakespearean truth, however, lies another
important thematic point: since the name is no longer directly
equivalent to the thing, we act at our peril. For just as one may
beat the wrong Cinna, so one may kill the wrong Caesar.

To kill the wrong Caesar is, of course, the fate of revolution-
ists and conspirators throughout Shakespeare, whether their
intended targets are Roman emperors or English kings. In *Julius
Caesar* the distinctions between *nomen* and *cognomen*, name
and addition, are first blurred, then lost, so that 'Julius' lies

bleeding while 'Caesar' escapes the conspirators' hands. Brutus feelingly invokes the doctrine of the king's two bodies:

> O, that we could come by Caesar's spirit,
> And not dismember Caesar! But alas,
> Caesar must bleed for it.   (II. i. 169–71)

But the result of his actions is ironically opposite to his intent. The initial confusion, however, and a willful one, is not Brutus' but Cassius' – since for reasons of both policy and nature, Cassius discounts the idea that names have power.

> Brutus and Caesar: what should be in that 'Caesar'?
> Why should that name be sounded more than yours?
> Write them together, yours is as fair a name;
> Sound them, it doth become the mouth as well;
> Weigh them, it is as heavy; conjure with 'em,
> 'Brutus' will start a spirit as soon as 'Caesar'.
>
>   (I. ii. 142–7)[13]

If this sounds a little like Edmund on astrology, or Iago's advice to Roderigo, that is because it is also part of Cassius' own ambitious plan. 'Brutus' and 'Caesar' do have the same number of syllables, and the same metrical stress – but then so does 'Cassius', the unspoken name behind this argument. Yet the irony again resides within the speaker's own rhetoric, for 'Caesar', unlike the others, can and does start a spirit – his own; his name alone has the power to conjure, as Cassius learns at last: 'O Julius Caesar, thou art mighty yet! / Thy spirit walks abroad, and turns our swords / In our own proper entrails' (v. iii. 94–6). Caesar's personal name of 'Julius' is used only twice in the play without the powerful addition: once by Mark Antony, and once by Brutus – both times, significantly, after he is dead. Caesar himself consistently speaks of himself in the third person:

> Caesar should be a beast without a heart
> If he should stay at home today for fear.
> No, Caesar shall not. Danger knows full well
> That Caesar is more dangerous than he . . .
> And Caesar shall go forth.   (II. ii. 42–8)

Yet there are of course two Caesars, the invincible ruler and the vulnerable man – a man who suffers from 'the falling sickness' and is hard of hearing:

I rather tell thee what is to be feared
Than what I fear; for always I am Caesar.
Come on my right hand, for this ear is deaf,
And tell me truly what thou think'st of him.

(I. ii. 211–14)

All the greater, therefore, is the conspirators' dismay when they discover that it is 'Julius' who lies bleeding at the Capitol, while Caesar is mighty yet – in fact, doubly mighty. The vengeful ghost stalks the battlefield, and a new Caesar, like a new phoenix, rises from the ashes of the old.

The stage is not long empty of a Caesar; the play's first mention of Octavius comes immediately after Antony's funeral oration. But Octavius is repeatedly described as 'young'; he is untried, an uninitiated novice, and there is in Antony's phrase 'no Rome of safety' for him yet (III. i. 289). It is not until the fourth act that he appears, still patronized by Antony: 'Octavius, I have seen more days than you' (IV. i. 18); in the third scene of that act 'young Octavius' is addressed or described by his novice's epithet no less than three times (92, 150, 165). But the next scene begins the fifth act, and with it his transition from boyhood to manhood, again manifested through a change of name. Antony, still condescending, instructs 'Octavius' to lead his troops to the left, but Octavius demurs; he will take the right. 'Why do you cross me in this exigent?' demands Antony, and the reply is worthy of the speaker's namesake: 'I do not cross you; but I will do so' (19–20). Only four lines later, we hear Antony for the first time address his colleague as 'Caesar', and 'Caesar' he remains, to Brutus (V. i. 56) and to himself (54). The 'peevish schoolboy' (61) has come of age, and the boast of 'always I am Caesar' is transferred to a new generation.

Julius Caesar thus offers its audience versions of the dangerous 'addition', the equally dangerous (because fallacious) belief in *nomen–omen*, and the initiation rite; of these it is the initiation rite which comes to occupy the most important position in the pattern of naming and renaming which animates so many of Shakespeare's plays.

In *Richard II*, for example, we can trace both a genuine pattern of initiation and a counterfeit of that pattern, as Richard and Bolingbroke each seek names which the other refuses to acknowledge. Bolingbroke progresses steadily through a sequence of names – Hereford, Lancaster, King Henry IV – insisting at each stage upon the perquisites of his title:

> *Berkeley*   My Lord of Hereford, my message is to you.
> *Bolingbroke*   My lord, my answer is – to Lancaster;
>   And I am come to seek that name in England.
>   (II. iii. 69–71)

Symbolically, on his return from exile, he chooses as his chief public complaint the fact that Richard has removed his engraved name from the buildings of the Lancaster estate: 'From my own windows torn my household coat, / Raced out my impresse, leaving me no sign . . . To show the world I am a gentleman' (III. i. 24–7). But Bolingbroke believes that kingship is a role, rather than an anointed right bestowed immutably on a chosen person; just as he can alter his behavior to suit the tastes of Northumberland on the one hand, and an oyster-wench on the other, so his progression from name to name is an act of expedience, culminating in a political objective. Neither the temporary loss of a name, nor the gaining of one, affects his nature and his confident sense of self; even when he has attained the kingship, his principal interest in 'name' is lineal, rather than personal, and centers on the dissolute behavior of his 'unthrifty son' (v. iii. 1). It is only at the close of the play, with a change in Richard's name rather than his own, that we see him truly moved, and determined for the first time to legitimize the stolen name of 'King'.

For Richard, of course, the quest for the name is vital, the more so because of his insistent denial that his name is lost. As we have already noted, his desperate cry of 'Arm, arm, my name!' (III. ii. 86) is greeted by the news that the citizens are deserting; for Richard the call to arms is, tragically, not metaphor but an articulation of literal truth – of the lost *nomen–omen* relationship in which he steadfastly believes. The impertinent Northumberland predictably takes a more harshly realistic view, in a revealing exchange with the Duke of York:

> *Northumberland*   Richard not far from hence hath hid his
>   head.

York   It would beseem the Lord Northumberland
   To say 'King Richard'. . . .
Northumberland   Your grace mistakes; only to be brief
   Left I his title out.
York   The time hath been
   Would you have been so brief with him, he would
   Have been so brief with you to shorten you,
   For taking so the head, your whole head's length.
                                        (III. iii. 6–14)

But that time is already long past. In the deposition scene (IV. i.)
it is Richard himself who finally disclaims the name, refusing the
courtesy title of 'my lord' offered by Northumberland, almost as
if he had overheard the conversation with York:

   No lord of thine, thou haught, insulting man,
   Nor no man's lord: I have no name, no title,
   No, not that name was given me at the font
   But 'tis usurped.   (IV. i. 253–6)

To his mind, in losing the title of 'King', he loses also the name
of 'Richard', and becomes, as Coriolanus will later become, 'a
kind of nothing, titleless' (*Coriol.* v. i. 13). His belief in the
nomen–omen relationship, the kingship of persona, compels
him to regard an 'unkinged Richard' as an oxymoron. As he
reasons in his soliloquy at Pomfret Castle, to 'play . . . in one
person many people' (v. v. 31) is, for him, to be 'nothing' (38); to
lose his title is also to lose his name.

   Yet Richard's name is not irretrievably lost, nor is its power
altogether gone. Like the ghost of Caesar, the corpse of the dead
Richard returns to confront his usurper, and the body of the
murdered king is for the first time given its full and proper
name:

   Great king, within this coffin I present
   Thy buried fear: herein all breathless lies
   The mightiest of thy greatest enemies,
   Richard of Bordeaux, by me hither brought.
                                        (v. vi. 30–3)

Exton's action and his pronouncement make Richard's name
into a word of power. 'Richard of Bordeaux', like 'Julius Caesar'
and 'Edgar and thy father's son', reunites the individual with his

lineage and heritage. Too late, Bolingbroke begins to realize that he, like the Roman conspirators, has chosen Richard's wrong name – seized the public name and not the secret or sacred one. He has appropriated a kingship, but the power of Richard of Bordeaux escapes him, and the name of King Richard, 'that sweet lovely rose' (*1HIV* I. iii. 173), comes inexorably to haunt his troubled reign.

Just as the name of the slain king haunts Brutus and Bolingbroke (as Henry IV), so his father's name haunts Hamlet. Claudius has usurped the kingdom, the queen, and the name of king, but Hamlet sees himself as a usurper as well – he bears his father's name, but feels unworthy of it. 'I'll call thee Hamlet, / King, father, royal Dane' (I. iv. 44–5), he apostrophizes the ghost; these noble additions should be the son's as well. But, like Edgar, he feels that he has been dispossessed of them. The *nomen–omen* fitness of the names of young and old Fortinbras taunts him; in that case the son is the image of the father, and though a novice, 'of unimprovèd mettle hot and full' (I. i. 96), young Fortinbras soon proves himself 'a delicate and tender prince' (IV. iv. 48), a destined ruler. But young Hamlet is persuaded that he bears no such resemblance to his father, the king. Like Edgar, therefore, he chooses a disguise, an 'antic disposition', which leads others to the same conclusion he has already drawn: that Hamlet *is not* Hamlet. His own inadequacies, as he sees them, coupled with Claudius' act of usurpation, have robbed him of his name.

Hamlet's reassertion of the lost name is, ironically, assisted by his school-fellows and age-mates, Rosencrantz and Guildenstern. Their failure becomes the means of his success. And the literal mark used to achieve that success is of particular interest, as Hamlet himself explains:

> I had my father's signet in my purse,
> Which was the model of that Danish seal,
> Folded the writ up in the form of th' other,
> Subscribed it, gave 't th' impression, placed it safely,
> The changeling never known.   (v. ii. 49–53)

With his father's ring he signs his name to the paper and the deed. In one uncalculated action ('Why, even in that was heaven ordinant' – 48) Prince Hamlet thus claims the authority of King

Hamlet, and exercises the prerogative of the royal seal, the king's official signature. 'Denmark', for him, like 'Egypt', for Cleopatra, is more than a country of origin – it is a surname, part of his identity and role; the play contains allusions to 'the main voice of Denmark' (I. iii. 28), and to 'jocund health[s] that Denmark drinks today' (I. ii. 125), both references to Claudius, while Gertrude implores Hamlet to 'look like a friend on Denmark' (I. ii. 69), again alluding to her present husband. Thus, by the act of using his father's seal, the emblem of Denmark, Hamlet lays claim once more to his name and its proper additions.

As we saw in *King Lear*, so also in *Hamlet* the importance of reclaiming the name is emphasized by a rearrangement of dramatic chronology, in order to place the literal moment of self-declaration at center stage. The shipboard incident with its account of the seal, like Edgar's tale of his talk with Gloucester, is presented to the audience at one remove – retold, rather than acted. Moreover, this incident, which occurs before the graveyard scene, is not retold until after it. The scene which therefore draws our attention, and which contains the crucial declaration, is the highly charged moment at Ophelia's graveside, when Hamlet challenges the grieving Laertes. As Edgar had unfolded himself, declaring, 'My name is Edgar, and thy father's son,' so Hamlet, suddenly revealing himself, steps forward to proclaim,

> This is I,
> Hamlet the Dane. (v. i. 257–8)

Private name and public name, personal name and surname, both long denied, come together at last in this self-assertion. The epithets addressed by a son to the ghost of his father are now worn as the son's own right; the dramatic tension which has extended from the initial address, 'I'll call thee Hamlet, / King, father, royal Dane' is resolved by the rightful appropriation of that address: 'This is I, / Hamlet the Dane.' Again the rite of passage has concluded with the gaining of a new name. If we need further corroboration of the importance of the name here, we may look to Hamlet's ensuing apology to Laertes, remembering that only once before in the play (IV. ii. 3) has he referred to himself by name at all:

Was't Hamlet wronged Laertes? Never Hamlet.
If Hamlet from himself be ta'en away,
And when he's not himself does wrong Laertes,
Then Hamlet does it not, Hamlet denies it.
                                        (v. ii. 235–8)

It is almost as if he enjoys, for the first time, the sound of his own name.

For Hamlet and Edgar, as to a certain extent for Richard and Bolingbroke, the experience of the naming ritual is the same: the novice begins with a personal name, but loses it or chooses to conceal it; he then passes some time in a nameless state, during which he is engaged in a quest or an initiation; having successfully undergone this rite, he acquires a new, public name, or else recovers his lost name with an 'addition' denoting family, rank, or social position. This is a basic pattern of maturation in Shakespeare's plays, and, as we have already noted, aspects of it can be found in many of the histories and tragedies. In *King Henry IV Part I*, for example, Prince Hal tries on a variety of names. Scornfully described by Hotspur as the 'sword-and-buckler Prince of Wales' (I. iii. 228) and the 'nimble-footed madcap Prince of Wales' (IV. i. 94), both belittlings of his right to office, he will later lay claim to that title through his actions in battle: 'And God forbid a shallow scratch should drive / The Prince of Wales from such a field as this' (v. iv. 9–10). As the play begins, we hear his father, the king, express the significant wish that his son be proved a changeling, swapped at birth for the valiant Hotspur, and many others suggest that this is in fact the case – that Hal is not his father's son. To become 'son Harry' (v. v. 39) he faces down his namesake on the field at Shrewsbury, in a formal scene of combat which once again marks a coming of age:

> *Hotspur*   If I mistake not, thou art Harry Monmouth.
> *Prince*   Thou speak'st as if I would deny my name.
> *Hotspur*   My name is Harry Percy.
> *Prince*   Why, then I see a very valiant rebel of the name.
>   I am the Prince of Wales, and think not, Percy,
>   To share with me in glory any more.   (v. iv. 57–62)

Hal, who by his previous behavior has indeed denied his name, here lays direct claim to both name and title. England cannot support two Harrys – so Hotspur must die. 'I am the Prince of Wales,' like 'This is I, / Hamlet the Dane,' joins together the sundered pieces of personal and public roles, and announces the change for which the regained name is a talisman. In the subsequent plays chronicling Hal's life and reign, this initiation pattern is twice repeated, each time accompanied by a further change of name. When Falstaff addresses the new monarch as 'King Hal' at the close of *Part II* (v. v. 41), we perceive the magnitude of his error, for that name and that title are irreconcilable. And when King Henry re-christens himself 'Harry le Roy' as he talks in disguise to the soldiers at Agincourt (*HV* iv. i. 49) we see a new kind of ruler fashioning himself to suit his changing country.

The love tragedies, too, include elements of the renaming ritual. Romeo's growth to maturity involves a change both in his own name and in that of his beloved. Prior to his meeting with Juliet he has exhibited all the symptoms of the classic Petrarchan infatuation: he roams the woods in darkness, and by day 'makes himself an artificial night' (i. i. 143), all for the love of the tantalizingly distant, maddeningly chaste lady Rosaline. Friar Lawrence calls this 'doting'. Despite his facility with quip and sword, Romeo is at this point still in many ways a child.

But the sight of Juliet brings about a change in his behavior and rhetoric which is confirmed by his willingness to change his name. 'Wherefore art thou Romeo?'; 'Deny thy father and refuse thy name'; 'What's Montague . . .?'; 'What's in a name?' (ii. ii. 33–43). Juliet's insistent questions are all in a way invitations to the quester to sever himself from his child's name or son's name, and to seek a new one through action and initiation. 'Romeo, doff thy name,' she urges, and unhesitatingly he consents to do so:

> Call me but love, and I'll be new baptized;
> Henceforth I never will be Romeo.   (50–1)

The new name he chooses for himself is appropriate; he is not only her love but for this moment 'Love' himself, Cupid, Eros, who 'with love's light wings' can o'erperch walls. The Romeo who doted on Rosaline has disappeared as effortlessly as the memory of Rosaline herself: 'I have forgot that name and that name's woe' (II. iii. 46). Unluckily for Romeo, however, his initiation involves not one but two actions associated with coming of age: in rapid succession he marries and he kills, and the second action dooms the first. Juliet's playful image of danger and loss now begins to come true:

> Bondage is hoarse and may not speak aloud,
> Else would I tear the cave where Echo lies
> And make her airy tongue more hoarse than mine
> With repetition of 'My Romeo!'   (II. ii. 161–4)

When she does call out his name repeatedly, at the news of his banishment and Tybalt's death, Romeo's first, histrionic response touches, likewise, on an ironic truth:

>   As if that name,
> Shot from the deadly level of a gun,
> Did murder her; as that name's cursèd hand
> Murdered her kinsman. O, tell me, friar, tell me,
> In what vile part of this anatomy
> Doth my name lodge? Tell me, that I may sack
> The hateful mansion.   (III. iii. 102–8)

Her forgiveness and her love are not enough. The tomb to which she is taken mocks the power of the name to summon its bearer, as Echo's cave mocks its own lonely inhabitant. To Juliet he is 'My Romeo', but he is also a Montague, and that is a name he can lose now only through his own death.

For Troilus and Cressida, the consequences of mingling love and war are, if possible, even more disastrous. In the play which tells their story, *nomen–omen* reappears in a malignant guise: 'Let all constant men be Troiluses, all false women Cressids, and all brokers-between Pandars!' (III. ii. 200–2). The archetypes predate the play, and are determinative; free will in names, as in actions, is 'slave to limit' (III. ii. 82). When the anguished Troilus observes the dalliance between Diomedes and Cressida, his confusion is directly related to the wish to make the name equal to the thing: 'This is, and is not, Cressid' (V. ii. 144). The meaning of 'Cressid' to him will not square with the facts as they appear.

The audience's familiarity with 'Troilus', 'Cressida', and 'Pandar' as archetypes or literary clichés gives these lines a curious doubleness in time, as if the play we are watching is or might be different from the story so often told before: against all reason we hold to the wish that for once Cressida will be faithful, and Troilus at last rewarded in his love. But Cressida's prayer, 'Make Cressid's name the very crown of falsehood / If ever she leave Troilus!' (IV. ii. 101–2) inevitably fulfills itself, and the play's characters are locked into their names and roles. Cressid *is* Cressid, despite Troilus' confusion; her 'secret' name is the name given her by legend, known to the audience and playwright, but not to Troilus – or to herself. Neither of them, of course, suspects that their destinies are fixed by history, and doubly sealed by their very names. The spectacle thus presented, of archetypes struggling blindly against their own defined identities, is – like the play itself – at once ironic and tragic.

We saw in *Romeo and Juliet* the beginning of the name quest, the novice's first step toward maturity, and in *Troilus and Cressida* the inexorability of the sacred or legendary name, together with the power wielded by those who know it. In *Antony and Cleopatra* we see Shakespeare coming to terms with the end of the quest for the name, the drama of the name regained. Cleopatra, of course, bears many names, among them Isis, Dido, Venus and the generic cognomen 'Egypt'. Like Bolingbroke, she knows the name game, and can shift from one role to another virtually at will. But from the first moment that we hear of Antony – and long before we meet him – he is presented as a man who has lost his name, and with it that name's power; as one of the Roman soldiers remarks,

> sometimes, when he is not Antony,
> He comes too short of that great property
> Which still should go with Antony.   (I. i. 57–9)

To this opinion Octavius likewise gives his assent; Antony, who was once a legend, now loses himself in dotage, and is 'not Antony'. The name of 'Antony' here carries a historical, almost a mythical weight; it is a category, and not merely a personal name – as we would say, 'a Hercules', or 'a Hitler'. And in his frustration, Antony himself is occasionally prone to this usage, as when he enters the throne room to find a messenger from Octavius kissing Cleopatra's hand:

> Authority melts from me. Of late, when I cried, 'Ho!'
> Like boys unto a muss, kings would start forth,
> And cry, 'Your will?' Have you no ears? I am
> Antony yet.   (III. xiii. 90–3)

There is pathos here, for this Antony no longer commands kings; his forces depleted, his troops deserting, he has shed most of the power which once was his. Yet he is hardly a novice. How then can we call this an initiation, or a self-discovery? If we can do so, it is, I think, by looking at the other meaning of 'Antony' – the Egyptian meaning, which is given so full an explication in Cleopatra's dream vision (v. ii. 74–100). In this reading, Antony is rather lover than soldier, his exploits in the field all confirmatory actions in the service of his lady. Much the same irony is present here as in *Troilus*: the Roman soldiers understand in 'Antony' the substance of a soldier and ruler; the audience, which knows the rest of the legend, perceives that he has only now become the true 'Antony', a warrior who gave all for love.

The voice in which he addresses her is that of a man on a quest:

> Dost thou hear, lady?
> If from the field I shall return once more
> To kiss these lips, I will appear in blood;
> I and my sword will earn our chronicle. . . .
>   Come,
> Let's have one other gaudy night.   (III. xiii. 172–83)

And Cleopatra, delighted at this restoration, replies,

> It is my birthday.
> I had thought t' have held it poor. But since my lord
> Is Antony again, I will be Cleopatra.   (185–7)

The two names are mutually sustaining and restorative. The mention of Cleopatra's birthday, which Shakespeare takes from Plutarch,[14] is here appropriately juxtaposed to an image of re-birth through the name. In short, the situation in *Antony and Cleopatra* bears a certain resemblance to a phenomenon we noticed in *Julius Caesar* and *Richard II*: the singling out of the wrong name. Cleopatra's Antony is in this moment restored, even as the Roman Antony prepares to die; at the end of this same scene, as if to emphasize the dichotomy, his Roman aide Enobarbus resolves to leave him. The death of Antony, when it comes, is tragically linked with Cleopatra's use (or misuse) of his name. Terrified of his anger after she has deserted his troops in battle, she takes refuge in the monument and sends the eunuch Mardian with a message:

> Mardian, go tell him I have slain myself:
> Say that the last I spoke was 'Antony.'
> And word it, prithee, piteously.   (IV. xiii. 7–9)

All too faithfully, Mardian performs his charge:

> The last she spake
> Was 'Antony! most noble Antony!'
> Then in the midst a tearing groan did break
> The name of Antony; it was divided
> Between her heart and lips: she rend'red life,
> Thy name so buried in her.   (IV. xiv. 29–34)

So effective is this piteous wording that it immediately realizes itself as truth. As the name of Antony is fictively broken and buried, so the living Antony resolves himself for death, as if the (supposed) destruction of his name wielded some magical power over the bearer of that name. 'Unarm, Eros. The long day's task is done, / And we must sleep' (35–6). Eros declines to stab his captain, and kills himself instead; yet if the soldier Eros is not his master's slayer, the fault may yet lie with his namesake: 'I will be / A bridegroom in my death, and run into 't / As to a lover's bed. . . . Eros, / Thy master dies thy scholar' (99–102). As it happens, Shakespeare did not invent the name of Antony's companion, nor did he choose the names of Cleopatra's hand-maidens, Iras and Charmian; yet it is clear that Antony dies in the company of love, and Cleopatra attended by her chief attri-butes of ire and charm. Thus in *Antony and Cleopatra* names become more than things – become powerful watchwords, easy to misinterpret, and tragic to misuse. Antony, long an initiate of war, remains almost throughout a novice in love; the triumph of regaining the name is followed immediately by the careless cursing of that name, at the direction of one whom Antony has acknowledged to be a 'witch' (IV. xii. 47).

Of all Shakespeare's heroes, perhaps the one who delights

most in his new-won name is Coriolanus; yet, as we have
already seen, it is his incautious use of that name which leads
directly to his death. Like Bolingbroke and Hal, Coriolanus
progresses through many names in the course of the play. When
we first meet him he is Caius Marcius, son of Volumnia, but
soon he earns the surname of 'Coriolanus', conqueror of the city
of Corioles. The way in which he wins and accepts that name is
worth our attention: declining any share of the spoils of war, he
consents to receive only his general Cominius' horse, and his
proclamation:

> from this time,
> For what he did before Corioles, call him,
> With all th' applause and clamor of the host,
> Caius Marcius Coriolanus.
> Bear the addition nobly ever!   (I. ix. 62–6)

But no sooner has he been given this honorific surname than the
audience is offered a chance to see what names mean, and do not
mean, to Caius Marcius. Like any hero, he has the right to beg a
favor of his generals, and this he promptly does, recalling that in
the city of Corioles lives a poor man who once gave him shelter.
'I request you', he says, 'To give my poor host freedom' (86–7).
'O, well begged!' cry the generals, and 'Marcius, his name?'
(87, 89). But Marcius has forgotten his name.

> By Jupiter, forgot!
> I am weary; yea, my memory is tired.
> Have we no wine here?   (90–2)

Personal names have no significance for him. Did the man live,
or die, because Marcius had forgotten his name – or was he ever
thought of again? Could knowing his name have saved him?
Things without names tend to slip from our memories, as
Marcius himself is shortly to learn.

In the middle of the play, Coriolanus undergoes a process of
stripping which is characteristic of the hero of Shakespearean
tragedy. From the man who has everything – mother, wife, son,
public honors, even briefly the consulate – he becomes a man
who has nothing – a man who, like Edgar, wears a disguise, and
temporarily lacks a name. Arriving at the home of his former
enemy, he is greeted by Aufidius, 'the second name of men'

(IV. vi. 126) in Cominius' phrase, and subjected to an insistent catechism:

> Whence com'st thou? What wouldst thou? Thy name?
> Why speak'st not? Speak, man. What's thy name?

In reply, Coriolanus unmuffles himself:

> *Coriolanus*   If, Tullus,
>   Not yet thou know'st me . . .
>   necessity
>   Commands me name myself.
> *Aufidius*   What is thy name?
> *Coriolanus*   A name unmusical to the Volscians' ears,
>   And harsh in sound to thine.
> *Aufidius*   Say, what's thy name?
>   Thou has a grim appearance, and thy face
>   Bears a command in't. . . .
>   What's thy name?
> *Coriolanus*   Prepare thy brow to frown. Know'st thou
>   me yet?
> *Aufidius*   I know thee not. Thy name!
> *Coriolanus*   My name is Caius Marcius, who hath done
>   To thee particularly, and to all the Volsces,
>   Great hurt and mischief; thereto witness may
>   My surname, Coriolanus. The painful service,
>   The extreme dangers, and the drops of blood
>   Shed for my thankless country, are requited
>   But with that surname. . . .
>   Only that name remains.
>   (IV. v. 57–77)

'Only that name remains.' Aufidius is right to wonder what this stranger in his camp may represent. In his own view, Coriolanus is no longer a man, but just a living name, or more properly a living surname. His addition of 'Coriolanus' replaces, and obliterates, all his other names and titles, leaving him no wife, no mother, no kin. In an earlier speech to the senators extolling the virtues of Coriolanus on the battlefield, Cominius described him in terms which were disturbingly machine-like: 'from face to foot / He was a thing of blood, whose every motion / Was timed with dying cries' (II. ii. 108–10). Now, newly ensconced in Corioles, this inhuman abstraction seems to be all that is left of Caius Marcius Coriolanus. On the one hand, his name has become a magic talisman to the Volscians; the 'soldiers use him as the grace 'fore meat' (IV. vii. 3). On the other hand, the man himself disclaims all names.

Coming to plead with him for mercy on behalf of Rome, Cominius finds that he has rejected even his surname:

> He would not seem to know me. . . .
> Yet one time did he call me by my name.
> I urged our old acquaintance, and the drops
> That we have bled together. Coriolanus
> He would not answer to; forbade all names;
> He was a kind of nothing, titleless,
> Till he had forged himself a name o' th' fire
> Of burning Rome.   (v. i. 8–15)

He will not be known by the proud title which commemorates a Roman victory; yet what title, what surname, could be awarded to the Roman general who conquers Rome? The concept is an oxymoron; the would-be conqueror remains, therefore, effectively dehumanized, 'a kind of nothing, titleless'. Characteristically, and with his usual charming obtuseness, the old counsellor Menenius when he goes to see him pleads from the other extreme, claiming exactly the kind of name Marcius has forbidden. 'My son Coriolanus' (v. ii. 63); 'thy old father Menenius' (70) – these are names that have long been rejected, long abandoned as too painful and vulnerable. The meeting between the two is framed by a scene that is at once painful and comic, as Menenius, sailing confidently into the Volscian camp, boasts to the watchmen of the power of *his* name:

> *Menenius*   My name hath touched your ears: it is Mene-
>   nius.
> *First Watch*   Be it so; go back. The virtue of your name
>   Is not here passable.   (v. ii. 11–13)

His name is not a magic word, a password, a shibboleth, despite what he may think. But Menenius presses further:

Menenius   Sirrah, if thy captain knew I were here, he would
use me with estimation.
First Watch   Come, my captain knows you not.
Menenius   I mean thy general.   (51–4)

Menenius has the wrong name, the wrong addition, yet again –
and he certainly has the wrong name when Coriolanus at last
appears: 'My son Coriolanus . . . O my son, my son!' (70). We
may be reminded of Falstaff's ill-chosen cry, 'God save thee, my
sweet boy!' (2*HIV* v. v. 43) addressed to the newly crowned
king. For Coriolanus has made up his mind: 'Wife, mother,
child, I know not' (81). He disavows all familial and lineal ties,
and his one word for Menenius is 'Away!' The watch, standing
at the fringes of this exchange, now has its inevitable revenge:

First Watch   Now, sir, is your name Menenius?
Second Watch   'Tis a spell, you see, of much power.
                                                              (94–6)

The magic power of names is completely denied by the world
into which Coriolanus has withdrawn. For if they know his
name, they will have power over him; and if he uses their
names, he admits to a relationship which makes him vulnerable.
To be nameless is to be unassailable, like a god.

But Coriolanus is not unassailable; he, too, has a secret name,
and when that name is pronounced he will respond. It is for this
reason that Volumnia approaches him as she does. She arrives
accompanied by his wife, Virgilia, who in turn produces their
son as a kind of stage property, an emblem of longevity: I
'brought you forth this boy,' she says, 'to keep your name /
Living to time' (v. iii. 126–7). But Volumnia knows that this
kind of lineal afterlife is less important to him than the afterlife
afforded by fame and reputation in which she has schooled him.
Skillfully, she begins to work on his feelings of history:

> if thou conquer Rome, the benefit
> Which thou shalt thereby reap is such a name
> Whose repetition will be dogged with curses,
> Whose chronicle thus writ, 'The man was noble,
> But with his last attempt he wiped it out,
> Destroyed his country, and his name remains
> To th' ensuing age abhorred.'   (142–8)

Here is a name over which Coriolanus will have no control. His new addition will be abhorrent and unpronounceable: the living paradox of a Roman conqueror of Rome. The key to Volumnia's strategy here lies in her dual role: she is both the mythic embodiment of Rome, the she-wolf who suckled Romulus and Remus, and the human mother of a particular man. Artfully now she turns from the civic to the personal – roles which have long been conflated in her tutelage of her son – appealing to him as a private man: 'There's no man in the world / More bound to's mother . . . yet. . . . / To his surname Coriolanus 'longs more pride / Than pity to our prayers' (158–71). And this reversal has its intended effect, though Coriolanus is perceptive enough to see that such pity is 'most mortal to him' (v. iii. 189). No longer an 'engine', who 'wants nothing of a god but eternity and a heaven to throne in' (v. iv. 23–4), in taking his mother's hand and reaffirming the lineal bond he seals his own doom. For Aufidius has been listening, and Aufidius now knows the secret name. The scene in which he makes use of that knowledge is one of the most painful in the tragedies, and one which shows us the initiation pattern reversed, the hero turned back, step by step, from *cognomen* to *nomen*, from maturity to childhood.

Ironically, the scene begins with Coriolanus marching for the first time with the commoners, a man who has at last acknowledged his bond with humanity. But Aufidius' jealousy is inflamed, and he unconsciously echoes the attack of the Roman tribunes, with the same chosen epithet of vilification:

Aufidius   tell the traitor in the highest degree
    He hath abused your powers.
Coriolanus   Traitor! How now!
Aufidius   Ay, traitor, Marcius!
Coriolanus   Marcius!
Aufidius   Ay, Marcius, Caius Marcius! Dost thou think
    I'll grace thee with that robbery, thy stol'n name
    Coriolanus, in Corioles?   (v. vi. 84–9)

This is a point which has probably never occurred to Coriolanus: that the inhabitants of Corioles might object to his surname, which signifies that he has conquered their city. But the worst is yet to come, as the indictment proceeds: 'at his nurse's tears,' continues Aufidius, 'He whined and roared away your victory'

(96–7). 'Hear'st thou, Mars?' erupts Coriolanus, calling upon
his namesake, and Aufidius' reply is the final straw: 'Name not
the god, thou boy of tears!' (100). Not Mars' man, Marcius, but
'boy' – his final name as well as his first name, and a name so
truly given that Coriolanus can do nothing but repeat it in
disbelief: ' "Boy!" O slave!' ' "Boy!" False hound!'

> If you have writ your annals true, 'tis there,
> That, like an eagle in a dovecote, I
> Fluttered your Volscians in Corioles.
> Alone I did it. 'Boy'?   (v. vi. 102, 111–15)

'Boy' is the true and hidden aspect of Coriolanus' nature, an
aspect which, once articulated, has the status of the ominous
'secret name' of ritual. It is a name which accords with his pride,
his vanity, his sense of war as a sexual event bonding man to
man, his choice of war over statecraft, his relative indifference to
his wife and child – and, above all, his passionate love for, and
submission to, his mother. Rendered vulnerable by all of these,
he is mercilessly stripped of the lineaments of adulthood. The
literal *sparagmos*, or tearing to pieces of the hero which is his
fate, follows directly from this loss of name; once again, those
who know the secret name of a king or priest are able to rob him
of his power. The killing of the name here results, not in a
symbolic death and rebirth, but in a real death, only partially
compensated – if at all – by the promise that 'he shall have a
noble memory' (v. vi. 152). The secret *nomen* of 'boy' returns
Coriolanus to the role of novice from which he began.

To be a 'novice' in Shakespeare's plays is to be one not yet
learned in his craft or art – or in his own nature. Octavius is
called a novice by Antony – 'Triple-turned whore! 'Tis thou /
Hast sold me to this novice' (*A&C* iv. xii. 13–14) – because of his
inexperience in war, and the slain Edward of Wales is described
as a 'princely novice' who never lived to rule (*RIII* i. iv. 225);
according to Petruchio his fellow suitors are novices in love (*Shr.*
ii. i. 304), and the virginal Isabella in *Measure for Measure* is
appropriately described as 'a novice of this place' both because it
is a nunnery, and because she is untried in the ways of generosity and compassion. As we have noted, the Shakespearean
novices who most directly undergo a process of maturation in
the course of their plays are often those who, in doing so, pass

through the concomitant stages of losing and regaining their names. The situation of Coriolanus is really a variation of the naming pattern rather than a contrast to it, just as the name-quest of Romeo, though it does not complete the full cycle exemplified by Edgar or Hamlet, nonetheless partakes of many of its aspects. In each case the basic rhythm of movement, from personal name to lost name to new name or name regained, can be felt as animating the life – and sometimes the death – of the hero.

If the play itself is in some sense a ritual, it contains within it echoes and vestiges of other rituals. Juliet seeks to know what's in a name; Hamlet impishly demands of Osric, 'What imports the nomination of this gentleman?' (v. ii. 129–30). Both pose a version of the initiate's question, identifying the name as riddle, spell and watchword, as well as title, rank and lineage. For the author of the 'Will' sonnets, once publicly calumnized as considering himself 'the only Shake-scene in a country',[15] the quest for the name and that name's meaning offers the dramatic ritual of initiation as yet another significant metaphor for the knowledge of self.

NOTES

1 Sir James Frazer, *The New Golden Bough*, Theodor H. Gaster (ed.) (1890; rpt. [abridged] New York: Mentor Books, 1964), p. 235. Frazer's chapter on 'Tabooed words', pp. 235–46 (sections 181–8), supplemented and revised by Gaster (esp. pp. 176, 271–2), is the major source of anthropological data in this paragraph.

2 Mircea Eliade, *Rites and Symbols of Initiation; The Mysteries of Death and Rebirth*, Willard R. Trask (trans.) (originally published as *Birth and Rebirth*) (New York: Harper & Brothers, 1958; rpt. Harper & Row, 1975), p. 74.

3 Sir Thomas Malory, *Le Morte d'Arthur* (1906; rpt. London: J. M. Dent & Sons [Everyman's Library], 1963), I, p. 10 (Bk. I, Ch. v).

4 Malory, II, p. 167 (Bk. XIII, Ch. iv).

5 Malory, II, p. 166 (Bk. XIII, Ch. ii).

6 Malory, II, p. 178 (Bk. XIII, Ch. xi).

7 Malory, II, p. 175 (Bk. XIII, Ch. ix).

8 Bernard Knox, 'Sophocles' Oedipus', in Cleanth Brooks (ed.) *Tragic Themes in Western Literature* (New Haven: Yale University Press, 1955; rpt. 1966), p. 13.

9 Knox, p. 20.

10 In accordance with the comedy of humors, the most interesting names in the comedies and the comic names in the tragedies and histories tend to be static and stereotypical rather than progressive and emblematic: consider Touchstone, Sir Toby Belch, Bottom, Doll Tearsheet, Ancient Pistol.

11 Cf. 'Nomen atque omen quantivis iam est preti,' Plautus, *Persa*, 625 ('That's a name and omen worth any price').

12 T. J. B. Spencer (ed.) *Shakespeare's Plutarch: The Lives of Julius Caesar, Brutus, Marcus Antonius and Coriolanus in the Translation of Sir Thomas North* (Middlesex, England, and Baltimore, Maryland: Penguin Books, 1964, rpt. 1968), p. 296.

13 The frequency and peculiarity of spoken names in *Julius Caesar* has been remarked by numerous critics, including Dowden, Granville-Barker, G. Wilson Knight, L. C. Knights, and Maurice Charney. Recently, Madeleine Doran, in *Shakespeare's Dramatic Language* (Madison: University of Wisconsin Press, 1976), has argued for a balance and pairing between 'Caesar' and 'Brutus' in the play, with the third name of 'Roman' bringing them into equipoise. See her essay, ' "What should be in that 'Caesar'?" – Proper names in *Julius Caesar*' (pp. 120–53), for a thoughtful discussion of the iterations and resonances of these names. For further analysis of proper names in the play, Doran cites especially R. A. Foakes, 'An approach to *Julius Caesar*', *Shakespeare Quarterly*, v (1954), 259–70, and M. W. MacCallum, *Shakespeare's Roman Plays and their Background* (London, 1910), pp. 228–32 and n. 1.

14 Spencer, p. 272.

15 Robert Greene, *Groats-worth of witte, bought with a million of Repentance* (1592), sig. F1^v.

4

PLAIN SPEAKING

'I TAKE THEE AT THY WORD'

⁕⁕⁕

> *Hieronimo*   Each one of us must act his part
> In unknown languages,
> That it may breed the more variety.
> As you, my lord, in Latin, I in Greek,
> You in Italian, and for because I know
> That Bel-imperia hath practisèd the French,
> In courtly French shall all her phrases be.
> *Bel-imperia*   You mean to try my cunning, then, Hieroni-
> mo.
> *Balthazar*   But this will be a mere confusion,
> And hardly shall we all be understood.
>

The Spanish Tragedy IV. i. 171–80

> . . . for mine own part, it was Greek to me.
>

Julius Caesar I. ii. 281

I

An infant, according to its etymology, is one who is unable to speak; the word comes from Latin *in*, meaning not, plus *fans*, the present participle of *fari*, to speak.[1] In Shakespeare's plays infancy is often defined in just this way, by its lack of speech; we may think of Jaques' 'infant, / Mewling and puking in the nurse's arms' (*AYLI* II. vii. 142–3), or Cassandra's 'Soft infancy, that nothing canst but cry' (*T&C* II. ii. 105). The most extensive mention of infancy in this connection, however, takes place, as we might expect, in *The Winter's Tale*, the one play in which an infant plays a central role. There Hermione reproaches Leontes for misinterpreting the motives of Polixenes, 'whose love had spoke, / Even since it could speak, from an infant, freely, / That it was yours' (III. ii. 68–70), and later Leontes, beholding the supposed 'statue' of his wife, invites it to

> Chide me, dear stone, that I may say indeed
> Thou art Hermione; or rather, thou art she
> In thy not chiding; for she was as tender
> As infancy and grace. (v. iii. 24–7)

Both references seem to depend, at least in part, upon a literal reading of 'infancy'. The point is made even clearer by Paulina, when she emerges from prison bearing the infant Perdita in her arms. She will show it to the king, she says, in hopes that he may relent:

> The silence often of pure innocence
> Persuades, when speaking fails. (II. ii. 40–1)

Not to speak, then, may be appropriate for a newborn child; for an adult, however, it is a different matter. Thersites describes the vaunting Ajax as one who is 'grown . . . languageless, a monster' (T&C III. iii. 262–3), and when Iago abdicates language, he abdicates the last vestiges of humanity: 'From this time forth I never will speak word' (Oth. v. ii. 303). Cordelia's famous 'Love, and be silent' (Lr I. i. 62) is an appeal to the pre-verbal bond between parent and child, but for that reason it is both culpable and vulnerable; in the fallen world of adulthood silence is a dangerously ambiguous kind of language, which often prompts misinterpretation. Hearing her sister Goneril speak glowingly of 'A love that makes breath poor, and speech unable' (60), Cordelia sees all language as tarnished beyond use. For her the language of love has been usurped, as for Hamlet the language of mourning has been usurped by the Claudius court; 'the trappings and the suits of woe' (I. ii. 86) seem to him capitulations to the prevailing rhetoric of hypocrisy, and to avoid the appearance of complicity he doffs his inky cloak and assumes the antic disposition of the fool – together with the fool's doubling language. But Cordelia's retreat to silence, like Hamlet's refuge in madness, places her greatly at risk; just as the infant Perdita fails to convert Leontes, Cordelia's silence only enrages Lear. We might say that her Shakespearean antitype is Lavinia in *Titus Andronicus*, who, though with 'her hands cut off, and her tongue cut out, and ravished' (II. iv. SD), is nonetheless able to 'speak' to her father and make herself understood – first by manipulating the pages of a book, and then by writing in the sand with a staff guided by her mouth and mutilated limbs.

In Shakespeare's plays learning to speak is a sign of responsible adulthood, yet another rite of passage – a coming of age – for the protagonist. In fact, language and humanity are often presented as mutually defining; the death of John of Gaunt, for example, is announced by reference to his loss of speech: 'His tongue is now a stringless instrument' (*RII* II. i. 149). In the same play Mowbray, hearing his sentence of banishment, likewise equates it with dying:

> The language I have learnt these forty years,
> My native English, now I must forgo,
> And now my tongue's use is to me no more
> Than an unstringèd viol or a harp. . . .
> I am too old to fawn upon a nurse,
> Too far in years to be a pupil now;
> What is thy sentence then but speechless death,
> Which robs my tongue from breathing native breath?
> (I. iii. 159–73)

Those who voluntarily abandon speech effectively dehumanize themselves, by denying the linguistic bond among men. Thus Pericles, believing that he has lost both wife and child, chooses to lose speech as well; when his ship arrives at Mytilene he is described as 'a man who for this three months hath not spoken / To anyone' (v. i. 25–6). His reawakening to life and language is accomplished, appropriately, by his daughter Marina, though neither at first recognizes the other. So profound is Pericles' despair that he turns rudely away from her ministrations, but when she begins to talk of her parentage a change takes place; she senses in his silence some deep attention:

> I will desist.
> But there is something glows upon my cheek,
> And whispers in mine ear, 'Go not till he speak.'
> (97–9)

When he does speak, in the very next line, the act marks a return to humanity and kinship: by questioning her, he finds his daughter, and himself.

At times the election of silence is a sign not of pain or weakness but of a kind of perverse strength. We have already noticed that Iago abandons the tool of language which has served him so malignly but so well, and thereby moves closer to the status of 'demi-devil' Othello imputes to him. Similarly in *Much Ado About Nothing* the Machiavellian Don John characterizes himself – and is characterized by others – as a man 'not of many words' (I. i. 153). A particularly striking instance of the dehumanizing power of silence occurs in the famous deposition scene of *Richard II*, for in that scene Richard talks almost without pause, though even he perceives that he has lost his onstage audience ('God save the king! Will no man say "Amen"? / Am I both priest and clerk? Well, then, amen' – IV. i. 172–3). Bolingbroke, on the other hand, confines himself to a few functional inquiries and commands, put forth with the utmost spareness: 'Are you contented to resign the crown?' (199); 'Go, some of you, and fetch a looking-glass' (267); and finally, 'Go, some of you, convey him to the Tower' (315). And when Richard's play has come to its melodramatic end with the breaking of the glass, Bolingbroke remains impassive and aloof: 'Mark, silent king, the moral of this sport' (289) implores Richard – but the play has different meanings for actor and spectator, and nothing demonstrates the futility of Richard's performance more strongly than the silence of the new king.

Sometimes, although speech is not lost, syntax is; the emotional pressures brought to bear on the individual result in a temporary loss of control which is mirrored by a loss of control over language. The clearest example here is perhaps Othello, whose formerly eloquent periods are reduced to gibberish under Iago's expert tutelage:

Handkerchief – confessions – handkerchief! – To confess, and be hanged for his labor – first to be hanged, and then to confess! . . . It is not words that shakes me thus. – Pish! Noses, ears, and lips? Is't possible? – Confess – Handkerchief? – O devil! (IV. i. 38–44)

The failure of syntax here is symptomatic: If the ability to speak demarcates that which is human, the fragmentation of language indicates a fall from full humanity, and from human dignity. The irony of 'it is not words that shakes me thus' is dual: Iago's false words have reduced Othello to this state, but his own words, and his inability to control them, are the signs of his reduced condition.

A further example can be found in the degeneration of Lear's speech, which like Othello's undergoes a process of extreme fragmentation. It would be foolhardy to deny that there is a kind of eloquence in 'kill, kill, kill, kill, kill, kill!' (IV. vi. 187), 'Now, now, now, now' (172), 'Howl, howl, howl, howl!' (V. iii. 259) or 'Never, never, never, never, never' (310), but it is an eloquence which emerges despite the language, rather than because of it. The strings of words each replicating the last, as if they could go on forever, draw a diagram of the speaker's unspeakable agony. It is impossible to parse such a sentence; like the wheel of fire, turning forever in hell, the words succeed one another without change or cease.

From here it is but a short jump to *Macbeth*, where

> Tomorrow, and tomorrow, and tomorrow
> Creeps in this pretty pace from day to day,
> To the last syllable of recorded time.   (v. v. 19–21)

The familiar metaphor is richly suggestive; to measure time by syllables is to draw a direct analogy between human life and human language. Here 'tomorrow' replaces 'howl' or 'kill', but the image is much the same – the future to Macbeth looks very like that line of future kings born of Banquo's seed, which seems to 'stretch out to th' crack of doom' (IV. i. 117).

At the other end of the linguistic scale, and in its way equally inexpressive, is the kind of ornate and obfuscating diction that characterizes figures like the chattering 'chough' Osric, or Don Armado, who will imminently 'turn sonnet', or the 'popinjay' with the 'pouncet box' who so irritates Hotspur. It is a style unwisely burlesqued by Kent, when Cornwall reproaches him for his plain speech: 'Sir, in good faith, in sincere verity, / Under th' allowance of your great aspect, / Whose influence, like the wreath of radiant fire / On flick'ring Phoebus' front – ' (*Lr* II. ii. 107–10). Here language may in fact be said to obstruct and prevent communication. The Shakespearean *locus classicus* for this mode of excess is *Love's Labor's Lost*, a play which is directly concerned with the problem of learning to speak. We could point to almost any passage in the play as an illustration here – from Costard's delighted discovery that a 'gardon' is worth elevenpence farthing more than a 'remuneration', to Boyet's 'translation' of the language of the 'Muscovites' from English to English, to Berowne's disavowal of ornate language which, inevitably, takes the form of a sonnet neatly concealed in the text.[2] Perhaps the most telling moment of all, however, is Marcade's announcement of the death of the King of France, which signals a coming of age not only for his daughter the princess, but also for Navarre and his lords. Significantly, in this play of languages, the news of the king's death is transmitted without words. The messenger's cautious preamble, 'The king your father – 'is interrupted by the princess: 'Dead, for my life!' – leaving him to reply only, 'Even so. My tale is told' (v. ii. 717–19). Once again the unspeakable remains unspoken. But even death seems not to educate Navarre, who pleads with the ladies to remain in a lengthy passage so rhetorically complicated that the audience must echo the princess's distress: 'I understand you not. My griefs are double' (750). Only at this point does Berowne express his plea for unadorned language in language sufficiently unadorned: 'Honest plain words best pierce the ear of grief' (751). But his initiation is not over; for a twelvemonth he must visit 'the speechless sick' and make them smile. Rosaline's homily, 'A jest's prosperity lies in the ear / Of him that hears it, never in the tongue / Of him that makes it' (859–61) is not only good moral sense but a sound articulation of the importance of plain talk in Shakespeare – the humanized communication between man and man.

A very similar development takes place in *Much Ado About Nothing*: with justice, Benedick calls Beatrice 'my Lady Tongue' (II. i. 265), while Beatrice observes that 'an excellent man' would be one whose qualities were midway between those of Don John ('too like an image and says nothing') and Benedick ('too like my lady's eldest son, evermore tattling' – II. i. 6–9). Again language threatens to prevent courtship rather than to make it possible, although it is ironically the lovers' similarity in speaking which signals to their friends – and to the audience – their suitability for one another. Happily both Beatrice and Benedick are compelled to listen rather than to speak by the ruses of their friends, and a last minute reversion to their earlier verbal sparring is silenced at last by a kiss: 'Peace! I will stop your mouth' (v. iv. 97).

We may notice that Berowne's reference to 'honest plain words' has a counterpart in *Much Ado*, when Benedick complains that Claudio has changed since he has fallen in love. 'He was wont to speak plain and to the purpose, like an honest man and a soldier; and now is he turned orthography; his words are a very fantastical banquet' (ii. iii. 17–20). Very frequently 'plain' is the word Shakespearean characters choose to denote appropriate and straightforward language. Because of the meanings imparted to that word by modern critics in their discussions of the sixteenth-century lyric, it may be useful – so as to avoid misunderstanding – to explore for a moment what Shakespeare appears to mean by 'plain'.

Yvor Winters, describing what he calls the 'native plain style' of Thomas Wyatt and others, defines a typical poem of that school as having 'a theme usually broad, simple, and obvious . . . a feeling restrained to the minimum required by the subject; a rhetoric restrained to a similar minimum, the poet being interested in his rhetoric as a means of stating his matter as economically as possible, and not, as are the Petrarchans, in the pleasure of that rhetoric for its own sake. There is also a strong tendency toward aphoristic statement.'[3] Clearly these are rigorous formal and stylistic criteria, derived inductively by observing a relatively small, homogeneous group of lyric poems. But it is worth noting that 'plain' was not a term chosen by poets or critics of the period to characterize these works. Moreover, what Winters means by 'plain' (and what C. S. Lewis, correspondingly, calls 'drab' verse) is somewhat different from the way in which Shakespeare uses the word.

For one thing, Shakespearean characters are usually not speaking of the lyric, or indeed of any formal structure. Berowne does associate lack of plainness with 'taffeta phrases' and Petrarchan sonnets, but there is a strong moral component to his self-reproach. 'Plain' for Shakespeare, as for Winters, can mean 'unembellished, not ornate' (*OED* iii. 8), but in the dramatic context, when it refers either to character or language, it more frequently means 'open in behavior; free from duplicity or reserve; guileless, honest, candid, frank' (*OED* IV. 11) or 'Free from ambiguity, evasion, or subterfuge; straightforward, direct' (*OED* IV. 12). Thus the *OED* cites Mulcaster in his pedagogical work *The Positions* (1581) as speaking of 'Such as have preferred plaine trueth before painted colours'. In other words, 'plain', either as a personal epithet or as a way of describing a character's language, is simultaneously a stylistic and a moral judgment. For example, Rosaline in *Love's Labor's Lost*, pretending to accept the fiction of the 'Muscovites', asks for an intermediary to discover their intentions: 'If they do speak our language, 'tis our will / That some plain man recount their purposes' (V. ii. 176–7). A 'plain man' here is someone who is trustworthy and direct, easy both to understand and to believe. Wittily, Rosaline chooses the dandified Boyet for this role, falling in with the spirit of the occasion, and thereby exposing a fundamental lack of 'plainness' on the part of the masquers. Whether used ironically, as here, or more directly, as in Henry V's assertion to Katherine, 'I speak to thee plain soldier', 'plain' in Shakespeare's plays carries these connotations rather than those elaborated by Winters, and in the discussion that follows the word will be considered – and analyzed – in its usual Shakespearean (and most frequent Renaissance) sense.

*

Benedick's 'tattling' and Armado's inclination to 'turn sonnet' represent one kind of pitfall for the Shakespearean speaker who wishes to make himself understood. Another, at the opposite end of the scale, is plainness itself, especially when carried to excess. We have mentioned Kent's linguistic debate with Cornwall, which lands him in the stocks. Cornwall's accusation, admittedly not offered by the most admirable of Shakespeare's critics of language, nonetheless expresses a prevalent point of view:

> This is some fellow
> Who, having been praised for bluntness, doth affect
> A saucy roughness, and constrains the garb
> Quite from his nature. He cannot flatter, he;
> An honest mind and plain, he must speak truth.
> And they will take it, so; if not, he's plain.

These kind of knaves I know, which in this plainness
Harbor more craft and more corrupter ends
Than twenty silly-ducking observants
That stretch their duties nicely.   (*Lr* II. ii. 97–106)

It may be remembered that Kent's initial bluntness was the cause of his banishment and disguise. We must all applaud the sentiments of his challenge to the king:

Be Kent unmannerly
When Lear is mad. What wouldst thou do, old man?
Thinkst thou that duty shall have dread to speak
When power to flattery bows? To plainness honor's bound
When majesty falls to folly.   (I. i. 145–9)

No less certainly, however, we must all observe the consequences of this mode of 'plainness' at work. No less than Cordelia, Kent is simultaneously to be praised and blamed. Without them Lear himself would undergo no anagnorisis; just as certainly, however, the choice of silence by one, and plainness by the other, is a radical – and ultimately tragic – reading of their audience. Unquestionably, Shakespeare invites us to admire and respect these two figures; with no less doubt, I think, he urges us to question the possibility of direct discourse in a tragic universe so entirely grammatized by solipsism.

Kent is not, of course, alone in the tragic company of plain speakers. Enobarbus, to his own loss, is similarly blunt with Antony, and in a significant exchange we can see yet another difference between Antony the hero, and Octavius the politician:

Antony   Thou art a soldier only; speak no more.
Enobarbus   That truth should be silent I had almost forgot.
Antony   You wrong this presence; therefore speak no more.
Enobarbus   Go to, then; your considerate stone.
Caesar   I do not much dislike the matter, but
The manner of his speech.   (*A&C* II. ii. 107–12)

Antony, disliking the matter as well as the manner, chooses not to hear; as a result, Enobarbus' repeated warnings are not heeded, and eventually he flees to the rival camp. An instructive contrast is offered in the same play by the messenger who comes to Cleopatra with news of Antony's marriage. Beaten at first for his tidings, he shortly changes his tone, though not his tune, and emerges from the audience with Cleopatra's accolade – and her gold. The lesson seems clear; plain speaking can be self-defeating, if the bluntness of the speaker disinclines his listener to hear. Plain speaking, in short, is not always synonymous with communication, but sometimes with its opposite. Indeed, Shakespeare has written an entire play about this subject – *The Tragedy of Coriolanus*.

There is, moreover, another kind of danger in plainness of speech, or rather in the claim to plainness. Often in Shakespeare's plays a character will use such a claim, with varying degrees of artfulness, to disguise or dissimulate a purpose which is far from plain. Hotspur, to take one example, is a comparatively naive advocate of plain speech. He continually mocks or rejects the arts of language, whether employed by Owen Glendower, or the 'nimble-footed madcap Prince of Wales', or his own wife. Glendower's famous 'I can call spirits from the vasty deep' (*1HIV* III. i. 52) elicits an equally famous reply which is a repudiation not only of magic, but also of magical or incantatory language: 'Why so can I, or so can any man; / But will they come when you do call for them?' (53–4). Yet Hotspur's own language is very different from the stripped and unsentimentalized diction he favors in others. The famous trait of 'speaking thick' (*2HIV* II. iii. 24) attributed to him by his wife has been much debated. On the stage, particularly in Germany, Hotspur has often been made to stutter, following Schlegel's translation of the word *thick* as *stottern*.[4] Michael Redgrave, interpreting 'thick' as 'guttural', produced a Hotspur with a Northumbrian *r*, while Laurence Olivier memorably performed the part with a speech defect which rendered him incapable of pronouncing the letter *w*, so that the deathbed line, 'food for – ' (v. iv. 84) was necessarily finished by Hal ('For worms, brave Percy' – 85). Much of this, however, seems to be the result of ingenuity rather than accuracy. The consensus of modern scholarship is that 'speaking thick' is merely speaking impetuously or quickly.[5] In fact, Hotspur's language is more than anything a Marlovian cadence, as his character is itself Marlovian; the 'honor' speech (i. iii. 199–205) and such sentiments as 'Doomsday is near. Die all, die merrily' (iv. i. 133) and

'if we live, we live to tread on kings' (v. ii. 85) have a distinct
smack of Tamburlaine, and the final confrontation of Hal and
Hotspur appears to replay the competition between Shakespeare
and Marlowe, with Hal-Shakespeare accorded the last, though
generous, word. As Hal completes Hotspur's last sentence,
literally taking the words out of his mouth, power and control
over language, as well as politics, passes from one to the other.

For Hotspur, though his own language is far from 'plain',
there is no division between what he intends to say and what he
actually says. When exploited by a skillful orator conscious of
his art, however, plainness may become a powerful weapon. The
full extent of that power can be seen in the Mark Antony of
Julius Caesar:

> I am no orator, as Brutus is;
> But (as you know me all) a plain blunt man
> That love my friend, and that they know full well
> That gave me public leave to speak of him.
> For I have neither writ, nor words, nor worth,
> Action, nor utterance, nor the power of speech
> To stir men's blood; I only speak right on.
> I tell you that which you yourselves do know,
> Show you sweet Caesar's wounds, poor poor dumb
>   mouths,
> And bid them speak for me. But were I Brutus,
> And Brutus Antony, there were an Antony
> Would ruffle up your spirits, and put a tongue
> In every wound of Caesar that should move
> The stones of Rome to rise and mutiny.
>
> (III. ii. 217–30)

This classic version of what Curtius calls the 'protestation of
incapacity'[6] means, of course, precisely the opposite of what it
says. Brutus, the plain – or plainer – man of the two, is made to
seem a schemer and an apologist for murder; the persona of the
'plain blunt man' provides a perfect cover for Antony, enabling
him to manipulate his audience with thoroughness and ease.
When he allows the mask to slip after the plebians have departed
– 'Now let it work: Mischief, thou art afoot' (261) – the offstage
audience, no less persuaded than its onstage counterpart, may
feel an unpleasant shock of surprise.

How complex this matter of 'plainness' can be is well illustrated by Rosalie Colie's comparison of Brutus' funeral oration with Antony's.[7] Brutus, she says, is a stoic, 'whose mode of speech is properly plain' or 'Attic', in contrast to the more 'Asiatic' Antony. Thus Brutus' oration is in prose, 'a device designed to show his relative directness and sincerity,' while Antony speaks in 'artful and insidious' verse. Yet, as Colie argues, 'in one sense, signalized by shifting syntax and broken tone, Antony's language is "plainer", answers more honestly to his mood, and is thus more "Attic" than Brutus'.' 'In *Julius Caesar*', she concludes, 'Shakespeare dealt in the problems of politics, as of character and motive; nothing is simple here – not even the rhetoric officially designated as "plain".'

*

When Antony's rhetorical ploy is turned to private use it produces equally devastating results. Richard III, confronting the hostile Woodvilles, takes shelter behind a facade of simplicity:

> Because I cannot flatter and look fair,
> Smile in men's faces, smooth, deceive, and cog,
> Duck with French nods and apish courtesy,
> I must be held a rancorous enemy.
> Cannot a plain man live and think no harm
> But thus his simple truth must be abused
> With silken, sly, insinuating Jacks?   (I. iii. 47–53)

Here we have the Osric-figure neatly turned inside out. Yet the snake is readily perceived in the grass, with the aural transformation of *simple* (52) into the spate of sibilants – *silken, sly, insinuating* – that insinuate themselves into the final line. Once again artlessness becomes the shield of artifice. This role of the plain man is one Richard will assume again and again throughout his play, from the opening soliloquy, in which he claims he 'cannot prove a lover / To entertain these fair well-spoken days' (I. i. 28–9), to the demeanor which leads Hastings to make Duncan's fatal mistake: 'For by his face straight shall you know his heart' (III. iv. 53). Significantly, Richard frequently adopts the pose of 'infancy' – linking an alleged childishness to his pretended inability to speak the language of love or policy. He is 'too childish-foolish for this world' (I. iii. 141); he '[does] not know that Englishman alive / With whom [his] soul is any jot at odds / More than the infant that is born tonight' (II. i. 71–3); even with his confederate Buckingham he is all submission: 'I, as a child, will go by thy direction' (II. ii. 153). Yet all those with whom he plays this part will shortly be his victims. As he perpetuates his own massacre of the innocents with the murder of the princes in the tower, he hides his deadly efficacy behind the smiling masks of infancy, the blunt and open posture of the self-proclaimed 'plain man'.

In such circumstances, 'plain' may become a code word, a warning sign for the attentive reader or listener. Just as those lovers who say that they 'dote' are liable to be found less than faithful, so speakers who call their language 'plain' invite our close attention. Those who insist most firmly on their plainness may well be concealing some darker purpose. True plain speaking in Shakespeare, then, is not so easily achieved or identified. Kent fails to communicate because he is, in a way, too plain. Richard fails because he intends to; he uses the guise of the plain man to replace, and to foil, all genuine human communication.

II

What I should like to argue here is that these pitfalls – whether of silence, syntactic disintegration, overelaborate rhetoric or deceptive plainness – are part of the test of the Shakespearean hero. To learn to speak well, and to communicate one's meanings, is to attain successful maturity in both a dramatic and a psychological sense. For many of Shakespeare's protagonists, the growth and change in their language is as significant as a shift of locale, clothing, or name: it is a change which confirms adulthood.

The most straightforward example is probably that of Prince Hal, whose education in the tavern is directly concerned with the study of a kind of foreign language. It is not sufficient for him to gain the admiration of his future subjects; in order to gain their confidence, he must learn their vocabulary, as he explains to Poins:

> Sirrah, I am sworn brother to a leash of drawers and can call them all by their christen names, as Tom, Dick, and

Francis . . . and when I am King of England I shall command all the good lads in Eastcheap. They call drinking deep, dyeing scarlet; and when you breathe in your watering, they cry 'hem!' and bid you play it off. To conclude, I am so good a proficient in one quarter of an hour that I can drink with any tinker in his own language during my life.

(*1HIV* II. iv. 6–8, 13–19)

A quarter of an hour may suffice for an introductory lesson, but the study of language and its speakers occupies King Henry V for most of his career. In *Henry IV Part I* Hal shows his skill in the language of tinkers and drinkers. In *Part II* his determination to learn languages is recognized as more serious and more self-conscious – as Warwick observes to the king:

The prince but studies his companions
Like a strange tongue, wherein, to gain the language,
'Tis needful that the most immodest word
Be looked upon and learned.   (*2HIV* IV. iv. 68–71)

By the time of *Henry V* it has become clear that the French are not the only enemies with whom England is at war; the internecine strife among British nationalities is underscored by the dialects of its soldiers. The regional accents of Captains Mac-Morris, Jamy, and especially the Welshman Fluellen are carefully indicated in the text, and the comic controversy between Fluellen and Pistol turns directly on the matter of language. As Pistol is forced to eat the leek of contrition, the king admonishes him for his error:

You thought, because he could not speak English in the native garb, he could not therefore handle an English cudgel. You find it otherwise.   (*HV* v. i. 76–9)

An earlier confrontation between Welsh and English, in a softer tone, had underscored the same division, for in *Henry IV Part I* we find Mortimer lamenting the difficulty of speaking with his wife, the daughter of the Welshman Glendower:

This is the deadly spite that angers me –
My wife can speak no English, I no Welsh.

(III. i. 188–9)

The problem is to some extent alleviated, though not solved, by the mediating influence of the lady's 'looks' (197), 'kisses' (201) and, above all, her song; Wales in the *Henry IV* plays, as later in *Cymbeline*, is pre-eminently a land of music and magic. In the same scene, however, we hear Hotspur's animadversions on 'mincing poetry' (130) and his good-humored invitation to his wife to leave 'in sooth' and swear 'a good mouth-filling oath' (252), like the lady she is. The two pairs, so entirely complementary, raise between them the question of the proper language for love and war, and anticipate the courtship between Henry and Katherine which concludes *Henry V*.

Katherine's rather comical language lessons in that play take up the theme once more, for even in the apparent safety of the princess's chamber danger lurks: the innocent terms 'pied' and 'robe', when rendered in the English tongue, are transformed into the vulgar words 'foot' and 'count', which bring a blush to a maiden's cheek – though she bravely resolves to pronounce them, nonetheless. Throughout *Henry V*, in fact, the king's continuing quest to speak and be understood is counterpointed by the adventures of Fluellen, on the one hand, and Katherine, on the other. With entire suitability, therefore, the final act is divided between them – the first scene presenting the discomfiture of Pistol, the second the wooing of Katherine, with the king present and active in both. His declaration of love is couched, yet again, in terms of plain language: he is a 'plain king' (127), a 'fellow of plain and uncoined constancy' (156); his pledge to his lady is 'I speak to thee plain soldier' (152). Henry's speeches here are prose, a form he has, for his three plays, used on the battlefield or in the tavern but never at court. He carefully reassesses the world of linguistic transformation and variety he has left behind, a world he now holds incompatible with the sober responsibilities of kingship. Each word, now, must mean precisely, and only, what it says:

> for these fellows of infinite tongue, that can rhyme themselves into ladies' favors, they do always reason themselves out again. What! A speaker is but a prater; a rhyme is but a ballad; . . . but a good heart, Kate, is the sun and the moon, or rather, the sun, and not the moon, for it shines bright and never changes, but keeps his course truly.   (158–67)

In the course of this final scene, the king speaks French as well as English, the princess English (of a sort) as well as French, and the betrothal is celebrated with a kiss in which King Henry finds 'more eloquence than in the tongues of the French council' (280–1). The play which began with a casuistic reading of a Latin phrase – 'In terram Salicam mulieres ne succedant' (I. ii. 38) – concludes with the union of French and English, Welsh and Scot, in a single, hopeful nation.

The techniques employed so successfully by Hal and others in the three *Henry* plays are also essayed by figures in other plays of the period, with more variable outcomes. The cowardly and loquacious Parolles in *All's Well That Ends Well*, whose very name means 'words', finds himself at a loss for them when he is blindfolded and hoodwinked by his fellow soldiers. Since 'he hath a smack of all neighboring languages' (IV. i. 16–17) they pretend to be an enemy regiment by inventing a gibberish of their own on the spot ('Throca movousus, cargo, cargo, cargo,' etc. – 66ff) and deprived of his only weapon Parolles is tricked into betraying them, fearing, as he says, that otherwise 'I shall lose my life for want of language' (72). At the other end of the scale of linguistic competence, but almost equally luckless, is Sir Andrew Aguecheek in *Twelfth Night*. Concluding that his suit for Olivia's hand is in vain, he announces his intention to depart, and Sir Toby Belch asks him 'pourquoi?' 'What is "pourquoi"?' replies Sir Andrew. 'Do, or not do? I would I had bestowed that time in the tongues that I have in fencing, dancing, and bearbaiting' (I. iii. 88–91). Yet had he done so Sir Andrew would have wasted his time. In Sir Toby's world of misrule the word 'why', in any language, has no meaning – until, when the revels are ended, Malvolio asks it three times, plaintively and in earnest, at the play's close ('tell me, in the modesty of honor, / Why you have given me such clear lights of favor, / . . . Why have you suffered me to be imprisoned, / Kept in a dark house, visited by the priest, / And made the most notorious geck and gull / That e'er invention played on? Tell me why' – v. i. 335–44).

As for the apparently inadvertent bawdiness of Katherine's experiments in English, such errors seem to have been a stock source of audience amusement, so broad that they hardly deserve the label of dramatic irony – but wherever they appear in Shakespeare's plays they serve a double function, coordinating the themes of the plot as they provide pleasure to the delighted spectators. William Page's Latin lesson in *The Merry Wives of Windsor* follows a pattern very similar to that in III. iv. of *Henry V*. The ignorant Mistress Quickly hears 'horum' as whore and 'pulcher' as 'polecats', or prostitutes, while the Latin master Evans's Welsh accent makes 'vocative' into the more suggestive 'focative', – especially when it describes the word 'caret', characterized by Mistress Quickly as 'a good root' (carrot). Evans himself seems to quibble on 'qui's', 'quae's', and 'quod's', (keys [penises], case [pudendum], and cods [testicles]), although he may well be unaware of his double entendre. As William Carroll has shown, the theme of language and its breakdown is central to the meanings of the play; 'proper English means, for the Windsorites, not only a plain but a native style as well.'[8]

A third instance of this kind of humor occurs in *Love's Labor's Lost* (v. i.), when Holofernes, Don Armado, and a willing but outclassed Costard engage in a lofty conversation touching on proximity 'ad dunghill' (Costard's mistake for 'ad unguem'), the smell of false Latin, the 'posteriors of this day', Armado's dallying with excrement (in the form of his moustache) and various 'eruptions and sudden breaking out of mirth' – 'but let that pass' (74–111). The recurrent scatological references have a lowering effect quite the opposite of what these hopeful linguists intend – and the implicit allegation of flatulence in language applies not only to them, but to their nominal 'betters' and employers, the king and his lords, who have commissioned the ill-fated Pageant of the Nine Worthies.

*

In the plays we have just been discussing, growth and change in language are major themes as well as techniques. That is to say, the plays are in one way or another *about* language, its use, misuse, and nature, and changes or aberrations in speech are directly relevant to the crux of the dramatic action. But for figures in some others of the plays, the process of growth is indicated not so much by a thematic discussion of language as by demonstrable shifts in the kind of language they speak. Often such figures establish a clear rhetorical pattern early in the play, and alter that pattern radically as the result of a crisis in personal development – whether that crisis is falling in love, achieving revenge, or committing a murder. Romeo, for instance, begins

by speaking in exaggerated Petrarchanisms and hackneyed
rhymes, as he declares his love for Rosaline. Love to him is
'a smoke', 'a fire', 'a sea', 'a madness', 'a choking gall' and 'a
preserving sweet', all in the course of five lines, and Rosaline
herself is described in the stalest possible terms, like a kind of
mail-order Stella:

> *Romeo*   O, she is rich in beauty; only poor
> That, when she dies, with beauty dies her store.
> *Benvolio*   Then she hath sworn that she will still live chaste?
> *Romeo*   She hath, and in that sparing make huge waste;
> For beauty, starved with her severity,
> Cuts beauty off from all posterity.
> She is too fair, too wise, wisely too fair,
> To merit bliss by making me despair.   (I. i. 218–25)

Shakespeare's sonnets, even those which are concerned with
procreation, sound nothing like this; Romeo's diction seems
clearly designed by the playwright to mirror his mental state.
But notice how quickly his metaphors and rhythms shift when
first he sets eyes on Juliet:

> O, she doth teach the torches to burn bright!
> It seems she hangs upon the cheek of night
> As a rich jewel in an Ethiop's ear –
> Beauty too rich for use, for earth too dear!
>
>   (I. v. 46–9)

The two passages begin identically – 'O, she is', 'O, she doth' –
and both are, remarkably, in couplet form – but the second
passage displays an energy and originality completely absent
from the first. From this moment, energy and originality will
animate, not only Romeo's speech, but also his action; the
change in his language is a sign of a change in character.

Like Romeo, Hamlet undergoes a startling shift in rhetoric at
a time of personal growth and change. As has often been noticed,
the soliloquies which are his most striking mode of utterance in
Acts I through IV are not present in Act V, which marks his
return from England. The soliloquies themselves are highly
inwrought structures, distinguished by long series of questions,
exclamations, maxims, and self-interruptions; the 'rogue
and peasant slave' speech alone (II. ii. 555–612) contains ten

questions and nine interjections ('And all for nothing!'; 'With Hecuba!'; 'Bloody, bawdy villain!', etc.). The jagged and eruptive syntax of his language in the early acts provides, once again, a counterpart for the troubled workings of his mind. Consider this single sentence from the first soliloquy:

Why, she would hang on him
As if increase of appetite had grown
By what it fed on; and yet within a month –
Let me not think on 't; frailty, thy name is woman –
A little month, or ere those shoes were old
With which she followed my poor father's body
Like Niobe, all tears, why she, even she –
O God, a beast that wants discourse of reason
Would have mourned longer – married with my uncle,
My father's brother, but no more like my father
Than I to Hercules.   (i. ii. 143–53)

Once again, it is impossible even to consider diagramming such a sentence.[9] But observe what happens to his language when he returns from England.

Up from my cabin,
My sea gown scarfed about me, in the dark
Groped I to find out them, had my desire,
Fingered their packet, and in fine withdrew
To mine own room again.   (v. ii. 12–16)

or again,

I had my father's signet in my purse,
Which was the model of that Danish seal,
Folded the writ up in the form of th' other,
Subscribed it, gave 't th' impression, placed it safely,
The changeling never known.   (49–53)

Notice the sudden appearance of strings of active verbs – *groped, had, fingered, withdrew, folded, subscribed, gave, placed.* This is a language of action, a literally transitive syntax, in which strong verbs and concrete identifiable objects replace abstraction, involution and indecision. In fact, the entire fifth act serves in a way as a lesson in plain speaking. We first encounter Hamlet in conversation with the gravedigger, learning his 'absolute' lesson on speaking 'by the card' (v. i. 138), or with precision. So 'absolute' is he, in fact, that intercourse with him is somewhat difficult; he speaks in a mode of language not far removed from riddle. Hamlet then moves to Ophelia's graveside, where he engages in a duel of hyperbolic words with Laertes ('Nay, an thou'lt mouth, / I'll rant as well as thou' – 283–4), and at this point there follow the passages I have just quoted, in which the verbs of action predominate. The appearance of Osric closes off this scene, for Osric embodies the opposite of plain speech. His language of flattery is not only unintelligible, but also self-defeating, since it requires full and constant annotation to be understood – what Horatio calls being 'edified by the margent' (v. ii. 158). Why does Shakespeare introduce such an idiosyncratic character at this late point in the play? I suspect that it is to underscore the necessity for plain speech, for language which says what it means, and thereby makes possible communication between man and man. Framed on the one side by the gravedigger, and on the other by Osric, Hamlet's change in linguistic style reinforces the change we have seen in his degree of self-knowledge. Significantly, although his dying words are 'the rest is silence,' he leaves an enlightened Horatio behind him to 'tell my story'.

III

To this point we have been largely considering cases of successful coming of age: characters like Hal, Romeo, and Hamlet – even Berowne and Benedick – whose pattern has been one of growth, and whose changes in language have reflected that growth. But there are in the Shakespearean canon examples of failed maturation as well. Caliban's accusation to Prospero is, 'You taught me language, and my profit on't / Is, I know how to curse' (*Tmp.* i. ii. 365–6). Caliban's persona and language are essentially childlike, appetitive, demanding; the lyrical passage that begins 'Be not afeard; the isle is full of noises' (iii. ii. 138–46) employs a childlike language, a childlike concern with things which 'give delight and hurt not', and the image of one who, like a child, wakes and cries to dream again. Caliban's attempted rape of Miranda contrasts sharply with Ferdinand's gentle courtship, which is accomplished, significantly, through their common tongue ('My language? Heavens! / I am the best of them that speak this speech, / Were I but where 'tis spoken' – I. ii. 431–3). In fact, it is Miranda's reply in that language which demonstrates to the enraptured Ferdinand that she is a woman, and not a goddess. Spirits in *The Tempest* may speak in song, or even in 'excellent dumb discourse' (III. iii. 39), but the condition of full humanity is clearly and repeatedly equated in the play with the proper use of speech.

It may seem fanciful to draw an analogy between Caliban and Coriolanus, yet both are child–men whose language, though sometimes lyrical, often reduces itself to a curse. Coriolanus is the Billy Budd of Shakespeare's plays, an essentially naive figure for whom a failure in language leads ineluctably to self-destruction. The safe path in *Coriolanus* is the path of Menenius, who uses language to beguile and, equally important, to let off steam: 'What I think I utter,' he explains, 'and spend my malice in my breath' (II. i. 54–5). But Coriolanus is unable to use language in this ameliorative way; whenever he addresses his adversaries he erupts into splenetic and fragmentary speech. Consider his very first words, addressed to the plebians whom Menenius has been at pains to placate:

> What's the matter, you dissentious rogues,
> That, rubbing the poor itch of your opinion,
> Make yourselves scabs?   (I. i. 166–8)

The moving silence between Coriolanus and his mother, indicated by the stage direction '*Holds her by the hand, silent*' (v. iii), re-establishes the filial bond, but at the cost of the son's adulthood, even his life. We may well be reminded of the silence between Cordelia and Lear, though formally the two are opposite: one coming at the beginning of the play, the other at the end; one inaugurating a breach between parent and child, the other contracting a peace, though one that invalidates all other contracts. For Coriolanus there is, tragically, no moment of attained maturity, but only a refusal of the burdens of adulthood.

Of all Shakespeare's characters, however, two in particular stand out as examples of a contrary linguistic pattern, a regression rather than a progression – a failure of maturation emblematized by a failure in language. Appropriately, they are characters whose careers, and even whose language, have afforded numerous other opportunities for comparison, as have the plays which contain them: Richard III and Macbeth.

Richard begins his play at the height of rhetorical power. He commands the stage in his opening soliloquy, not only because he appears alone before us, but also because of a superb oratorical style by which he manipulates the offstage audience as easily as he will, in the next scene, manipulate the Lady Anne. The soliloquy itself is a masterpiece of syntactical organization. Its fundamental shape is that of logical argument, a sort of negative syllogism which returns insistently to the vocabulary of proof. The tripartite division of 'Now' (1), 'But' (14), 'And therefore' (28) is reinforced by strategically placed cue words of an escalating power: 'Now' (1), 'Now' (5), 'And now' (10); 'But I' (14), 'I' (16), 'I' (18), 'Why, I' (24), 'And therefore, since I cannot prove' (28), 'I am determinèd to prove' (30).

Even within this elaborate framework, syntactical divisions and repetitions are precise, calculated, and effective. Notice, for example, the compelling result Richard achieves by combining two stylistic devices: (1) parallel phrases, signalled as such by the repetition of an initial word, with the second and subsequent phrases compressed into half the time of the first; and (2) the recurring use of participial constructions.

> Now *is* the winter of our discontent
> *Made* glorious summer by this sun of York;
> And all the clouds that loured upon our house
> In the deep bosom of the ocean *buried.*
> Now *are* our brows *bound* with victorious wreaths,
> Our bruised arms *hung up* for monuments,
> Our stern alarums *changed* to merry meetings,
> Our dreadful marches to delightful measures.
>
> (I. i. 1–8)

Parallelism is emphasized here by the repetitions of both *now* (ll. 1, 5) and *our* (1, 3, 5, 6, 7, 8). The deceptively leisurely and discursive pace of the first four lines is replaced in the next four by a series of rapid rhetorical strokes, each a complete thought in a single line, culminating in the understood gerundive verb of the last ('Our dreadful marches to delightful measures'); by implication, the point is now so self-evident that no separate verb is needed. A similar progression takes place in lines 16–23, with a similar effect:

> I, that *am* rudely *stamped*, and want love's majesty
> To strut before a wanton ambling nymph;
> I, that *am curtailed* of this fair proportion,
> *Cheated* of feature by dissembling nature,
> *Deformed, unfinished, sent* before my time
> Into this breathing world scarce half made up,
> And that so lamely and unfashionable
> That dogs bark at me as I halt by them.   (16–23)

Again there is both parallelism and an insistent acceleration, a pile-up of verbal forms which seem to urge the manifest truth of what is being said. Richard, it appears, scarcely has breath enough to enumerate all the reasons for his just anger and resentment. The personal aside in lines 20–23 is a stroke of genius, seeming to show for a moment the speaker's genuine vulnerability, and thereby enlisting a sympathy which might have been withheld from too dazzling an orator. His very first lines had offered a diabolically equivocal enjambment ('Now is the winter of our discontent / Made glorious summer'), and the final resolution carries all the conviction of an argument fully demonstrated: 'therefore, since I cannot prove a lover . . . I am determinèd to prove a villain' (27–8).

I have dwelt on the syntactical and rhetorical structure of this speech in order to emphasize its speaker's astonishing degree of control – for what is most remarkable about the opening soliloquy is that it is entirely a tour de force: its self-portrait is demonstrably a lie, and a lie exposed by Richard's own eloquence. The man who cannot prove a lover, and who is neither fair nor well spoken, will in the next scene woo and win the wife of his most recent victim, in the presence of her father-in-law's corpse. Shortly thereafter, with quick-tongued intervention, he will turn Queen Margaret's curse back upon her, ending her list of imprecations with 'Thou detested –' 'Margaret' (I. iii. 232–3). He assures the doomed Clarence, with wry justice, that his imprisonment will not be long; he outwits the credulous Hastings by a trick of syntax, turning his 'If' from a conditional ('If they have done this deed, my noble lord' – III. iv. 72) into a subjunctive indicating a condition contrary to fact, and thus damns him out of his own mouth. The opening soliloquy, in short, is Richard's notice to the audience that he can use language to entrap and imprison. Its rigidly logical format contains a wholly illogical and untrue premise which, nonetheless, like so much of his language, persuades.

However, when Richard attains his objective, and thus turns from antagonist to protagonist, his power – and his language – begin to fail him. The breakdown starts slowly; the play he has designed in order to win the support of London's citizens unaccountably fails of its object. We may be reminded of that later and more poignant scene, the deposition of the king in *Richard II*. 'The citizens are mum, say not a word' (III. vii. 3), Buckingham is forced to report. He himself has been the vehicle of Richard's language, instructed and rehearsed by his mentor.

> *Buckingham*   And when my oratory drew toward end,
>   I bid them that did love their country's good
>   Cry, 'God save Richard, England's royal king!'
> *Richard*   And did they so?
> *Buckingham*   No, so God help me, they spake not a word,
>   But like dumb statues or breathing stones
>   Stared on each other and looked deadly pale.   (20–6)

A second subterfuge, which significantly employs an initially silent Richard between two bishops, works, not perfectly, but well enough. But no sooner does Richard become king than language is turned against him for the first time. His mother, the long-suffering Duchess of York, confers on him the excommunication of silence, exiling him from humanity and kinship:

> Hear me a word;
> For I shall never speak to thee again.   (IV. iv. 181–2)

And those upon whom he has practiced his puns and wordplay, deceiving and entrapping them, now begin to find fault with his choice of words. To Richard's feigned indignation, 'You speak as if that I had slain my cousins!' (IV. iv. 222), Queen Elizabeth replies, 'Cousins indeed, and by their uncle cozened' (223), and when he protests to her, 'know that from my soul I love thy daughter' (256), she plucks out his word 'from', showing it to mean 'apart from', and leaving him to remonstrate, 'Be not so hasty to confound my meaning' (262).

Most significantly, although Richard is persuaded that he succeeds, in fact his wooing fails. The queen sees through his rhetoric of persuasion, and the marriage he seeks will not take place. When we compare this scene to the earlier (and successful) wooing of Anne, to which it is structurally parallel, we can readily see what a falling-off has happened here. That Richard does not see this – he comments to himself as she leaves the stage, 'Relenting fool, and shallow, changing woman!' (431) – is part of the play's dramatic irony, and further evidence of his decline.

It is at Bosworth Field, however, that the ultimate degeneration of Richard's spirit and speech takes place. The scenes at Bosworth are a fascinating mix of old and new dramaturgy, working in complementary ways to paint a picture of human dissolution and despair. The famous dream sequence, with the ghosts of Richard's victims visiting first his tent, and then Richmond's, derives much of its power from the medieval pageant of virtues and vices on which it is modeled. But set next to that scene, and in startling contrast to it, is a speech of such psychological realism and immediacy that it seems almost to come from a different play. If we call to mind the seductive mellifluousness of the opening soliloquy, we can have no doubt that Richard's control of the external world – and of his own emotions – has undergone a severe deterioration.

> What do I fear? Myself? There's none else by.
> Richard loves Richard: that is, I am I.
> Is there a murderer here? No. Yes, I am.
> Then fly. What, from myself? Great reason why!
> Lest I revenge. What, myself upon myself?
> Alack, I love myself. Wherefore? For any good
> That I myself have done unto myself?
> O no! Alas, I rather hate myself
> For hateful deeds committed by myself.
> I am a villain. Yet I lie, I am not.
> Fool, of thyself speak well. Fool, do not flatter.
>
> (v. iii. 183–93)

The fragmentation of thought and structure here is almost complete. Eleven 'I's, nine 'myself's, and one reflexive thyself' burden these eleven lines, which are as chopped and

contradictory as any in Shakespeare.[10] Once the master of persuasion, Richard now has difficulty sustaining his language the
length of a line. His telling verbal ambiguities have been replaced
by a debilitating ambiguousness in his sense of self.

The decline in Richard's language and character from gran-
diloquence to stammering self-confutation is fairly direct. In the
case of Macbeth, the pattern is more intricate and more various.
We are never really shown a Macbeth in full control of his own
speech; from the first, Shakespeare shows us a man whose
diction betrays his distress of mind. Thus the tortured syntax
which reflected Hamlet's indecision is even more pronounced in
Macbeth's:

> If it were done when 'tis done, then 'twere well
> It were done quickly. If th' assassination
> Could trammel up the consequence, and catch,
> With his surcease, success. . . .   (I. vii. 1–4)

The equivocation of the balanced clauses which seem to lead to
no conclusion is exacerbated by the hissing sibilants ('assassin-
ation', 'consequence', 'surcease', 'success') which render this
speech as difficult to pronounce as it is to decipher. And nowhere
in Shakespeare's plays, perhaps, is syntax more eloquent of
emotion than in Macbeth's final weighing of the murder of
Duncan. Only once before in the play has he used the word
'murder', and then only to assert defensively that his murder
is 'yet but fantastical' (I. iii. 139), imagined. Now he is faced
with the deed itself, and though time will not permit him to
delay further, syntax will:

> Now o'er the one half-world
> Nature seems dead, and wicked dreams abuse
> The curtained sleep; witchcraft celebrates
> Pale Hecate's offerings; and withered murder,
> Alarumed by his sentinel, the wolf,
> Whose howl's his watch, thus with his stealthy pace,
> With Tarquin's ravishing strides, toward his design
> Moves like a ghost.   (II. i. 49–56)

Subordinate clause after subordinate clause retards both the
conclusion of the speech and the conclusive, fearful action.

'Withered murder', the subject of Macbeth's sentence and his contemplation, is separated from its verb by three entire lines of verse – until finally the inevitable verb 'Moves' makes its tardy appearance. With that verb, there can be no more delay. The bell rings, the murder is done, and Macbeth's language undergoes a radical alteration.

Theatrically, the change is unmistakable, for it is a change from knotty involution to nakedness and disorientation; words are dropped singly into the silence like stones echoing one by one down a well:

> *Lady Macbeth*   Did not you speak?
> *Macbeth*   When?
> *Lady Macbeth*   Now.
> *Macbeth*   As I descended?
> *Lady Macbeth*   Ay.
> *Macbeth*   Hark!
>   Who lies i' th' second chamber?
> *Lady Macbeth*   Donalbain.
> *Macbeth*   This is a sorry sight.   (II. ii. 16–20)

This linguistic diminuendo signals a new phase. Now Macbeth begins to be concerned about things he could *not* say – 'wherefore could I not pronounce "Amen"?' (30) – and finds himself, for the first time, unable to complete a thought. The postponed verb of the previous passage is followed by a passage which contains no verb at all, the reverse of Hamlet's progress toward a union of verb and action:

> Methought I heard a voice cry 'Sleep no more!
> Macbeth does murder sleep' – the innocent sleep,
> Sleep that knits up the raveled sleave of care,
> The death of each day's life, sore labor's bath,
> Balm of hurt minds, great nature's second course,
> Chief nourisher in life's feast –   (II. ii. 34–9)

Lady Macbeth's impatient interjections, 'What do you mean?' and 'Who was it that thus cried?' (39, 43), interrupt a sequence of appositives which otherwise threatens to continue without end. For a moment Macbeth is reduced to 'infancy', that is, to virtual speechlessness; and, as Cleanth Brooks long ago pointed out, it is as a child that he is treated by his wife from this time forward.[11]

But there is yet another change of diction on Macbeth's part, which is once again consonant with his emotional state – and this change becomes evident at the time that the murder is discovered. Where his language was at first tortured, and then naked, his public tone, as he announces the death of Duncan, is if anything over-finished, highly decorative, ornate – the language of an Osric or an Armado. Duncan's two sons are awakened, and demand to know what is the matter, and to them Macbeth replies,

> The spring, the head, the fountain of your blood
> Is stopped; the very source of it is stopped.
>
> (II. iii. 98–9)

Luckily, Macduff is present to offer a translation: 'Your royal father's murdered.' But Macbeth goes on, to describe the body itself, though he is speaking to the bereaved sons of the dead man:

> Here lay Duncan,
> His silver skin laced with his golden blood.
>
> (II. iii. 111–12)

This is the image of a device, a statue or a tapestry, a fictional death rather than a real one. Macbeth's metaphor is doubly self-betraying – first because of its palpable artificiality, and second because it directly violates a crucial canon of heraldry, one that teaches that metal is not to be placed on metal: 'Metal on metal is false heraldry'[12] – a proverbial saying that Shakespeare would surely have known. Like the fanciful picture of the daggers in bloody trousers – 'unmannerly breeched with gore' (116) – this language declares its own untruth. Especially in comparison with the plain-spoken Macduff, Macbeth's rhetoric in this scene is transparently false – and suggests both another 'false face', or attempt to deceive his hearers, and a belated and ineffectual attempt to deceive himself. The syntactical wilderness of the 'tomorrow and tomorrow' speech will only confirm the distance he is here beginning to place between himself and genuine human discourse.

IV

Macbeth's 'tomorrow', like T. S. Eliot's 'whimper', suggests a debasement of utterance to the point where it no longer holds communicative value. If we ask the question, when is speech not speech, one possible phenomenological answer would be, when it is not understood. Recently a number of scholars in widely divergent fields have addressed themselves to matters that bear upon this question, and the results of some of their studies may serve as a useful coda to this discussion.

A fascinating medical case reported in 1977 involved a pair of twin six-year-old girls in San Diego, California. The girls, Virginia and Grace Kennedy, were placed by their parents in a school for retarded children because they were unable to speak intelligently in any known language, although they apparently understood both English (their father's language) and German (their mother's) as well as a smattering of Spanish. They communicated with one another by means of what seemed to be unintelligible gibberish. But psychologists at the school maintained that the twins were in fact of normal intelligence, and that the sounds they spoke to one another might well be a kind of private language. As the principal therapist in the case suggested, 'their jabberwocky may be really a comprehensive private language with a structured syntax.'[13] Only one similar case is recorded in the medical literature of the last fifty years – a case involving triplets in Germany. The scientists who studied the Kennedy twins hypothesized that theirs might be one of the very rare instances of what is known as 'idioglossia', or twin speech. If so, as one psycholinguist observed, there might be 'tremendous implications for suggesting that there is an innate endowment for language in humans'.[14] Whatever the outcome of these researches – and all observers agreed that more data was necessary before a conclusion could be drawn – the situation of the Kennedy twins is highly suggestive. When it was thought that they could not speak in such a way as to be understood, they were classed as subnormal; once it became clear that they communicated with one another and in fact invented words, perhaps even linguistic structures, to suit their experiences and needs, the girls were reclassified as normal children, and new efforts were made to communicate with them and to teach them those codes we recognize as 'languages' today. In other words, the capacity to speak and be understood was used as a defining principle of human behavior, and the adult futures of the twins will depend in large part upon their continued growth toward a more socially acceptable form of speech.

When we turn from medicine to social science, we will find some of the same kind of investigation going on among folklorists, anthropologists, and psychologists. To take only one example, Bruno Bettelheim in *The Uses of Enchantment* examines the Grimm brothers' fairy tale known as 'The Three Languages' and discerns in it the rudiments of adolescent maturation: discordant human tendencies are integrated by the hero 'until all coalesce within him, as is necessary for gaining full independence and humanity'.[15] The tale offers a useful analogy to the patterns we have been noticing. A young man, sent out into the world by his father to study with a famous master, returns after a year to report that he has learned 'what the dogs bark'. His father, disgusted, sends him for another year to another master, from whom he learns 'what the birds speak'. A third year, and a third master, yields only 'what the frogs croak', and the furious father orders that his son be taken to the forest and killed. By the kindness of servants, however, he escapes, and his subsequent adventures in the world of adulthood make predictably crucial use of the three languages. Eventually he becomes Pope, and is able to conduct a Mass although he does not know the words, through the assistance of two white doves which settle on his shoulders and whisper in his ear.

Bettelheim's analysis of the tale is of considerable interest. He argues that dogs, as land animals, 'represent the ego of man',[16] that birds, 'which can fly high into the sky . . . stand in this story for the superego',[17] and that frogs, denizens of the water, are emblems of sexuality and of the id. The boy's progressive mastery of the three languages thus emblematizes his mastery of the complex needs and drives of human nature. 'I know of no other fairy tale', Bettelheim concludes, 'in which the process of an adolescent reaching his fullest self-actualization within himself and also in the world is described so concisely.'[18] The basic pattern of language acquisition is here made into a powerful, though deliberately simplified, metaphor for the process of attaining successful maturity.

Viewed from another perspective, the son's adventure might be seen as a chronicle of political education or anthropological inquiry into the patterns of an alien culture. In this way his mastery of unvalued foreign tongues resembles that of Prince Hal, and is put to a similarly expeditious use. A plausible modern analogue is John F. Kennedy's political coup in declaring himself a Berliner in Berlin. Four simple German words, in the midst of a speech otherwise entirely delivered in English, captivated a nation and made favorable headlines around the world.

Since yesterday's fantasy so frequently becomes today's reality, it is not entirely surprising to encounter an intriguing converse of 'The Three Languages' in the annals of modern science – specifically, in the experimental work of animal behaviorists. In recent years, under their patient tutelage, dolphins, gorillas, and chimpanzees have been taught to 'speak'. Whether by means of actual vocalic sounds, sign language, or lexigrams typed on an electronic keyboard, these animals have been able not only to indicate wants and needs, but also in some cases to construct actual sentences, even affective ones expressing pleasure or interest. What is especially striking here is the willingness of psychologists, behaviorists, and the general public to equate linguistic capability with 'humanness'. In the case of Koko, a gorilla, funds were raised by public subscription to obtain her 'release' from the San Francisco Zoo, enabling her to live with her trainer–teacher, a graduate student in psychology. A creature who could talk did not, in many people's estimation, belong in a cage. As the trainer expressed it, at a time when it seemed that enough money would not be collected to meet the zoo's demand, 'to take her away from her family, her environment, to throw her in a cage with a bunch of gorillas [sic] – it could kill her.'[19]

Koko, who had achieved a vocabulary of over 300 words and was estimated to have an IQ equivalent to that of a five-year-old child, even acquired a lawyer – a law professor who specialized in animal rights. He maintained that even if the funds could not be raised, Koko no longer belonged to the zoo. 'The gorilla doesn't exist anymore,' he said.

Under normal circumstances, the only thing this animal doesn't have that we do is language. Now you have changed it. When you give it the conceptual apparatus for conscious reasoning, for mobilizing thought, you have radically altered it. You have given it the pernicious gift of language. If it has never been one before, it is an individual now. It has the apparatus for the beginning of a historical sense, for the contemplation of self.

'In this case', he added, 'you have an ape that has ascended.'[20] By acquiring the ability to speak, Koko had – in the lawyer's view at least – become 'human', and should be accorded her human rights.

Recent scholarship on animal 'speech' has tended toward a more skeptical view of the subject. Herbert Terrace, a psychologist, concludes in his 1979 book *Nim*[21] that so-called incidents of 'language' were actually only clever tricks devised by the apes to obtain rewards; and in *Speaking of Apes*[22] Thomas Sebeok, a linguist, and his wife Donna Jean Umiker-Sebeok, an anthropologist, contend that the animals are actually exhibiting what is known as the 'Clever Hans effect'. (Hans, a German performing horse at the turn of the century, appeared to be able to compute and analyze by tapping out answers with his hoofs, but was discovered to be picking up unintentional signals from his handler.) Noam Chomsky – after whom Terrace playfully named his chimpanzee 'Nim Chimpsky' – is similarly dubious, asserting in a magazine interview, 'It's about as likely that an ape will prove to have a language ability as that there is an island somewhere with a species of flightless birds waiting for human beings to teach them to fly.'[23] But whatever the outcome of this debate among scientists, both the attempt to teach apes to speak and the hotness with which the issue of animal 'language' is debated underscore the degree to which human beings associate 'humanness' with the powers of syntactical speech.

If this definition of 'humanness' seems disputable, naive or even slightly comical, it is nonetheless one that has been given widespread credence over the years. Shakespeare's contemporaries would have found lively literary examples of the same popular belief in Ovid's *Metamorphoses*, where in a remarkable number of cases the poet emphasizes loss of language as a key element in transformation. Inability to speak, rather than change of shape, constitutes the real isolation from humanity.

Thus Kallisto, transformed into a bear by Juno because she is pregnant with Jove's child, is deprived of speech lest her entreaties move the goddess to pity. A harsh, terrifying growl is all that is left her, although, as Ovid is careful to remind us, *mens antiqua manet*[24] – her human feelings remained.

Echo, who similarly displeased Juno by detaining her in talk while Jove disported himself among the nymphs, is given a punishment to fit her crime: as Golding translates, 'that toong that hath deluded me shall do thee little good; / For of thy speach but simple use hereafter shalt thou have'.[25] Actaeon, too, loses the capacity for speech. Having come upon Diana and her nymphs bathing, he is changed into a stag, and in Ovid's account the metamorphosis seems deliberately designed to prevent him from reporting what he has seen: 'Now make thy vaunts among thy mates, thou sawst Diana bare, / Tell if thou can.'[26]

Most interesting, perhaps, is the case of Io, whom Jove changed to a heifer in order to conceal her from Juno; the goddess then cleverly requested the heifer as a gift. Io tried to express her complaints, but was only able to moo, so that her own voice frightened her. When she came to the banks of her father's stream, he fed her but did not recognize her in her altered form. 'She would have told hir name and chance and him of helpe besought / But for because she could not speake, she printed in the sand / Two letters with hir foot, whereby was given to understand / The sorrowfull changing of hir shape.'[27] Io's inventive substitution of writing for speech is remarkably similar to that of Lavinia in *Titus Andronicus*, and may have influenced Shakespeare in his framing of that scene. But it may not be too fanciful to compare these actions, as well, to that of the chimpanzee who types out words since she cannot speak them. The imperative need in each case is communication. The story of Io differs from the others we have been considering in that Io, unlike Kallisto, Echo, or Actaeon, is restored to her former shape. Moreover, the restoration, like the bestial metamorphosis, turns upon and emphasizes the change in speech. Io first fears to speak lest she moo instead, but gradually regains her former language. The power of human speech is the final element in the transformation. In essence, Io's language defines her humanity.

In Shakespeare's plays, language frequently takes on a comparably defining role. Those who are willfully silent, those who obfuscate, those who babble of green fields, set themselves apart from the world of full human communication, while others, like Hal and Hamlet, confront and explore the very nature and purpose of speech. The Shakespearean world contains neither a Babel nor a Pentecost; unlike Hieronimo's play, in which each player speaks a different language, there is never in Shakespeare a total loss of understanding – nor is there ever a single, universal, apostolic tongue understood by all. It is precisely because of this medial and mediating role that language becomes a gauge of maturity; for Shakespeare's characters, as for his audience, plain, effective speaking demarcates a rite of passage, separating the self-knowledgeable adult from those capable only of inexplicable dumb shows and noise.

NOTES

1 For a persuasive discussion of *infans* in its relationship to the poetry of George Herbert, see Rosalie L. Colie, *Paradoxia Epidemica: The Renaissance Tradition of Paradox* (Princeton: Princeton University Press, 1966), pp. 201ff.

2 O, never will I trust to speeches penned,   a
  Nor to the motion of a schoolboy's tongue,   b
  Nor never come in vizard to my friend,   a
  Nor woo in rhyme, like a blind harper's song!   b
  Taffeta phrases, silken terms precise,   c
  Three-piled hyperboles, spruce affectation,   d
  Figures pedantical – these summer flies   c
  Have blown me full of maggot ostentation.   d
  I do forswear them; and I here protest   e
  By this white glove (how white the hand, God knows!)   f
  Henceforth my wooing mind shall be expressed   e
  In russet yeas and honest kersey noes.   f
  And to begin, wench – so God help me, law! –   g
  My love to thee is sound, sans crack or flaw.   g

                                                                                         (v. ii. 403–16)

3 Yvor Winters, *Forms of Discovery* (Chicago: Alan Swallow, 1967), p. 3.

4 C. J. Sisson, *New Readings in Shakespeare* (Cambridge: Cambridge University Press, 1956), ii, pp. 45–6.

5 The Arden editor, A. R. Humphreys, cites *Cymbeline* III. ii. 58–60, 'say, and speak thick . . . how far it is / To this blessed Milford', as a parallel instance of usage.

6 E. R. Curtius, *European Literature and the Latin Middle Ages*, Willard Trask (trans.) (New York: Harper & Row, 1953; rpt. 1963), pp. 409–12.

7 Rosalie L. Colie, *Shakespeare's Living Art* (Princeton: Princeton University Press, 1974), pp. 170–5.

8 William Carroll, ' "A received belief": Imagination in *The Merry Wives of Windsor*', *Studies in Philology*, LXXIV, 2 (April 1977), 200. See also the Arden edition, H. J. Oliver (ed.) (London: Methuen, 1971), IV. i. 45n, and the Signet edition, William Green (ed.) (New York: Harcourt Brace Jovanovich, 1965), IV. i. 76n.

9 J. Dover Wilson, *What Happens in Hamlet* (Cambridge: Cambridge University Press, 1935; 3rd edition, rpt. 1970), pp. 41–2, and Madeleine Doran, *Shakespeare's Dramatic Language* (Madison: University of Wisconsin Press, 1976), p. 47, both comment on the way in which this sentence 'turns and turns upon itself' (Wilson) or 'circle[s] round and round' (Doran).

10 For a contemporary example from another Elizabethan poet, though in a much different spirit, compare Sidney's sonnet 74, in which the breakdown of language becomes the subject of the poem.

11 Cleanth Brooks, 'The naked babe and the cloak of manliness', in *The Well Wrought Urn* (New York: Harcourt, Brace & World, 1947), pp. 22–49.

12 John Woodward and George Burnett, *A Treatise on Heraldry British and Foreign*, new introduction by L. G. Pine (Rutland, Vermont: Charles E. Tuttle, 1969; rpt. from 1892), p. 102. I am indebted to G. Evelyn Hutchinson for bringing this maxim to my attention.

13 Everett R. Howes, 'Twin speech: A language of their own', *The New York Times* (11 September 1977), 54.

14 Howes, p. 54.

15 Bruno Bettelheim, *The Uses of Enchantment: The Meaning and Importance of Fairy Tales* (New York: Alfred A. Knopf, 1976), p. 97.

16 Bettelheim, p. 100.

17 Bettelheim, p. 101.

18 Bettelheim, p. 102.

19 Francine 'Penny' Patterson, a graduate student in psychology at Stanford University, quoted in Harold T. P. Hayes, 'The pursuit of reason', *The New York Times Magazine* (12 June 1977), 79.

20 Theodore Sager Meth, a Newark attorney and Seton Hall law professor, quoted in Hayes, 23–4.
21 Herbert Terrace, *Nim* (New York: Plenum Publishing Company, 1979).
22 Thomas Sebeok and Donna Jean Umiker-Sebeok, *Speaking of Apes* (New York: Alfred A. Knopf, 1980).
23 Noam Chomsky, quoted in *Time* magazine, cxv, 10 (10 March 1980), p. 57.
24 *Metamorphoses* ii, l. 485. Citations are from Ovid, *Metamorphoses*, Frank J. Miller (ed.), 2 vols, 2nd edition (Cambridge, Mass.: Harvard University Press, 1921; rpt. 1971).
25 *Met.* iii, ll. 366–7. *The xv Bookes of P. Ovidius Naso: Entitled Metamorphoses*, Arthur Golding (trans.) (London: John Danter, 1593).
26 *Met.* iii, ll. 192–3, Golding (trans.).
27 *Met.* i, ll. 647–50, Golding (trans.).

5

WOMEN'S RITES

'AS SECRET AS MAIDENHEAD'

❧❧ ❧❧

I

The history of the family, sex and marriage, long of interest to playwrights and novelists, has lately been the subject of several illuminating studies by demographic historians. Drawing upon such evidence as parish registers, diaries, autobiographies, household listing, family correspondence and church court records, scholars like Lawrence Stone, Peter Laslett and the Cambridge Group for the History of Population and Social Structure have attempted to survey the domestic relationships and sexual habits of previous generations in England. Stone, in particular, has sought to draw conclusions and establish trends from the data he has collected, creating what one reviewer called a 'typology'[1] of changes in social behavior over the period 1500–1800.

In approaching the predominant patterns of sexual and marital behavior in Shakespeare's plays, it will be useful to consider some of this material, as a way of understanding both what the playwright might have inherited and observed from his times, and how he changed it to conform to his own dramatic purposes. The plays reflect contemporary social history as well as the writings of Elizabethan historians, and the canons of the church courts are sources in some ways as germane to our inquiry as the novelle of Lodge and Greene.

Before Lord Hardwicke's clarifying Marriage Act of 1753, the rite of marriage itself was quite ambiguously defined in England, consisting as it did of no less than five separate steps: (1) a written financial contract between the parents; (2) the spousals, or contract, a formal exchange of oral promises; (3) the proclamation of banns three times in the local church of one of the parties; (4) the wedding ceremony in church; and (5) the sexual consummation. This sequence was further complicated by the existence of two kinds of spousals, the contract *per verba de futuro* and the contract *per verba de praesenti*. As their names imply, the contract *per verba de futuro* involved promises to marry in the future, and the contract *per verba de praesenti* promises couched in the present tense (as, 'I do take thee for my wife'). This second kind of promise, in the present tense, was considered by ecclesiastical law to be a binding legal marriage, which would invalidate a later church wedding to another person. The contract *per verba de futuro* also became binding if it was followed by sexual consummation.[2]

Bearing this information in mind, we can, for example, see more clearly into the complexities of *Measure for Measure*. Claudio has been imprisoned for the sin of sexual intercourse with his fiancée, in a judgment which echoes the disapproval of the church; yet by that church's law he is nonetheless (because of that act) now legally married to Juliet. Angelo, in the same play, has apparently engaged at least in a contract *per verba de futuro* with Mariana. According to the duke,

> She should this Angelo have married; was affianced to her by oath, and the nuptial appointed: between which time of the contract and limit of the solemnity, her brother Frederick was wracked at sea, having in that perished vessel the dowry of his sister.   (III. i. 213–17)

In the shipwreck Mariana lost not only her brother and her dowry, but also her 'combinate husband' (222), for Angelo then abandoned his vows, and accused her falsely of dishonor. The 'bed trick' arranged by the duke thus adds sexual consummation to the oral contract, and neatly completes the marriage. It is from this tangled ambiguity of terms and steps that Mariana derives the riddle of her status as 'neither maid, widow, nor wife' (v. i. 177–8).

The matter of contract and precontract is also raised in *King Lear*, where Albany ironically intercedes in Regan's claim to Edmund's hand: 'For your claim, fair sister,' he declares,

I bar it in the interest of my wife.
'Tis she is subcontracted to this lord,
And I, her husband, contradict your banes.
If you will marry, make your loves to me;
My lady is bespoke.   (v. iii. 85–90)

This was indeed the purpose of the banns, to allow allegations of precontract to be heard; Albany deliberately mocks the process, calling into question yet another one of the play's problematic 'bonds'. Edmund himself will take up the figure as he lies mortally wounded, when, receiving news of the sisters' death, he announces 'I was contracted to them both: all three / Now marry in an instant' (230–1). The familiar Renaissance pun on 'die' is here combined with the language of contractual marriage to produce an effect that is doubly disconcerting.

Elsewhere in the plays we hear Falstaff boasting that he has conscripted 'contracted bachelors, such as had been asked twice on the banes' (1HIV iv. ii. 16–17) – and who are thus presumably eager to buy their freedom – and we witness Katherine's anticipation of her shame when Petruchio fails to appear: 'to be noted for a merry man, / He'll woo a thousand, 'point the day of marriage, / Make friends, invite, and proclaim the banns, / Yet never means to wed where he hath wooed' (Shr. iii. ii. 14–17). The aborted marriage ceremony of Claudio and Hero in Much Ado about Nothing, which to Benedick 'looks not like a nuptial' (iv. i. 67), is an instance of the denial of contract at the stage of the church wedding, on grounds similar to those feigned by Angelo: the dishonorable conduct of the bride.

In an attempt to regularize and control marital proceedings which seemed to encourage lax behavior, the Anglican canons of 1604 laid down strict rules about the times and places of church weddings. They were to occur only between the hours of 8 a.m. and noon, in the local parish of one of the partners – again, we assume, to ensure that no conflicting precontract existed. Marriages performed in secular places like inns, or at inappropriate times, such as night, would incur serious penalties for the clergyman. The hedge-priest Sir Oliver Mar-Text in As You Like It is a good example of the kind of clergyman the canons wished to discourage, for reasons which are made clear in an exchange between Jaques and Touchstone:

Jaques   And will you, being a man of your breeding, be
married under a bush like a beggar? Get you to church,
and have a good priest that can tell you what marriage
is. This fellow will but join you together as they join
wainscot; then one of you will prove a shrunk panel,
and like green timber warp, warp.

Touchstone   [*Aside*] I am not in the mind but I were better to
be married of him than of another; for he is not like to
marry me well; and not being well married, it will be a
good excuse for me hereafter to leave my wife.

(III. iii. 81–92)

In the event, Touchstone is persuaded, and rejects the services of
Sir Oliver to join instead in the 'blessed bond of board and bed'
(v. iv. 142) presided over by Hymen, the god of 'high wedlock'
(144).

Olivia in *Twelfth Night* is clearly more amenable to the idea of
permanence in marriage, persuading Sebastian to 'go with me
and with this holy man / Into the chantry by' (IV. ii. 23–4), the
nearby parish chapel. The ceremony there performed, 'a contract of eternal bond of love' (v. i. 155), is probably a contract *per
verba de praesenti*, given Olivia's impatience and eagerness; in
any case she subsequently addresses Viola–Cesario (to whom
she thinks she is contracted) as 'husband' (v. i. 141). On the
other hand, in both *The Winter's Tale* and *The Tempest*, the
contract seems clearly *per verba de futuro*: Florizel speaks of
'that nuptial, which / We two have sworn shall come' (*WT*
IV. iv. 50–1), and asserts his resolute chastity, while Prospero
enjoins Ferdinand not to 'break [Miranda's] virgin-knot before
/ All sanctimonious ceremonies may / With full and holy rite be
minist'red' (*Tmp*. IV. i. 15–17).

Another common situation the canons of 1604 sought to
correct was that of precipitate early marriage; marriages between persons less than twenty-one years of age were in that
year prohibited without the consent of parents or guardians. Yet
once again, although a clergyman performing such a ceremony
was liable to punishment, the marriages so performed were
deemed both valid and irrevocable. The problem, of course,
predated the attempted solution, and Shakespeare touched on it
in the situation of Romeo and Juliet. The place of their secret

marriage is acceptable – the friar's cell – and the time equally so – it is something after half-past-nine in the morning (II. v. 1–2); these particulars might be seen as emphasizing the spiritual legitimacy of the marriage. Yet the subsequent suggestion made by Juliet's Nurse, that having seen Romeo banished she should consent to marry Paris, is more outrageous to modern sensibilities than it would have been to a contemporary audience. Bigamy was a frequent occurrence, which usually went unpunished and even undetected; it was not until 1603 that it became a civil offense.[3] As early as the first act the Nurse had expressed the ambiguous desire to 'see thee married once' (I. iii. 61), leaving the door open for more; her pragmatic observation 'Your first is dead – or 'twere as good he were / As living here and you no use of him' (III. v. 226–7) gave voice to a common sentiment, particularly among the lower classes – though needless to say not one that Shakespeare urged upon his hearers.

The greatest violation committed by Romeo and Juliet, however, was in marrying without their parents' permission – for this action struck at the core of the entire social system. The objectives of marriage were the consolidation and safeguarding of family property, the acquisition of further property or other financial advantage, and the continuity of the family lineage and name through procreation. It was an accepted fact of sixteenth-century life that marriages were arranged by the parents, based upon these economic considerations, and without regard to ties of affection or personal choice. Indeed Dr Johnson, writing two hundred years later, could still express the conviction that 'marriages would in general be as happy, and often more so, if they were all made by the Lord Chancellor, upon a due consideration of the characters and circumstances, without the parties having any choice in the matter'.[4] The doctrine of filial obedience in the sixteenth century was based firmly upon the Fifth Commandment, as stressed by both Protestant clergymen and spokesmen for the state,[5] but its roots were as much economic and political as they were moral. Thus Lawrence Stone suggests:

> To an Elizabethan audience the tragedy of Romeo and Juliet, like that of Othello, lay not so much in their ill-starred romance as in the way they brought destruction upon themselves by violating the norms of the society in which they

lived, which in the former case meant strict filial obedience and loyalty to the traditional friendships and enmities of the lineage. An Elizabethan courtier would be familiar enough with the bewitching passion of love to feel some sympathy with the young couple, but he would see clearly enough where duty lay.[6]

Naturally enough, the economic considerations were most visible, if not necessarily most important, among the great families and the nobility. The opening scene of *King Lear* is not only an abdication and a division of the kingdom, but also, by design, a betrothal. Cordelia is courted by two men of noble lineage, who are significantly described by epithets of property: 'to [her] young love / The vines of France and milk of Burgundy / Strive to be interest' (i. i. 83–5). But once 'her price is fallen,' (197) Burgundy refuses her hand: 'Election makes not up on such conditions' (206). The gallant rejoinder of France, 'She is herself a dowry' (241), expresses a satisfying sentiment from the vocabulary of romantic love, but remains a most untypical point of view for an Elizabethan monarch. Cordelia's corresponding idealism ('Peace be with Burgundy. / Since that respects of fortune are his love, / I shall not be his wife' – 247–9) underscores the fact that this attitude is an unusual and symbolic departure from the social norm, germane to Shakespeare's dramatic purposes, and deliberately contrary to accepted political and economic custom. The norm would probably be represented more nearly by Angelo's rejection of the dowerless Mariana, or by Bertram's refusal to have a 'poor physician's daughter' as his wife (*All's Well* ii. iii. 116).

But then Shakespeare is not exclusively concerned with portraying norms. The elements of social realism in his plays rather serve as a background for the emblematic patterns he devises, and as counterpoint to his central characters and their actions. The concept of romantic love, celebrated by courtiers in England since the twelfth century and fostered in Shakespeare's time by both poets and playwrights, offered a beguiling literary alternative to the cold facts of sexual and marital behavior. The nobles and the upper classes must have known both fact and art, and perhaps – like the lords in *Love's Labor's Lost* – allowed the latter to influence the former. But despite the appeal of a conceit like love at first sight, 'falling in love' as it was popularized by Petrarch and depicted in Shakespearean comedy remained very much a minority experience, especially among the propertied classes.[7]

The pragmatic approach to marriage and family planning had its counterpart in the process of child-rearing itself, and notably with the personage of the wet-nurse. Infants of the upper classes were routinely separated from their mothers after birth and sent out to wet-nurses, where they spent, on average, the first eighteen months to two years of life. Thus, as we shall see, Leontes taunts Hermione by declaring himself glad that she did not nurse their son, the prince. In some wealthy families the nurse became a permanent member of the household, remaining on as the child's friend and confidant after the weaning process had been completed. Juliet's Nurse is one such figure, demonstrably closer to her charge than are the elder Capulets. We hear of her own daughter Susan, now dead, who was born at the same time as Juliet, and of Juliet's weaning eleven years ago (at the age of three!), when she tasted wormwood on the Nurse's nipple, and proceeded to 'fall out with the dug' (I. iii. 32). It is not clear whether Marina's nurse Lychorida is a wet-nurse, but she is manifestly the strongest personal influence on Marina from birth to puberty, since Pericles, believing his wife dead, has placed his infant daughter into the care of foster parents, the King and Queen of Tharsus. Euriphile, the nurse of Cymbeline's sons, stole them from the king at the behest of the aggrieved Belarius, and the young men grew to manhood regarding the couple as their natural parents; so also Perdita believes herself the child of the shepherd and his wife. In fact, one psychological outgrowth of the practice of wet-nursing was a not infrequent identity crisis on the part of many adults, as reflected in the popular changeling fairy tales of the period. It was perhaps natural to imagine that a wet-nurse whose wealthy charge had died might substitute a child of her own for the missing infant, so as to avoid punishment.[8]

Nor were the children of the period permitted much more access to their parents as they grew older. The practice of 'fostering out', whereby young people left the home at an early age – about ten – for school or work elsewhere, was extremely common in the sixteenth century. Among its other effects, fostering out led to a concept of adolescence (or 'youth') as a separate stage of human development between sexual maturity in the teen years and marriage in the middle twenties. Lawrence Stone nicely observes that the shepherd in Shakespeare's *Winter's Tale* 'must have struck a familiar chord when he remarked, ''I would there were no age between sixteen and twenty-three, or that youth would sleep out the rest; for there is nothing in the between but getting wenches with child, wronging the ancientry, stealing, fighting.'' '[9] To this category of 'youth' we may assign the young bloods who travel with Romeo, as well as Prince Hal's tavern friends, and, allowing for some difference in class, Rosencrantz and Guildenstern – perhaps even Laertes. It may be noticed that this list of 'youth' is composed almost exclusively of secondary characters; if Romeo and Hal and Hamlet are adolescents, they are so in a very special sense, and their progress toward adulthood is deliberately played off against that of their peers. But the very device of 'playing off' is made possible, in part, by the existence of historical norms and historical practices, familiar to the audience, against which the playwright could counterpoise his characters and his plot.

The concept of 'youth' as the shepherd describes it did not, of course, apply to the young women of the period, although typically they too passed a considerable time between the onset of puberty and the entry into marriage – if indeed they married at all. From the thirteenth through the early sixteenth century, when English nunneries flourished, it was not uncommon for fathers to pledge their daughters to the religious life in order to avoid the expense of a large dowry.[10] The situation of Hermia, forced to choose between an arranged marriage and the cloister, is likewise certainly not without precedent in fact. Yet the suppression of Catholicism and the abolition of the nunneries in England, while greatly increasing the number of women who married, rather constricted than expanded the options open to them. Before the Reformation a well-born woman ambitious of personal power often found the freedom she sought rather as the head of a nunnery than as a wife, however important her husband – nor did the rigors of convent life apparently prevent her from indulging a taste for personal luxuries.[11] Unlike the case of

Shakespeare's deliberately reclusive nuns, such as Emilia in *The Comedy of Errors*, the convent for some of these women was a way of entering the world even as they were by convention dead to it.

But with the coming of the Protestant ascendancy a new emphasis was placed upon the wife's duty and subjection to her husband, and upon the 'feminine' domestic arts. It is true that during the central decades of the sixteenth century a brief movement toward classical education for women was given impetus by such humanists as Vives and Erasmus. Queen Elizabeth was herself one of the women affected by this trend. She spoke fluent Latin, Greek, French and Italian, and could boast to Essex of confounding an impertinent Polish ambassador with extempore remarks in Latin – a tongue which had 'lain long rusting' since her schooldays.[12] As late as 1580 Richard Mulcaster still endorsed the idea of women's education, writing in praise of the many women in the country 'so excellently well trained and so rarely qualified in regard both to the tongues themselves and to the subject-matter contained in them'.[13] But even as he wrote, education in the classics was being replaced by a return to the traditional courtly graces: the needlework in which we find Hermia, Helena and Marina so well skilled, the 'music, instruments and poetry' which delight the docile Bianca in *The Taming of the Shrew* (i. i. 92), and the dancing so deftly performed by the ladies of *Love's Labor's Lost*. The older, more 'masculine' model would perhaps have been more to the taste of other Shakespearean women, like Beatrice, Portia and Kate. But pressures from Protestant clergymen strongly urged a return to the concept of docility in women and wives. Luther's view that women should mind the house and bring up the children was echoed and supported by Protestant theologians and lay persons throughout England. The Homily on Marriage, which was to be read out periodically in all Anglican churches from 1562 onwards, plainly asserted the inferiority of women:

> The woman is a weak creature not endued with like strength and constancy of mind; therefore, they be the sooner disquieted, and they be the more prone to all weak affections and dispositions of mind, more than men be; and lighter they be, and more vain in their fantasies and opinions.[14]

Still, there was a woman on the throne, and clergymen, like poets and playwrights, were well advised to walk carefully. Bishop Aylmer, in a sermon before Elizabeth, spoke of two kinds of women, some 'wiser, better learned, discreeter, and more constant than a number of men', the others 'fond, foolish, wanton, flibbergibs, tattlers, triflers, wavering, witless, without council, feeble, careless, rash, proud, dainty, tale-bearers, eaves-droppers, rumour-raisers, evil-tongued, worse-minded, and in everyway doltified by the dregs of the devil's dunghill'.[15] Whether Gloriana was mollified by this politic distinction is not certain. Without doubt, however, the situation of the Virgin Queen created special problems. On the one hand, women were almost universally thought to be inferior, unworthy of holding property, in law and theology alike subjugated to the will of their husbands, basically valuable for the dowries they brought with them and the children they produced. On the other hand, the sovereign was not only a woman but an unmarried woman, without husband or heirs. One member of Parliament in 1559 spoke for them all when he opined that 'nothing can be more contrary to the public respects than that of the Princess, in whose marriage is comprehended the safety and peace of the Commonwealth, should live unmarried, and as it were a Vestal Virgin'.[16]

Elizabeth herself was not unmindful of this conventual parallel. At one point, early in the reign, she dramatically drew her coronation ring from her finger and held it aloft to declare herself England's nun: 'behold the pledge of this my wedlock and marriage with my Kingdom'.[17] Certainly she was as aware as any medieval abbess that her power in some ways derived from her single state – that to marry would inevitably be to subjugate herself to both a husband and a king. Nor could she have forgotten the fate of her mother or that of her father's other wives, forced to surrender not only autonomy but sometimes life itself in Henry's relentless quest for a male heir to his throne. Elizabeth's repeated assertions that she preferred a virgin life were almost surely colored by politics as well as by personal preference,[18] but whatever the reason she elected not to marry, her rhetoric of virginity remained to be dealt with by her citizens and courtiers – side by side with her lifelong taste for flirtation and courtship. Throughout her long career Elizabeth remained a paradox for her times, the foremost of Knox's 'monstrous regiment of women' – a keenly intelligent, highly educated, strong-minded, single woman, ruling England absolutely, submissive only to God.

Yet despite the dazzling example of the Virgin Queen, the philosophers and the theologians of the age were turning away from the medieval ideal of chastity and toward the concept of 'holy matrimony', marriage as a condition decidedly preferable to the celibate life of the cloister. In 1523 Erasmus had written that lifelong virginity was a flower which 'hathe her bryghte beautye, her fayre fragrancy, her grace and dignities in *this world*'[19] – incorporating the priest, monk or nun into the mainstream of life. However, a hundred years later the tide had shifted. Cardinal Bellarmine still held to the Pauline view that marriage was for those who could not resist the weakness of the flesh: 'marriage is a thing humane, virginity is angelical'.[20] But the celebrated Protestant preacher William Perkins took a different stance: marriage, he asserted, was 'a state in itself far more excellent than the condition of a single life'.[21] In 1549 Archbishop Cranmer had added to his new Prayer Book a third motive for marriage, joining it to the ancient purposes of avoiding fornication and bearing legitimate children; now 'mutual society, help and comfort' was also deemed an acceptable reason to marry. The idea of 'holy matrimony' was coupled with that of 'matrimonial chastity', moderation of sexual passion within marriage – a phrase that sounds curiously like the problematic 'married chastity' of Shakespeare's Phoenix and Turtle, which resulted in their 'leaving no posterity'. (*P&T* 59–61). What 'matrimonial chastity' and 'holy matrimony' meant for the development of social institutions in England was an inevitable clash between the old practice of arranged marriages and strict filial obedience, and the new doctrine, encouraged by Protestant theologians, of personal choice in wedlock. Lust was as unacceptable in marriage as out of it, but the claims of affection and preference were growing stronger. In the later seventeenth century the cause would be taken up by numbers of prominent Protestants and Puritans; Jeremy Taylor would compare marital love to the purity of light and the sacredness of a temple, and Milton would claim that the chief purpose of marriage was neither procreation nor civil order, but 'the apt and cheerful conversation of man with woman, to comfort and refresh him against the solitary life'.[22]

*

For Shakespeare, himself coming of age as a dramatist in this period of consolidation and change, the prevailing beliefs of the time about marriage, virginity, chastity and child-rearing were essential materials for his art. In the history plays he deals vividly with the question of marriages arranged for political purposes and personal gain. The surrogate wooing of Suffolk, the cynical marital politics of Richard III, and Henry V's moving attempt to express his love for Katherine as a personal need over and above the needs of the state – all these are placed against the background of historical custom. The deep affection between Richard II and his queen is yet another evidence of Richard's primary identity as a private person rather than a public monarch – and it is useful to remember here that Shakespeare changed history in order to make the queen a grown woman. Laertes' assertion to Ophelia that Hamlet is a prince, and therefore 'may not, as unvalued persons do, / Carve for himself' (*Ham.* I. iii. 19–20) touches upon the same theme, as (on the level of the squirearchy) do *A Midsummer Night's Dream*, *Romeo and Juliet* and *Othello*. The figure of the tyrant father, defender of patriarchy and patrimony, is everywhere in his work, from Egeus to Shylock.

Yet Shakespeare was by no means, of course, merely the creature of his time. In comedies, tragedies and histories alike, he describes love in affective terms which for the most part go beyond even the courtly expectations of romantic love. As we shall see, his characters are often vividly aware of their own sexuality. His women, in particular, are frequently outspoken about their sexual feelings, as well as about the quality of their love. Certainly they are not the tattlers and triflers of Bishop Aylmer's diatribe; rather, time and again, they show themselves wiser and more capable than their lovers and husbands. In short, much as we should expect, Shakespeare uses the beliefs and practices of the world around him to inform his own dramatic vision, not as a copyist but as an interpreter, making of social custom a thematic instrument to reveal the nature of his characters and their situations.

The rites of passage which demarcate sexual growth to maturity are explored in the plays in considerable detail, in terms which are at some times literal, at others metaphorical or emblematic. To observe them more closely, it will therefore be useful to divide our topic into three phases: sexual self-knowledge as manifested in attitudes towards virginity, chastity and sexuality; actual rites, like marriage, defloration, child-bearing and nursing; and symbolic or metaphorical representations of sexual themes.

II

In the opening scene of *A Midsummer Night's Dream*, Theseus cautions Hermia to consider her choices carefully: if she does not marry Demetrius, she must either die, or 'abjure / Forever the society of men'.

> Therefore, fair Hermia, question your desires;
> Know of your youth, examine well your blood,
> Whether, if you yield not to your father's choice,
> You can endure the livery of a nun,
> For aye to be in shady cloister mewed,
> To live a barren sister all your life,
> Chanting faint hymns to the cold fruitless moon.
> Thrice-blessèd they that master so their blood.
> To undergo such maiden pilgrimage;
> But earthlier happy is the rose distilled,
> Than that which, withering on the virgin thorn,
> Grows, lives, and dies in single blessedness.
>
> (I. i. 65–78)

Despite his perfunctory praise for the 'blessed' condition of virginity, Theseus – himself shortly to become a bridegroom – clearly regards a life of cloistered celibacy as not very different from the alternative punishment of death. His choice of words – 'endure', 'barren', 'faint', 'cold', 'fruitless', 'withering' – creates a vivid picture of denial and consequent deterioration. By contrast the rose is 'earthlier happy' because it is distilled, transmuted to a perfume which lingers and gives pleasure.

In fact, cloisters, monasteries and nunneries in the plays are not seen as productive parts of 'this world' at all. We have already noted that the abbesses in *The Comedy of Errors* and *Pericles* both emerge from seclusion to resume their social roles as wives and mothers, and that Hamlet's injunction to Ophelia to 'get thee to a nunnery' underscores Ophelia's persistent refusal of adult responsibility. In a similar way Friar Lawrence proves an unfit counsellor for Romeo and Juliet precisely because of his unworldliness, his lack of experience. His bromidic advice to 'love moderately' is wholly at odds with the precipitousness of their youthful passion and its language of lightning and excess. Moreover, when pressed by circumstances, he forgets his own conviction that 'They stumble that run fast' (ii. iii. 94) and intervenes with unwonted haste – performing the secret marriage, administering the sleeping potion, posting a letter to Romeo that is never delivered, and finally stumbling himself, both literally and figuratively, in the graveyard. Though he is pardoned by the Prince of Verona – on the grounds that 'We still [i.e. always] have known thee for a holy man' (v. iii. 271) – this holy unworldliness is precisely his problem, and his naive attempt to apply the *sententiae* of the cell to the world of love and action is in large measure responsible for the play's tragic outcome.

A complementary pattern is exemplified by the duke in *Measure for Measure*, himself very much a man of 'this world', who takes on the fictive identity of 'Friar Lodowick' to observe and control corruption in Vienna. Lucio's description of him as a 'meddling friar' (v. i. 127) fits Friar Lawrence as aptly as Friar Lodowick, but the duke's manipulations are founded in a wiser and less absolute understanding of human nature. Both friars attempt to direct the course of events in the plays of which they bear a part – indeed, the duke has often been compared to a playwright, as well as to God. Structurally, Friar Lawrence's devices might merit the same comparison, except for the important fact that his plans inevitably miscarry, leading at last not to 'wedding cheer' but to a 'sad burial feast' (*R&J* iv. v. 87). The functional distinction between the two men is pre-eminently that of experience in the world. Like Emilia and Thaisa, the duke enters his monastery as a temporary refuge, and emerges from it at the play's end to preside over several marriages, including – perhaps – his own.

Together with *All's Well*, *Measure for Measure* probably

stands as the most direct Shakespearean exploration of the psychological effects of celibacy. In that play Angelo, a self-declared Puritan, reveals himself as a sensualist and 'virgin-violator' (v. i. 41), while Isabella, who is about to enter a convent, can utter the chilling sentiment that 'More than our brother is our chastity' (II. iv. 184) at the same time that she describes the loss of virginity in terms both sexual and pathological:

> Th' impression of keen whips I'd wear as rubies,
> And strip myself to death as to a bed
> That longing have been sick for, ere I'd yield
> My body up to shame.   (II. iv. 100–3)

For both Angelo and Isabella, virginity has itself become a mode of excess, as dangerous in its way as the licentiousness of Lucio, and much more damaging to personal development than the sin of impregnation for which Claudio lies under sentence of death. Isabella, too, is under sentence – a self-imposed one – for she is denying the very process of growth and life. The scene (I. iv.) in which Lucio tells her of her brother's sentence adroitly juxtaposes her uncompromising view with its polar opposite. For Isabella has chosen the order of St Clare, a sisterhood noted for its strictness – and she would prefer a yet 'more strict restraint' (4). Here again her attitude toward the virgin life is one of almost self-indulgent excess. Only because she is as yet unsworn is she permitted to speak to Lucio and receive his message – a message couched in lyrical and sensuous terms sharply at odds with the spare diction of the rest of the scene, and indeed the rest of the play. This is one of those passages in which the poet Shakespeare seems to speak through (instead of in) his character, for the language is not really appropriate to Lucio; rather, its presence in the scene seems a clear contro-version of the 'strict restraint' Isabella would impose upon life and speech:

> Your brother and his lover have embraced;
> As those that feed grow full, as blossoming time
> That from the seedness the bare fallow brings
> To teeming foison, even so her plenteous womb
> Expresseth his full tilth and husbandry.   (40–4)

The prolific agricultural metaphor, the richness of descriptive detail, even the double meaning of 'husbandry' here emphasize the fruitful and productive value of sexuality and child-bearing. We may recall Theseus' contrasting language of fruitlessness in discussing the life of a 'barren sister' – as well as Isabella's own call for restraint. When, shortly thereafter, Lucio characterizes Lord Angelo as 'a man whose blood / Is very snow-broth' (57–8), the contrast of seasons and temperaments is even more clearly drawn.

As we have seen, Isabella's metaphorical identification of Juliet as her 'cousin' serves to emphasize the contrast between the two young women. Where once they were virtually inter-changeable, another set of Shakespearean twins, one 'cousin' is now entering a convent, the other bearing a child. Later in the play, the appearance of Mariana as a medial figure will help to fill out the continuum of women's roles. Isabella refuses sexuality and thus denies life both to herself and to her brother; Mariana, a virgin when the play begins, sleeps with Angelo and consum-mates their marriage, postponed when her own brother died and lost her dowry at sea; Juliet fulfills the promise of marriage in her pregnancy, and asserts to the duke that the act of love was 'mutually committed' (II. iii. 27), the responsibility of both lovers equally. She thus associates herself with those other Shakespearean women (like her namesake Juliet and like Desde-mona) who actively declare their own sexual identities and desires.

It may be well at this point to emphasize that the repre-sentation of virginity in Shakespeare's plays is by no means entirely negative. Prospero's concern that Ferdinand not 'break [Miranda's] virgin-knot before / All sanctimonious ceremonies' (IV. i. 15–16) is represented as both natural and appropriate, the king in *All's Well That Ends Well* promises Diana a husband 'If thou be'st yet a fresh uncroppèd flower' (v. iii. 326), and Marina is able to transform the clients of a brothel into men who prefer to hear the vestals sing. All three of these women are virgins – but all will also shortly be brides. It is when the condition of virginity becomes a stasis rather than a stage that the plays invite us to regard it with a disapproving eye. Spenser's Brito-mart is a militant virgin, whose power derives in part from her virginity, although she too progresses toward marriage. In

Shakespeare's plays the only militant virgins are Isabella, in whom the desire for lifelong celibacy is represented as almost pathological, and Joan La Pucelle, who as she approaches the stake declares that she is pregnant – whether by the Dauphin, or the King of Naples, or the Duke of Alençon. Marina comes as close as any Shakespearean woman to the ideal of the virgin endowed by her condition with special powers, and indeed I think we never quite find her betrothal to Lysimachus believable. However, the romance genre of *Pericles*, and in particular the play's stress on a virtuous love between father and daughter contrasting with the incestuous passion of Antiochus, help to set her aside as a special case outside the general pattern.

In general, then, those Shakespearean characters who adopt a rule of celibacy in adulthood do so in defiance – or ignorance – of their own natures. The lords in *Love's Labor's Lost* proudly swear to 'war against [their] own affections / And the huge army of the world's desires' (I. i. 9–10) – and at once fall most inconveniently in love. Their 'little academe' is a secularized version of the monastery, even less admirable because it is dedicated not to the worship of God but to their own vain quest for fame. The stylized courtship and covert sonneteering to which these lords are reduced is neatly counterpointed by Costard's overtly sexual interest in the wench Jaquenetta and his artless defense of natural sexuality: 'Such is the simplicity of man to hearken after the flesh' (I. i. 216–17). In this respect, the character of Costard, though much more attractive, looks forward to the plain-spoken advocates of sexual freedom in the dark comedies: Pompey the bawd in *Measure for Measure*, who advises Escalus that young men 'will to't' unless 'your worship mean[s] to geld and splay all the youth of the city' (II. i. 228–31), and Parolles in *All's Well That Ends Well*.

In fact, the most extended argument against virginity in the plays is offered by the frankly unamiable figure of Parolles, who is rightly described by Helena as a liar, a fool and a coward. But in his own way Parolles is one of Shakespeare's realists, a figure akin to Emilia in *Othello* and Enobarbus in *Antony and Cleopatra*; as he says, simply the thing he is shall make him live. His voice provides a necessary counterpoint to the romantic idealism of both Helena and Bertram, as for example when, having inquired whether Helena is 'meditating on virginity', he offers a meditation of his own:

> Loss of virginity is rational increase, and there was never virgin got till virginity was first lost. . . . 'Tis too cold a companion. . . . There's little can be said in't; 'tis against the rule of nature. To speak on the part of virginity, is to accuse your mothers. . . . Besides, virginity is peevish, proud, idle, made of self-love. . . . Off with 't while 'tis vendible . . . your old virginity is like one of our French withered pears: it looks ill, it eats drily; marry, 'tis a withered pear.
>
> (I. i. 130–65)

What is missing from this dispassionate summary is, of course, any sense that sexual relationships are founded on idealism and love, and Helena quite properly responds with a spirited defense of her particular love for Bertram, to whom she wishes to be 'a mother, and a mistress, and a friend . . . a guide, a goddess, and a sovereign' (169–71).

While Parolles is advocating license, his appraisal of virginity has striking affinities with other, more sympathetically expressed sentiments on the subject elsewhere in Shakespeare's plays. For example, he shares with Theseus the view that virginity is 'cold' and 'withered' – a life-denying state – though he omits the balancing praise of marriage essential to Theseus' speech. His materialistic injunction, 'Off with't while 'tis vendible', which reduces love to a commodity, at the same time calls to mind Rosalind's much more appealing – but equally unromantic – admonition to the love-struck Phebe: 'Sell when you can, you are not for all markets' (*AYLI* III. v. 60). And his association of virginity with pride and self-love is exemplified in *Twelfth Night* by both the self-cloistered Olivia and the Puritan Malvolio. Parolles' speech confirms the audience's sense that he, like Pompey in *Measure for Measure*, is a severely limited human being, but his pronouncement that virginity is 'against the rule of nature' is nowhere contradicted in Shakespeare's works. Even the churlish hero of *Venus and Adonis*, who disdains 'sweating lust' and the determined advances of the goddess of love herself, is held up in comic contrast to his more amorous and self-knowledgeable – and in this way more human – horse.

Adonis may be assumed to be a virgin in the same sense as Isabella; indeed, his protestations are amusing in part because, in defiance of the usual sexual stereotype, he seems to be defending his virtue, while Venus offers the habitual *carpe diem* arguments of the male seducer (ll. 745–68). As a rule, however, refusals of sexuality (and consequently of adulthood) in Shakespeare are divided, as we should expect, along lines of gender, women (like Isabella) protesting against the loss of literal virginity, men (like the Navarrese lords) imposing upon themselves an unnatural abstinence. In *A Midsummer Night's Dream* Hermia resists Lysander's invitation to lie beside him in the wood, though he protests that his intentions are honorable:

> gentle friend, for love and courtesy
> Lie further off, in human modesty.
> Such separation as may well be said
> Becomes a virtuous bachelor and a maid,
> So far be distant.   (ii. ii. 56–60)

This decision has important dramatic consequences: Lysander's eyes are anointed by Puck, who reads the separation of the pair, not unnaturally, as a sign of his indifference to her: 'She durst not lie / Near this lack-love, this kill-courtesy' (76–7). As a result, he wakes to declare his allegiance to the first woman he sees, who happens to be Helena. Hermia then awakens alone, remembering with terror a dream in which she is attacked by a snake, while Lysander sits by and smiles – a dream which seems very like a metaphor for her sexual fears. Hermia's prudery is in striking contrast to the active and energetic quest for love by Helena, whom Demetrius upbraids for her boldness:

> You do impeach your modesty too much,
> To leave the city, and commit yourself
> Into the hands of one that loves you not,
> To trust the opportunity of night
> And the ill counsel of a desert place
> With the rich worth of your virginity.   (ii. i. 214–19)

Helena's instant reply, 'Your virtue is my privilege' (220), is a direct inversion of Hermia's response to Lysander, and suggests a distinction between the two women which is borne out by the development of the plot. From this point Helena's fortunes will

rise and Hermia's fall, until Hermia too realizes something of
the pain and risk which are intrinsic to love. The elopement into
the wood is not enough; only through solitude is Hermia forced
to confront her emerging identity as a lover – and as a woman. In
a play which begins and ends with reminders of sexual eagerness
– 'how slow / This old moon wanes! She lingers my desires'
(I. i. 3–4); 'to wear away this long age of three hours / Between
our aftersupper and bedtime' (v. i. 33–4) – acceptance of the
sexual aspects of love is an essential prerequisite for successful
adulthood and marriage.

A timidity similar to Hermia's appears to afflict Hero in *Much
Ado about Nothing*. Hero's submissiveness to her father is made
clear early in the play, when he tells her of Don Pedro's supposed
suit for her hand and apparently receives her consent; after the
error is discovered and corrected, she is equally willing to wed
Claudio. Yet on the eve of her wedding she displays a real
reluctance even to talk about sex and lovemaking. Margaret's
jests about being 'heavier soon by the weight of a man' (III. iv. 26)
are met only by 'Fie upon thee! Art not ashamed?' (27), and the
audience must feel some sympathy for Margaret's ensuing
defense of marriage – sex and all – as an 'honorable' estate. We
may think that Hero pays an excessively great price for the small
vices of prudery and passivity, but the pattern she follows here is
a familiar one, differentiating her in crucial ways from those
bolder female spirits who defy their fathers' wishes and express a
positive wish for sexual fulfillment.

For male characters facing similar problems of sexual self-
knowledge the consequences can be even more acute, since they
typically respond not with passivity but with precipitous and
ill-conceived action. In the case of Othello, marriage comes
before the confrontation with sexual desire, with disastrous
results. Like Coriolanus, Othello has come of age in war without
pausing to learn the nature of love; his explanation of how he
came to care for Desdemona is ominously expressed in terms of
hero worship:

> She loved me for the dangers I had passed,
> And I loved her that she did pity them.   (I. iii. 166–7)

This is not at all how Desdemona sees their relationship; she
'saw Othello's visage in his mind,' she says, and she 'love[s] the

Moor to live with him' (247, 243), as an equal and a sexual
partner, not an admiring audience: 'if I be left behind, / A moth
of peace, and he go to the war, / The rites for why I love him are
bereft me' (250–2). Yet the consummation of the marriage is
repeatedly deferred. There is a bitter irony in Iago's spate of
sexual images – 'an old black ram / Is tupping your white ewe'
(I. i. 85–6); 'your daughter and the Moor are making the beast
with two backs' (112–14); 'the gross clasps of a lascivious Moor'
(123) – for twice we see Othello roused from his nuptial bed
to attend upon state business; once in Venice, in the council
chamber, and a second time at Cyprus. Even there, though Iago
informs us that 'he hath not yet made wanton the night with
her' (II. iii. 15–16), he leaves Desdemona's bed to silence the
brawling troops: "tis the soldiers' life', he tells her, 'To have
their balmy slumbers waked with strife' (255–6). Moreover, he
goes out of his way to insist that his feelings for her are not
carnal, assuring the duke that he wants her company in Cyprus

> not
> To please the palate of my appetite,
> Nor to comply with heat – the young affects
> In me defunct – and proper satisfaction;
> But to be free and bounteous to her mind.
>
> (I. iii. 256–60)

The general, we may think, protests too much. In his attempt to
be more civilized even than the native Venetians, Othello denies
his own sexual nature: 'The tyrant Custom, most grave senators, / Hath made the flinty and steel couch of war / My thrice-
driven bed of down' (226–8). Once again we may compare this to
Desdemona's frank acknowledgment of 'the rites for why I love
him'. Othello's fall, when it comes, is a direct consequence of his
denial of the primacy of love, both emotionally and sexually.
That he can believe Desdemona unfaithful to him on the slight-
est of hints from Iago – indeed, that he trusts his ancient more
than his wife – derives in large part from his resolute rejection of
the claims of private life. Convinced at last of his wife's infidelity, he laments that 'Othello's *occupation's* gone!' (III. iii. 354) –
his *occupation*, not his marriage. Everything is referred to the
world of war, until the violence of his repressed sexual feelings
takes the displaced form of murder. Significantly, the supposed

'proof' of Desdemona's guilt is the handkerchief spotted with strawberries, which becomes in Othello's mind an unconscious but powerful metaphor for the wedding sheets stained with hymeneal blood. Cassio possesses the handkerchief – therefore, Cassio must have possessed his wife. The wedding sheets themselves, placed on the bed at Desdemona's request, are finally stained not by love but by death, as Othello vows his revenge: 'Thy bed, lust-stained, shall with lust's blood be spotted' (v. i. 36). The confusion of sexual and martial impulses which has characterized him from the beginning is nowhere more tragically evident than in this final scene, when, the 'cold' and 'chaste' Desdemona lying dead before him, Othello can declare, with bitter bravado, 'Behold, I have a weapon; / A better never did itself sustain / Upon a soldier's thigh' (v. ii. 259–61). His refusal to accept his own sexual feelings and to acknowledge the place of sexuality in human life lies at the root of his tragedy.

When a similar situation occurs in a romantic comedy, the outcome is predictably less serious, but tragic possibilities are never far away. Count Claudio in *Much Ado about Nothing*, though described by a jealous rival as – like Cassio – a 'most exquisite' Florentine, also exhibits, oddly enough, certain resemblances to Othello. He has distinguished himself in war 'beyond the promise of his age' (i. i. 13), and, partly in consequence, he has no experience in love. Before the recent war, he says, he 'looked upon [Hero] with a soldier's eye, / That liked, but had a rougher task in hand / Than to drive liking to the name of love' (i. i. 291–3). When he turns his mind to courtship, he is at first uncertain of his own success, seeking an intermediary to plead his suit. Most ominously, he shows a willingness to part from his wife immediately after the wedding. When his commander, Don Pedro, declares his intention to stay only 'until the marriage be consummate', Claudio immediately offers to accompany him to Aragon, and is reproved: 'Nay, that would be as great a soil in the new gloss of your marriage as to show a child his new coat and forbid him to wear it' (iii. ii. 5–7). The simile echoes Juliet's affirmation of sexual longing:

So tedious is this day
As is the night before some festival

> To an impatient child that hath new robes
> And may not wear them.   (*R&J* III. ii. 28–31)

But where Juliet breaks the bounds of modesty to acknowledge her desires, Claudio, like Othello, represses them in a show of civility, subjugating personal to public motives. It is not entirely surprising, then, that like Othello he is easily persuaded of his bride's guilt. Again, the situation in the two plays is structurally similar: where Iago had led Othello to a place from which he could see – and misinterpret – a meeting between Cassio and Desdemona, the Iago-like Don John leads Claudio to the orchard to observe what appears to be a clandestine meeting between Hero and another man. The device of a waiting woman dressed in Hero's clothes is successfully deceptive, and Claudio publicly denounces Hero at the altar:

> Would you not swear,
> All you that see her, that she were a maid,
> By these exterior shows? But she is none.
> She knows the heat of a luxurious bed;
> Her blush is guiltiness, not modesty.   (IV. i. 37–41)

Hero is a 'rotten orange' (31), fair to look upon, but diseased within. Her subsequent swoon and apparent death, like the death of Desdemona – and the later swoon and 'death' of Hermione – symbolically replace and displace the sexual 'death' which should have consummated her marriage. Accused of 'dying' falsely with a lover she must, in the Friar's words, 'die to live' (252), or else face the familiar alternative of banishment to 'some reclusive and religious life' (241). Claudio's education in the nature of love, to the extent that it takes place, is a result of serendipity (the watch has overheard the conspirators) and belated contrition (having killed Hero, he consents to wed her 'cousin', whom he has never seen), rather than a real growth in character; but his willingness to undertake a marriage on faith ('I'll hold my mind, were she an Ethiope' – v. iv. 38) is at least the outward sign of an intimated change. Within the play's comic framework his accusation of Hero has indeed been much ado about nothing, and is easily undone; but the play's title might serve with equal appropriateness as a subtitle for *Othello*, where a failure to accept and understand sexuality converts 'trifles light as air' into proofs of sin and a rationale for murder.

As we have begun to see, for Shakespeare's characters a rejection of sexuality or a denial of its importance can often signal the presence of other serious flaws or failures in self-knowledge. There are, however, occasions in which such behavior is part of a fundamentally sound convention – when it is acknowledged as a stage in human development, rather than asserted as the ultimate ideal of conduct. Romantic lovers in the plays, for example, often include a declaration of their chaste desires as a necessary prelude to marriage. Thus Florizel compares himself favorably to those gods who have transformed themselves for love: 'since my desires / Run not before mine honor, nor my lusts / Burn hotter than my faith' (*WT* iv. iv. 33–5). Similarly, Ferdinand assures Prospero that

> the strong'st suggestion
> Our worser genius can, shall never melt
> Mine honor into lust, to take away
> The edge of that day's celebration
> When I shall think or Phoebus' steeds are foundered
> Or Night kept chained below.   (*Tmp.* iv. i. 26–31)

The masque presented to the lovers, while it includes both Juno, the goddess of marriage, and Ceres, the patroness of fertility, contains only a scathing reference to Venus and Cupid, who are described as intending 'some wanton charm upon this man and maid' (95) to make them break their chaste vows. This propriety of behavior is certainly approved, rather than condemned, in the plays, but there is evidence that Shakespeare wished to balance the picture. The masque of Juno and Ceres is interrupted by Prospero's remembrance of Caliban and his plot – and Caliban is, of course, the play's one unmistakable figure of lust, who (like Ferdinand) desires Miranda, and 'didst seek to violate / The honor of [Prospero's] child' (i. ii. 349–50). In the same way, Florizel's respectful disavowal of lust is complemented almost immediately by the arrival of Autolycus and his bawdy ballads. In *The Winter's Tale* the pre-nuptial event is a sheepshearing feast rather than a pageant, but in both ceremonies – as in both plays – the effect is the same: the young suitor, virtuously praising restraint, is reminded at the moment of his betrothal of the

power and importance of sexual energy. Passing from bachelor-
hood to marriage, he is made to recognize the complexity of an
adult relationship between man and woman. In these two plays,
interestingly, the emblem of sexuality is a fantastic and symbolic figure – Caliban, Autolycus – who differs in kind from the
more realistically drawn lovers; as a result, emphasis is placed
upon the human dilemma of the initiate, the youth on the
threshold of maturity.

When similar figures appear in other plays, providing an
emblematic infusion of sexual energy, they tend likewise to be
privileged, if not by nature then by class or occupation, and thus
to offer a counterpoint to the human drama of choice. Costard
and Pompey are both lower-class figures, who may speak with
freedom and frankness of hearkening after the flesh. The fairy
queen Titania and the ass-headed Bottom (whose elongated ears
and nose suggest corresponding endowments of a sexual nature)
each come from a world apart from that of the Athenian court.
Theirs is the only amorous relationship in the play that does not
lead to marriage, and it clearly represents lust. In this case
reason and love keep no company at all, for as Puck points out,
'My mistress with a monster is in love' (*MND* iii. ii. 6).

In *As You Like It*, another play in which pairs of lovers
contrast vividly with one another in their attitudes toward love,
the irruptive element of sexual energy is provided by Touchstone, who 'press[es] in . . . among the rest of the country
copulatives, to swear and forswear, according as marriage binds
and blood breaks' (v. iv. 56–8). Without Touchstone and his
Audrey – whose name, as he reminds us, rhymes so easily with
bawdry – the dialogue of love in the play would tend, despite
Rosalind's realism, toward the merely literary and the over-
romantic. One reason Rosalind retains her disguise in the wood
once she has found Orlando is surely to educate Orlando in the
complexities of love, and guide him away from the hackneyed
Petrarchan practice of hanging poems on trees. But if Orlando is
too literary, Silvius and Phebe are too romantic – comic star-
crossed shepherd lovers whose rhetoric is as hyperbolic as their
self-knowledge is limited. Touchstone, with his insistence that
shepherds earn their livelihood not by writing poems but by the
copulation of cattle, 'betray[ing] a she-lamb of a twelve-month
to a crookèd-pated old cuckoldly ram, out of all reasonable

match' (III. ii. 79–82), is a constant and necessary corrective to the prevailing tone. 'Will you be married, motley?' asks the solitary Jaques, and Touchstone's reply is once again a reminder of Costard:

> As the ox hath his bow, sir, the horse his curb, and the falcon her bells, so man hath his desires; and as pigeons bill, so wedlock would be nibbling. (III. iii. 77–81)

'We must be married, or we must live in bawdry' (95). Once again a privileged speaker asserts the importance of sexuality in human love. Touchstone's exaggerated insistence on the centrality of sex (like the similar extremes represented by Autolycus and Caliban) helps to balance the romanticism of the other lovers, and provides both for them, and for the audience in the theater, a more mature and self-knowledgeable view of marriage.

Moreover, the situation of Phebe in the same play offers yet another kind of corrective, for Phebe's infatuation with Ganymede–Rosalind is not only blind but also by definition fruitless. This misdirection of sexual desire, doting on a disguised member of one's own sex, is often used by Shakespeare as an indication of self-indulgence and consequent immaturity in love. Rosalind instructs Phebe in no uncertain terms, 'mistress, know yourself. Down on your knees, / And thank heaven, fasting, for a good man's love' (III. v. 57–8). Yet Phebe's transfer of affections from the illusory 'Ganymede' to the importunate Silvius is stylized at best, occurring only as a result of Rosalind's last-minute self-revelation: 'If sight and shape be true, / Why then, my love adieu!' (V. iv. 120–1). Her error of judgment is a metaphorical commentary on Orlando's partial blindness, rather than a focal point of actual growth and change.

In *Twelfth Night*, however, a greater emphasis is placed upon the substitution of an appropriate love object for an impossible one. When we first hear of Olivia we are told that she has sequestered herself away from the world for a period of seven years:

> like a cloistress she will veilèd walk,
> And water once a day her chamber round

With eye-offending brine: all this to season
A brother's dead love.   (I. i. 29–32)

The words 'season' and 'brine' here suggest that Olivia wishes to
preserve and prolong, rather than to pass through, her feeling of
grief. Characteristically, Orsino admires rather than deplores
this self-annihilating behavior, intending to build upon her filial
affection and fashion out of it a love for himself. But it quickly
becomes clear that both are principally enamored of themselves. Olivia's subsequent infatuation with the supposed
'Cesario' thus represents a considerable step in the right direction – that is, away from the safe and childlike identification with
a sibling and an equally childlike narcissism. Yet her choice of a
woman in disguise suggests that this first stage, of personal risk
and unaccustomed openness, must for her be only transitional.
In essence she progresses from the self-love and self-pity of an
Isabella to the sisterly love of Rosalind and Celia; like Celia
accompanying Rosalind into the forest, she will learn first to
risk, and then to love. The substitution of Sebastian for Viola,
which is often criticized as unacceptable dramatic opportunism,
is prepared for by the sequence of Olivia's development, and
may perhaps be usefully compared to the lightning transformations in some fairy tales. Just as learning to love a tame bear
prepares Snow-White (in 'Snow-White and Rose-Red') to love
the Prince who has been imprisoned in that form, so learning to
love the energetic but indubitably feminine Viola allows Olivia
to develop as a woman, until she is ready to meet her husband in
Sebastian. Both Phebe and Olivia take refuge, initially, in traditional female postures of sexual avoidance: Phebe as an unattainable (though slightly déclassé) Petrarchan beloved, Olivia as a
kind of secular nun. Their choice of false or intermediary objects
of desire represents the middle stage in a progression from auto-
erotic to homoerotic and thence to fully adult, heterosexual,
erotic identity. It may be useful here to call to mind Freud's
observations on the sexual theories of children, in which he cites
the first false (but suggestive) theory commonly held by them
as a 'neglect of the differences between the sexes'.[23] In an Elizabethan theater in which all women's parts were played by
men, this gender distinction would be even more complex, since
Olivia's task is to single out the man-playing-a-woman-

playing-a-man from the men-playing-men. Sebastian neatly summarizes the result of her experiences when at last the truth is disclosed:

> So comes it, lady, you have been mistook.
> But nature to her bias drew in that.
> You would have been contracted to a maid;
> Nor are you therein, by my life, deceived:
> You are betrothed both to a maid and man.
>
> (v. i. 258–62)

Not only Nature, the goddess, but human nature as well has led to Olivia's maturation. She will never be as self-knowledgeable as Viola – but then Orsino will never reach the human wisdom of Sebastian. Shakespeare's concern is not to indicate a single plateau of perfection – neither Phebe nor Audrey will ever rival Rosalind – but rather to suggest a pattern of progress toward maturity.

III

When we shift the focus of our attention from sexual awareness and acceptance to actual sexual behavior, or, in other words, from 'rights' to 'rites', we can see that the sexual rites undergone by women in the plays span the entire sequence of marriage acts: from initiation and defloration, through pregnancy, child-bearing and nursing. The act of defloration itself is not often commented upon, for reasons which may relate as much to dramatic feasibility and to delicacy as to the playwright's degree of interest. We do have the two aubade scenes, one in *Romeo and Juliet*, the other in *Troilus and Cressida*; in both the lovers are seen together immediately after a night of love-making, having been aided in the secrecy of their arrangements (and teased for their eagerness) by the very similar figures of the Nurse and Pandarus. In each case the song of the morning lark is heard and noted by the man, the end of night rejected or wished away by the woman, and the encounter ends with what will prove to be a final parting from the place of love. But if the two women rise from their beds in a similar mood, they approach them very differently, in accordance with the very different tones of the plays. Juliet abandons 'compliment', or conventional decorum, as early as the orchard scene, and she is already in that scene able to address Romeo with a mixture of flirtatiousness and naiveté. The question she flings to him from the unreachable height of the balcony, 'What satisfaction canst thou have tonight?' (II. ii. 126) is not wholly innocent of sexual implications, nor, I think, does she intend it to be. On the day of her marriage, as we have seen, Juliet impatiently sues for the coming of night, when she and Romeo will 'lose a winning match, / Played for a pair of stainless maidenhoods' (III. ii. 12–13). Even on her deathbed in the tomb, she converts suicide into an allusively sexual act: failing to find poison left in Romeo's cup – a conventional female symbol – she instead stabs herself with his dagger: 'This is thy sheath,' she says to it, 'there rust, and let me die' (v. iii. 171).

For Cressida, of course, the situation is very different. She is not married to Troilus, and does not seem to expect to be. Her position in Troy is extremely tenuous, and she accepts it at first with a cool realism. Certainly she is from the first aware of the bargaining power inherent in her virginity, and she articulates a sexual mercantilism rather uncharacteristic of Shakespeare's women, though entirely consonant with the dark inequities of the play:

> Women are angels, wooing;
> Things won are done, joy's soul lies in the doing.
> That she beloved knows nought that knows not this:
> Men prize the thing ungained more than it is;
> That she was never yet, that ever knew
> Love got so sweet as when desire did sue.   (I. ii. 293–8)

Yet significantly, Cressida violates her own prudent maxim, and yields to her love and desire for Troilus. She, too, abandons compliment, knowing the risks as she does so:

> Prince Troilus, I have loved you night and day
> For many weary months. . . .
> But though I love you well, I wooed you not;
> And yet, good faith, I wished myself a man,
> Or that we women had men's privilege
> Of speaking first.   (III. ii. 113–28)

In the somber world of *Troilus and Cressida* women do not have 'men's privilege', either in speaking or in a choice of life;

Cressida's hopeful entry into the world of sexuality leads not to fruitful marriage but to her branding as a 'daughter of the game'. But the act of sexual initiation itself is a moment of affirmation which not even her later faithlessness will entirely obscure.

Other instances of defloration or references to it in the plays frequently include a reminder of the physical evidence of that act. We have already noted the multiple significances of the spotted handkerchief in *Othello*, which comes by a series of transferences to seem a symbol of Desdemona's defloration, whether by Othello or (as he fears) by Cassio. An actual bloody garment appears in the Pyramus and Thisby play of *A Midsummer Night's Dream*, where Pyramus interprets the 'mantle good, / What, stained with blood!' as evidence that 'lion vile hath here deflow'red my dear' (v. i. 280–1, 290). It is difficult, as always, to know where we are with Pyramus' choice of words; 'deflow'red' may well be a metaphor of sorts, but in view of the play's earlier images of animal sexuality in the woods, the choice by Shakespeare (if not by Bottom–Pyramus) is significant. Once again, the contiguity – even interchangeability – of defloration and dying carries with it not only the force of the usual Renaissance pun, but also a somewhat different meaning, increasingly familiar to the Shakespearean audience, in which death becomes an alternative or substitute for love. A third instance, not unrelated to the theme of the bloody garment, is that of the beheading of Cloten, who has disguised himself in Posthumus' clothing and set out to 'enforce', that is, to rape, Imogen (*Cymb.* IV. i. 17). His subsequent decapitation at the hands of Guiderius, once again a symbolic castration, substitutes one 'bloody' act for another. Significantly Imogen, awakening, describes the dead trunk as an unwelcome 'bedfellow' (IV. ii. 295), and comes quite naturally to the conclusion that it is her husband Posthumus who lies beside her.

The most obscure, and for that reason perhaps the most arresting, appearance of the bloodstained token in the plays takes place in *As You Like It*, when Orlando sends a 'bloody napkin' to 'the shepherd youth / That he in sport doth call his Rosalind' (IV. iii. 154–5) – that is, of course, to Rosalind herself. Receiving it she swoons, agrees with Oliver that she lacks 'a man's heart', (163), and confesses, accurately enough, 'I should have been a woman by right' (173–4). The entire scenario is curious. Oliver, the tyrannous older brother, tells a tale of lying asleep in the forest, a 'green and gilded snake' wreathed about his neck, who 'with her head, nimble in threats, approached / The opening of his mouth' (108–9). The snake is frightened away by the approach of Orlando, only to provoke 'a sucked and hungry lioness' (125) with 'udders all drawn dry' (113) to launch her own attack. Orlando, first inclined to abandon his brother to a well-deserved fate, instead gives battle to the lioness and kills her, but not before she can inflict a wound. The blood-stained handkerchief is offered as an explanation for his absence and a sign that he had not forgotten his appointment with 'Rosalind'.

When we compare this account to that in Lodge's *Rosalynde*, we will at once be struck by the nature of Shakespeare's innovations. Lodge describes the sleeping man, but omits any reference to a snake, and the lion of his story is clearly male: it is described with masculine pronouns, and there is certainly no mention of suckling. Nor does the episode of the 'bloody napkin' have its counterpart in the source.[24] The enrichment of detail in Shakespeare's version adds in general to the fairy-tale tone of the work, to the Edenic echoes and to the wonderfully various fauna and flora who inhabit the literary forest of Arden. But it is also clear that the modifications have to do with gender, with sexuality and with initiation. Oliver, an unnatural brother and the unworthy son of a noble father, is menaced by two female animals, one of them a nurturant mother, the other a female (but at the same time unmistakably phallic) snake. Orlando, the male lover, participates in a symbolic ritual exclusively associated with women, offering a cloth spotted with his own blood as a sign of his purity and fidelity in love.

What are we to make of this striking confluence of sexual initiation symbols? Why, indeed, are so many female symbols associated with the two brothers? It seems clear that we are not (seriously) being asked to question the masculinity of either Oliver or Orlando – although we would do well to keep in mind that Orlando is 'wooing' a person he believes to be a man. But the phallic snake, and the supine, vulnerable and classically 'feminine' posture of Oliver, evoke the central symbols of what must be seen as an identifiable and explicit rite – the deflowering.

of a young woman. So resonant are the symbols of this particular rite that they are at hand to be used to signal less explicit
transformations – Oliver's self-described 'conversion' (IV. iii.
135) from unnatural to natural brother, Orlando's change from
vengeance to forgiveness and brotherly love. The displaced
presence of these sexual symbols in this play is perhaps less
jarring than would be the case in almost any other, since
As You Like It deals so centrally and consistently with the
alternation of male and female roles: the heroine spends most
of the play dressed as a man, and the hero courts her in this
disguise.

What we have in the incident of the 'bloody napkin' and the
elements that surround it is, then, another version of the sexual
rite of passage from childhood to maturity. Immediately following his rescue and 'conversion', Oliver falls in love with 'Aliena'
– so quickly that even Orlando is surprised. Orlando, for his
part, tires of the courtship games he is playing with 'Rosalind',
and declares, 'I can live no longer by thinking' (v. ii. 50). He now
seeks a real woman, and a real marriage, to parallel the love his
brother has found, and which is so deftly described by Rosalind:
'they [have] made a pair of stairs to marriage, which they will
climb incontinent, or else be incontinent before marriage: they
are in the very wrath of love, and they will together; clubs
cannot part them' (37–41). The theme of sexual fulfillment,
previously represented only by Touchstone and Rosalind, now
attaches itself to Orlando. Through Rosalind's teaching, but also
through the act of rescuing his brother, he too has come of age,
abandoning the play courtship of a supposed 'youth' for the
adult roles of husband and householder. His love for the
androgynous Ganymede has made possible the renewal of his
love for Oliver, as well as a deeper and less self-indulgent love
for Rosalind. In a complementary way, by attaining the condition of filial love previously lacking in his education, Oliver too
gains the capacity to love a woman. His transformation is remarkably swift, passing through filial bonding to sexual love in
an hour, but it corresponds to a process we have seen before. The
symbolically threatening 'rape' of Oliver, and the symbolic
'deflowering' of Orlando, which at first seemed so strangely and
inappropriately female, now fit more easily into the play's larger
pattern of education in love. The two brothers have been

liberated into a world of mature sexuality; the lioness, who reminds us not only of Oliver's failed nurturance and the possible
results of deflowering, but also of the remnants of childlike behavior in both young men, now lies dead.

*

For a dramatist of his time Shakespeare is unusually interested
in the whole cycle of marital behavior, but perhaps particularly
in the fruits of marriage. We have noted elsewhere that
Shakespearean children are often disturbingly precocious, but it
is equally true that they are portrayed as dearly loved. The
bearing of children and their nurture is uniformly described in
the plays as a fulfillment of life's promise, and the imagery
surrounding pregnancy and childbirth is, as we should expect,
closely associated with fruitfulness in nature. There is, in fact, a
distinctive lyricism in many of Shakespeare's depictions of pregnant women. In addition to the 'teeming foison' and 'blossom-
ing time' ascribed to Juliet in *Measure for Measure*, we have
Titania's evocative portrait of her former votaress, the mother of
the Indian changeling boy who is the cause of her dispute with
Oberon. 'On Neptune's yellow sands,' she recalls,

> we have laughed to see the sails conceive
> And grow big-bellied with the wanton wind;
> Which she, with pretty and with swimming gait
> Following – her womb then rich with my young squire –
> Would imitate, and sail upon the land,
> To fetch me trifles, and return again,
> As from a voyage, rich with merchandise.
>   (*MND* II. i. 128–34)

Here, as in the Juliet passage, a metaphor of fecundity in the
external world becomes elided with a literal description of
human pregnancy, and provides a brief glimpse of a world of
mellow fruitfulness. The dispute about the changeling itself
suggests once more the vital connection in these plays between
progeny and natural fertility, while Titania's eventual surrender
of the child may perhaps be viewed as an acknowledgment of his
masculine identity: in order that he may fulfill his promise as a
man, rather than remain forever a (step-)mother's child, she
allows Oberon to make him a 'Knight of his train, to trace the

forests wild' (II. i. 25), abandoning her own instinct to 'withhold'
him from the world, '[Crown] him with flowers, and [make] him
all her joy' (26–7).

The fate of the Indian changeling is usefully contrasted with
that of Mamillius in *The Winter's Tale*, whose mother, Hermione, is likewise described in highly 'natural' terms. We hear
that Hermione 'rounds apace' (II. i. 16), like the moon or the
seasons of the year – though Leontes can only sneer that
Polixenes has made her 'swell thus' (62), choosing his metaphor
from the language of disease rather than healthful growth.
Mamillius' name, substituted by Shakespeare for Greene's
'Garinter', suggests a connection with Latin 'mamilla', the nipple of the female breast, though it is interesting that Leontes
explicitly states that his son was not suckled by his mother.
'Give me the boy,' he demands of Hermione,

> I am glad you did not nurse him;
> Though he does bear some signs of me, yet you
> Have too much blood in him. . . .
> Bear the boy hence, he shall not come about her.
>   (II. i. 56–9)

As he does so often, Leontes here misinterprets the evidence at
hand; we have already seen that although Hermione did not
literally nurse her son he was not denied her nurturance, the
primal bond between mother and child. Indeed, separated from
her he at once begins to sicken and die, behavior Leontes ob-
tusely construes as a sign of 'nobleness'; 'Conceiving the dishonor
of his mother, / He straight declined, drooped, took it deeply'
(II. iii. 13–14). 'Conceiving', which of course here carries the
primary meaning of 'comprehending', also suggests pregnancy,
and is ironically juxtaposed to declining, drooping and lan-
guishing. While thus falsely envisaging his son as a kind of
Hamlet, responding to his mother's dishonor, Leontes also imagines himself prospectively as a Lady Macbeth, as he vows 'The
bastard brains [of Perdita] with these my proper hands / Shall I
dash out' (139–40). The odd circumstance of a boy called
'Mamillius' who is *not* nursed by his mother is, in fact, entirely
consonant with the major themes of the play, reminding the
audience of claims of love which transcend the merely biological,
and thus preparing the way for the adoption of Perdita by the

shepherd and the clown, and the transformation of those worthies into 'gentlemen born':

> The king's son took me by the hand and called me brother; and then the two kings called my father brother; and then the prince (my brother) and the princess (my sister) called my father father; and so we wept; and there was the first gentle-manlike tears that ever we shed.   (v. ii. 143–8)

Even when not expressly lyrical, the depiction of pregnancy in the plays is associated with larger patterns of fertility. When we learn of the wench Jaquenetta in *Love's Labor's Lost* that 'she's quick; the child brags in her belly already' (v. ii. 674–5), the news interjects a renewed element of fertile energy into a play otherwise dominated by coy flirtatiousness and entirely verbal encounters between the sexes. Moreover, the juxtaposition of Jaquenetta's 'quick-ness' to the death of the King of France, which is announced a few lines later in the same scene, offers a striking actualization of the thematic conflicts with which the play has all along been concerned, and leads directly to the final fruitful songs of winter and spring. A more dramatically ener-gized aspect of the same motif is developed in the character of Cleopatra, whose children seem virtually numberless, if we are to believe the fastidious (and fascinated) Octavius: 'Caesarion, whom they call my father's son, / And all the unlawful issue that their lust / Since then hath made between them' (*A&C* III. vi. 6–8). Agrippa's less psychologically perturbed account ('He plowed her, and she cropped' – II. ii. 230) and the continued association of Cleopatra with the teeming Nile ('the seedsman / Upon the slime and ooze scatters his grain, / And shortly comes to harvest' – II. vii. 22–4) again draws a close connection between the child-bearing woman and the fertile landscape. And when, on her deathbed, Cleopatra herself perverts the rituals of nurture by placing an asp at her breast, the effect is not to deny her fruitful-ness or her maternal role, but rather to demystify death itself:

> Peace, peace!
> Dost thou not see my baby at my breast,
> That sucks the nurse asleep?   (v. ii. 308–10)

In essence, this is the feminine version, superbly dramatized, of a simile Shakespeare frequently uses for *men* in the plays of this same period: that of the dying man who runs to death as the bridegroom to his bed.[25] For Cleopatra the action is not one of capitulation, but rather of triumph:

> she looks like sleep,
> As she would catch another Antony
> In her strong toil of grace.   (345–7)

Just as pregnancy is associated with fulfillment in the plays, barrenness becomes, as we should expect, a sign of spiritual deprivation. It has frequently been noted that lost children in the romances are equated with a loss of fertility in the land, and even with the spiritual death of the parent/king. But the most striking instances of infertility occur in the tragedies. The first words we hear from Julius Caesar are his reminder to Calphurnia that she should stand in Antonius' way on the feast of the Lupercal, in order for him to touch her in the chase and thus help 'shake off [her] sterile curse' (JC I. ii. 9). Plutarch mentions this superstition in his *Life of Caesar*, but not Caesar's interest in it, or Calphurnia's barrenness; in his account the Lupercal is merely an excuse for Antony to offer Caesar a crown.[26] Shakespeare's modification of the source and, in particular, the fact that he places this detail at the very start of the play invite the audience to speculate about how the childlessness of the ruler (whether a Caesar or an Elizabeth) may leave the land open to threats of civil war. Caesar does not, of course, die entirely without heirs. He leaves his gardens and parks to the general populace, as Antony shrewdly announces in his funeral oration; his political position is soon to be filled by his nephew Octavius, who will himself ultimately claim the title of Caesar. Yet neither nephew nor citizens can wholly replace the longed-for son, and Calphurnia's barrenness, so prominently highlighted by its dramatic placement, casts over the entire play an initial aura of loss and doom.

By the time of *King Lear*, barrenness has become a vivid metaphor for the quintessence of the unnatural. Lear's curse on Goneril is explicit:

> Into her womb convey sterility,
> Dry up in her the organs of increase,
> And from her derogate body never spring
> A babe to honor her.   (*Lr* I. iv. 280–3)

'If she must teem', the heir he wishes upon her is a 'child of spleen' who will teach her what it is to have a thankless child. But Goneril shows no sign of teeming, and the play that began with the image of a betrothal between Cordelia and the 'vines of France' or 'milk of Burgundy' (I. i. 84) quickly degenerates into images of cannibalism, the converse of parturition and nurture. Within a hundred lines of her first appearance Cordelia becomes as unwelcome to her father as 'he that makes his generation messes / To gorge his appetite' (I. i. 117–18). Later Lear will excoriate his children as 'pelican daughters' who feed upon their parent's blood (III. iv. 74), while Albany peers darkly into the future:

> It will come,
> Humanity must perforce prey on itself,
> Like monsters of the deep.   (IV. ii. 49–51)

These cannibalistic images, involving as they do the feeding of parent upon child or child upon parent, imply not only the disorder concomitant upon such role reversal, but also a more specifically sexual dysfunction. The parent, who should give life, devours; the womb becomes transformed into a consuming mouth, the *vagina dentata* of psychology and anthropology.

In *Titus Andronicus*, of course, the depiction of cannibalism extends beyond the bounds of metaphor. Titus, dressed 'like a cook', presides over a banquet at which Tamora's sons are served up to their mother:

> Why there they are, both bakèd in this pie,
> Whereof their mother daintily hath fed,
> Eating the flesh that she herself hath bred.
>   (V. iii. 60–2)

In a sense, this pathological inversion of childbirth, in which the parent takes the child back into her body, is prepared for by an earlier moment in the play, when Lavinia, soon to be ravished by those same sons, pleads with them for mercy:

> O, do not learn her wrath; she taught it thee.
> The milk thou suck'st from her did turn to marble;
> Even at thy teat thou hadst thy tyranny.
>   (II. iii. 143–5)

That human nature is derived from human nurture, and character is transmitted through the act of suckling, is a common figure
of the period; thus Juliet's nurse crows to her charge, 'Were not I
thine only nurse, / I would say thou hadst sucked wisdom from
thy teat' (R&J I. iii. 67–8). But Tamora's sons suck tyranny,
not wisdom, and when they are horridly reingested by their
mother, they complete the pattern of inversion that her malign
nurturance began.

One of the most psychologically peculiar uses of the language
of suckling and nursing occurs in Coriolanus, a play whose
protagonist is consistently described as a man who was denied
sustenance and love at his mother's breast – and who will in turn
deny sustenance in the form of corn to the citizens of Rome. His
mother Volumnia defends her actions in sending Coriolanus to
war 'When yet he was but tender-bodied . . . when for a day of
kings' entreaties, a mother should not sell him an hour from her
beholding,' because she 'was pleased to let him seek danger where
he was like to find fame' (I. iii. 6–13). She hopes that he will
return from combat against the Volscians with a bloody brow,
since – as she tells his fearful wife – 'the breasts of Hecuba, /
When she did suckle Hector, looked not lovelier / Than Hector's
forehead when it spit forth blood / At Grecian sword, contemn-
ing' (I. iii. 40–4). Later she will remind her son that 'thy valiant-
ness was mine, thou suck'st it from me' (III. ii. 129). Significantly Coriolanus borrows his mother's metaphor when he
defects to the Volscian camp, proclaiming himself to Aufidius as
one who has 'Drawn tuns of blood out of thy country's breast'
(IV. v. 103). But the perverse substitution of blood for
nourishing milk does not, as Volumnia hopes, produce an invul-
nerable hero. Indeed the final discomfiture of Coriolanus comes
at the moment when Aufidius sneers to the Volscian troops that
'at his nurse's tears / He whined and roared away your victory'
(V. vi. 96–7). Here the socially derogatory 'nurse' instead of
'mother' adds insult to injury, while the allusion to suckling
(and the half-implied suggestion that Coriolanus is not yet
weaned) links with the foregoing imagery to complete the
portrait of a man–child still helplessly dependent upon his
mother.

Volumnia is one version of the destructive nursing mother;
another, even more malignant, is Lady Macbeth, who petitions

the spirits of murder to 'Come to my woman's breasts, / And take my milk for gall' (I. v. 47–8). Her exhortation to her wavering husband to be steadfast is memorably couched in terms of motherhood:

> I have given suck, and know
> How tender 'tis to love the babe that milks me:
> I would, while it was smiling in my face,
> Have plucked my nipple from his boneless gums,
> And dashed the brains out, had I so sworn as you
> Have done to this.   (I. vii. 54–9)

Ironically, we have just heard her muse that Macbeth's nature is 'too full o' th' milk of human kindness' (I. v. 17) to contemplate murder, and shortly, with equal irony, we will hear his praise of her: 'Bring forth men–children only; / For thy undaunted mettle should compose / Nothing but males' (I. vii. 72–4). Macbeth, who will later protest that he is not a female child, 'the baby of a girl' (III. iv. 106), becomes in fact the man–child his wife will bring to birth – and dash to shards.

The proverbial question, 'How many children had Lady Macbeth?', has perhaps been unfairly maligned: the play is as urgently concerned with dynasty, offspring and succession as any in Shakespeare, and against that background Lady Macbeth's relationship to maternity stands out in sharp relief. Duncan's two sons, Banquo's Fleance, Macduff's 'pretty chickens' (IV. iii. 218) all exemplify the leading characteristics of their parents; in fact, Macduff's young son, of whom his mother remarks 'Fathered he is, and yet he's fatherless' (IV. ii. 27) resembles his father even in this paradoxical parenthood, since Macduff, 'from his mother's womb / Untimely ripped' (v. viii. 15–16), was thus 'none of woman born' (IV. i. 80). Moreover, Lady Macduff herself, a fruitful wife and the mother of numerous children, provides the most vivid possible contrast to Lady Macbeth's own barrenness and faulty nurture. Even the 'temple-haunting martlet' that nests in the crenelations of Macbeth's castle contributes to this sense of contrast, for 'the pendent bed and procreant cradle' of the breeding birds offers an ironic antithesis to the destructive energies of the human occupants within. The irony is heightened by both the dramatic situation and the placement of these lines, since Banquo speaks them to

Duncan, unwarily supporting the view that one can find the mind's construction in the face, and the scene in which they are spoken (I. vi.) is immediately followed by that which contains not only the 'I have given suck' speech, but also Macbeth's references to 'men–children only' and 'pity, like a naked newborn babe'.

The puzzle of Lady Macbeth's maternity is never solved in the play, since no child – save Macbeth himself – is ever seen or mentioned. But the active malignity of a mother who would nurse her infants with gall and pledge to dash their brains out is, perceptually, much greater than the merely passive picture of a barren Calphurnia or a determinedly virginal Rosaline. The opposite of Cleopatra, who poetically transmutes the poison of snakes into mother's milk, Lady Macbeth in her animadversions on motherhood provides the play with one of its most striking continuing images, an image which will resound anew in Malcolm's fictive pledge of iniquity:

> Nay, had I pow'r, I should
> Pour the sweet milk of concord into hell.
>
> (IV. iii. 97–8)

IV

The representations of sexual behavior in the plays are not, of course, limited to those acts explicitly shown or mentioned. At the same time that Shakespeare's characters are explicitly concerned with problems of virginity, marriage, child-bearing and the like, the symbolic language of imagery and action reinterprets and enriches these concerns. In some cases these dramatic symbols seem to be the hidden psychological counterparts of visible acts and audible thoughts; in other cases such symbols appear to serve as counterpoint to, or even as ironic commentary upon, developments in the plot.

The specific image of 'deflowering', for example, occurs from time to time in Shakespeare's works in a variety of contexts. Although some poets of the fourteenth century did use 'flower' as a synonym for virginity,[27] this metaphorical connotation seems to have been quickly lost. The earliest definition of 'deflower' itself in the OED is 'To deprive (a woman) of her virginity; to violate, ravish (1382)', with no explicit connection to 'flower' at all. Characteristically, Shakespeare renews or reconstructs the floral metaphor, with interesting results. Although he will occasionally use 'deflower' without any allusive sense (e.g. *Titus* II. iii. 191; *Measure* IV. iv. 21), as early as *The Rape of Lucrece* he has Tarquin vow to himself 'I must deflower' (348) and then inform Lucrece, 'I see what crosses my attempt will bring, / I know what thorns the growing rose defends' (491–2). Likewise, Old Capulet, discovering Juliet apparently dead, laments to Paris, 'O son, the night before thy wedding day / Hath Death lain with thy wife. There she lies, / Flower as she was, deflowerèd by him' (*R&J* IV. v. 35–7). As we have already noted, the king in *All's Well* seeks Diana's assurance that she is 'yet a fresh uncroppèd flower' (v. iii. 326). Theseus' view in his charge to Hermia that the 'rose distilled' is 'earthlier happy' than that left 'withering on the virgin thorn' is yet another, slightly more oblique, instance of this same figure. To these merely allusive or verbal references, however, we can add two with more far-reaching dramatic consequences: the flower-giving scenes of Ophelia and Perdita.

One change is already apparent: where we have been speaking of deflowerers or flower-takers, we now have flower-givers, women who 'de-flower' themselves. This is, of course, exactly what Ophelia is repeatedly cautioned not to do. Hamlet's insistent mention of the nunnery is the third such warning she has received. Polonius, who will shortly aver that 'drabbing' is no disgrace for his son, commands his daughter to 'Be something scanter of [her] maiden presence' (I. iii. 121), and, in fact to avoid Hamlet altogether, while Laertes' icily practical (and at the same time oddly prurient) advice includes an inverted echo of Theseus on the fate of a 'barren sister': 'The chariest maid is prodigal enough / If she unmask her beauty to the moon' (I. iii. 36–7). In this same speech Laertes alludes to infected flowers, 'the infants of the spring' galled by the cankerworm 'before their buttons [i.e. buds] be disclosed' (39–40), and Ophelia counters, with uncharacteristic spirit, by warning him to avoid 'the primrose path of dalliance' (50). Both images obliquely equate virgins with flowers, and predatory males with flower-pickers, in much that same way that Milton will later describe Proserpina as a flower 'gathered' by gloomy Dis.[28]

In the mad scene, however, it is Ophelia who plucks the flowers and gives them away. As with Hermia's dream of the snake, this gesture is a displacement; in Freudian terms it might be considered an action undertaken by the unconscious to express what has been repressed by the conscious mind. Ophelia's song is, of course, a ballad of lost virginity, couched in a language most untypical of her usual chaste persona:

> Then up he rose and donned his clothes
>   And dupped the chamber door,
> Let in the maid, that out a maid
>   Never departed more. . . .
> Young men will do't if they come to't,
>   By Cock, they are to blame.
> Quoth she, 'Before you tumbled me,
>   You promised me to wed.'

He answers:

> 'So would I'a' done, by yonder sun,
>   And thou hadst not come to my bed.'
>   (IV. v. 52–67)

Excluded from the normal pattern of sexual initiation by her own filial submissiveness as well as by Hamlet's action, she becomes instead a symbolic self-deflowerer, whose death is perforce both a consummation and a source of renewed fertility: 'from her fair and unpolluted flesh / May violets spring!' (v. i. 239–40). The violet, a traditional emblem of faithfulness, is associated with Ophelia's affections from Laertes' first cautionary speech (Hamlet's favor is 'A violet in the youth of primy nature' – I. iii. 7) to Polonius' death ('they withered all when my father died' – IV. v. 184–5) and beyond that to her gravesite; but in her dying moments violets are replaced by garlands of another purple flower, significantly described by Gertrude: 'long purples, / That liberal shepherds give a grosser name, / But our cold maids do dead men's fingers call them' (IV. vii. 169–71). The demure violet becomes the phallic early purple orchid,[29] a sign at once of sex and death.

The flower-giving ceremony in *The Winter's Tale* seems at first glance very different from Ophelia's, yet formally they have much in common: a young virgin distributes floral emblems to appropriate recipients according to one or another language of flowers. ('Rosemary, that's for remembrance. Pray you, love, remember.' – *Ham.* IV. v. 175–6; 'flow'rs / Of middle summer, and I think they are given / To men of middle age' – *WT* IV. iv. 106–8).[30] And once again, one kind of flower is missing. Ophelia's sheaf lacked violets, Perdita's lacks 'flow'rs o' th' spring' (113) to bestow upon her suitor, Florizel, and the shepherdesses 'That wear upon your virgin branches yet / Your maidenheads growing' (115–16). This may be an oblique reference to the incipient presence of fall (and fallenness) in the apparently paradisal landscape, but it also seems an apt reminder of Perdita's own liminal state. She is easily able to gratify old and middle-aged men who represent neither a sexual threat nor an analogy to her own sexual condition: she *wishes* she could give flowers to Florizel, but cannot. Indeed, her expressed desire 'To strew him o'er and o'er' (129) not unnaturally leads Florizel to ask 'What, like a corse?' once again implying a substitution of death for sexual love. Moreover, some of the metaphors in which Perdita describes flowers, both those she has and those she lacks, are oddly preoccupied with the very subject of deflowering. 'The marigold that goes to bed wi' th' sun, / And with him rises, weeping' (105–6) is an image of fearful and unhappy sexual initiation, and 'pale primroses, / That die unmarried ere they can behold / Bright Phoebus in his strength (a malady / Most incident to maids)' (122–5) offers a picture of the unhappy alternative, spinsterhood and death. We might perhaps view Perdita's flower-giving as a therapeutic version of Ophelia's, since it does result in fulfilled love and marriage. But Perdita's maiden fearfulness emerges in the metaphors she chooses, as well as in her gesture itself – and, as we have already seen, it is not until the arrival of Autolycus that sexual energies are fully acknowledged or accepted in the world of the sheepshearing feast.

Just as the fragility and beauty of the virginal condition is emblematized as a flower, so its preciousness is connoted by another frequent emblem, that of the treasure. Thus Laertes warns Ophelia not to 'lose your heart, or your chaste treasure open / To his unmastered importunity' (*Ham.* I. iii. 31–2). As this example suggests, the treasure is an apt metaphor not only because it represents value, but also because it is enclosed: the treasure chest becomes a womb, the deflowerer becomes a thief.[31] In *Cymbeline* this image comes dramatically to life, as Iachimo persuades Imogen to store in her bedchamber a trunk ostensibly containing plate and jewels. In fact, the trunk contains Iachimo himself, who by this stratagem is able to violate Imogen's bedchamber and obtain false evidence that he has made love to her.[32] In a variant of this same figure, the virgin beloved is seen as a miser, hoarding up unspent riches. Romeo rails against Rosaline's 'strong proof of chastity' (i. i. 213), complaining that

> she is rich in beauty; only poor
> That, when she dies, with beauty dies her store.
>
> (218–19)

The so-called 'procreation sonnets' (1–17) argue essentially the same point, especially sonnet 4, in which the beloved is addressed as 'unthrifty loveliness' (1), 'beauteous niggard' (5) and 'profitless usurer' (7). Sexuality becomes an investment, which brings returns not only in the form of pleasure, but also of children.

The fullest application of this metaphor, of course, occurs in *The Merchant of Venice*, which rings the changes on many of these themes. Shylock, who early on speaks of money as something to 'breed' (i. iii. 93), locks in his house both his virgin daughter and his hoarded ducats, but both escape and are ultimately given to Lorenzo.[33] He laments the loss of daughter and ducats with indiscriminate grief, showing perhaps a slight preference to the ducats, and visualizes both as re-enclosed under his power: 'I would my daughter were dead at my foot, and the jewels in her ear! Would she were hearsed at my foot, and the ducats in her coffin!' (iii. i. 84–6). Once again, death is imagined as a substitute for marriage, while the coffin symbolically preserves the virginity which will in fact be lost. Manifestly, Portia's three caskets are also in this sense womb or virginity emblems. Throwing the treasure down from her father's window, Jessica had enjoined Lorenzo to 'catch this casket; it is worth the pains' (ii. vi. 33). Likewise Portia, whose fate in marriage depends upon her father's test, invites Bassanio to try his luck with the caskets of gold, silver, and lead: 'I am locked in one of them; / If you do love me, you will find me out'

(III. ii. 40–1). Once he selects the right casket and finds her portrait within (an inversion of the physical reality, that the casket is inside her body), the marriage is solemnized by the exchange of rings. The casket having been opened, there is no longer need for a functional symbol of virginity: the ring now comes to represent married chastity, an unbroken circlet penetrated only by the chosen spouse.

This image of the ring placed upon the outstretched finger as a symbol of intercourse is familiar from folkloric and mythic sources as well as from popular and vulgar tradition.[34] In *The Merchant of Venice* the substitution of the open ring for the closed casket as the emblem of the female sexual organs marks an important turning point. The treasure, once locked away, is now put to use as a medium of exchange. Rings are repeatedly associated throughout the play with women of marriageable age. Shylock's ring, a turquoise (a stone thought to 'take away all enmity, and to reconcile husband and wife')[35] was given to him 'when [he] was a bachelor' (III. i. 117–18) by the woman who would become his wife. Jessica, the rightful inheritor of the ring in both a legal and a sexual sense, takes it away with her and is reported to have traded it for a monkey, proverbially one of the most promiscuous of animals. In Shylock's view, this is exactly what she has done: traded her virginity, which should remain locked up, for a licentious relationship with Lorenzo. What we actually see of Jessica seems not to accord with this flighty behavior. The episode, which is described to Shylock by a fellow Jew, instead serves the play symbolically in a dual fashion, emphasizing Jessica's repudiation of her father's values and offering a psychological insight into Shylock's mind. (We may perhaps compare this association of Lorenzo with a monkey to Hermia's conflation of Lysander with an equally sexual, equally distasteful snake – with, of course, the crucial difference that the immature or warped sexual imagination here belongs to the father and not the young girl herself.)

The central 'ring trick' in the play, however, is played by Portia and Nerissa, who bestow rings upon their husbands at the time of betrothal, exacting a promise that they never be removed. Disguised as the learned 'doctor' and his 'clerk', they then mischievously obtain the rings from their reluctant spouses, as the only acceptable payment for the confounding of

Shylock. Back home, in their own persons, the ladies proceed
to accuse their husbands of unfaithfulness, equating ring and
sexual fidelity in straightforward terms:

> Portia Since he hath got the jewel that I loved,
> And that which you did swear to keep for me,
> I will become as liberal as you;
> I'll not deny him anything I have,
> No, not my body nor my husband's bed. . .
> I'll have that doctor for mine bedfellow.
> Nerissa And I his clerk.   (v. i. 224–34)

Since Portia and Nerissa *are* the doctor and the clerk, this
promise can easily be kept, without the breaking of the marriage
vow.

Variations of the 'ring trick' appear in several other plays, and
whereas in *The Merchant of Venice* the link between ring and
cervix is elaborated in a somewhat expository fashion, elsewhere
the identification seems virtually taken for granted. Olivia,
smitten with the boy 'Cesario' who is Viola in disguise, sends
him a ring, claiming that he left it behind him. Viola, while
asserting to Malvolio that 'She took the ring of me. I'll none of
it' (II. ii. 12), privately muses 'I left no ring with her. What
means this lady?' (17) and comes instantly to the correct conclusion: 'She loves me sure' (22). The ring is not Viola's offer of
sexuality, much less Orsino's, but rather Olivia's gift of herself.
Recalled to her house, Viola once again refuses Olivia's affections and is, significantly, presented with a new token: 'here,
wear this jewel for me; 'tis my picture' (III. iv. 213). The pattern
reverses that in *The Merchant of Venice*: the open ring is
succeeded by the closed locket or pendant, in which the maiden
Olivia remains sealed. Only when she meets and marries Sebastian does she once again acquire a ring, as is made clear by the
priest who performs the ceremony:

> A contract of eternal bond of love,
> Confirmed by mutual joinder of your hands,
> Attested by the holy close of lips,
> Strength'ned by interchangement of your rings.
>   (v. i. 155–8)

For Helena in *All's Well That Ends Well*, the problem is

somewhat different: not how to give a ring, but how to get one. Her husband, the unlovable Bertram, who prefers 'Wars . . . To the dark house and the detested wife' (II. iii. 294–5), flatly declares 'I will not bed her,' and sends instead an ultimatum:

> When thou canst get the ring upon my finger, which never shall come off, and show me a child begotten of thy body that I am father to, then call me husband; but to such a 'then' I write a 'never'.   (III. ii. 58–61)

The sequence of 'ring' and 'child' is self-explanatory in view of the other ring references we have noted; moreover, the play, as if to underscore the point, uses 'ring-carrier' as a synonym for 'bawd' (III. v. 90) – the only instance of that term in all of Shakespeare. Helena's stratagem, by which a virgin aptly named Diana will pretend to surrender to Bertram in exchange for his ring, prompts a conversation which once again makes the implicit explicit:

> *Diana*   Give me that ring.
> *Bertram*   I'll lend it thee, my dear, but have no power
>   To give it from me. . . .
>   It is an honor 'longing to our house,
>   Bequeathed down from many ancestors,
>   Which were the greatest obloquy i' th' world
>   In me to lose.
> *Diana*   Mine honor's such a ring.
>   (IV. ii. 39–45)

And when Helena, in substitute for Diana, obtains Bertram's ring, she gives him hers, assuring the denouement before the king. The double proof of ring and pregnancy finally resolves the case, fulfilling the seemingly impossible conditions of Bertram's initial demand.

Moreover, not only rings but also other jeweled circlets play this role in Shakespeare's plays. In *The Comedy of Errors* Antipholus of Ephesus, annoyed at his wife's conduct, promises to give a gold chain designed for her to a courtesan instead. On the strength of this promise, the courtesan herself bestows a diamond ring upon Antipholus of Syracuse, whom she mistakes for his twin. In *Cymbeline*, Imogen and Posthumus exchange tokens as he embarks upon his exile. She gives him a diamond ring, he offers a bracelet, a 'manacle of love' (1. i. 122). In the course of his nocturnal espionage, Iachimo steals the bracelet, and by its evidence convinces Posthumus that he has enjoyed Imogen's sexual favors. In both of these cases the sexual symbolism is muted, but in neither is it absent. The 'golden gifts' (*Err.* III. ii. 184) accompany and emblematize a pledge of fidelity, but they are also expressly related to actual physical love.

Of all the symbols Shakespeare uses to denote sexual activity and sexual rites of passage in the plays, the most traditional of all is the walled garden. Significantly, such a garden unites the image of the flower with that of the treasure, casket or ring, since it is an enclosure which contains flowers. An entire – and familiar – medieval heritage lies behind this figure, from the *Romance of the Rose* to Domenico Veneziano's painting of *The Annunciation*, a work in which all the iconography of the trope is present. In it the Virgin stands, head bowed, in a porticoed room which opens on to a walled garden, visible only as a corridor framed by vines and foliage. At the further end of the corridor is a double wooden door, bolted shut. The Virgin's blue robe is draped over what at first appears to be part of a bench, but which on closer examination proves to be an enclosed chest. Across the room, the angel Gabriel kneels and, holding out a cluster of lilies in one hand, reverently raises the index finger of the other. This is the Annunciation; it is also the act of conception, taking place before our eyes. Room, chest, garden, all signify the womb; the passageway is at the same time anatomical and geographic, the bolted doors (and the lilies) suggest the virgin state, the raised finger is unmistakably, though subtly, phallic.

Such symbolism, while familiar, is more frequently found in poetry and painting than it is in drama; yet Shakespeare makes full and intriguing use of its possibilities, grafting them onto a secular context. The traditional biblical description of the bride as a *hortus conclusus*, a 'garden inclosed' (Song of Songs 4 : 12), becomes in his plays a geographical emblem of virginity and a locus for sexual initiation. The terms 'garden' and 'orchard' at this period both refer to an enclosed plot of land devoted to horticulture; 'orchard' derives etymologically from Latin *hortus* and Anglo-Saxon *yard*. It is in such settings in the plays, almost inevitably, that love is sworn and affections given. Thus Troilus walks in the orchard waiting for Cressida's approach, and is then invited into her house. Olivia, who has sequestered herself like a 'cloistress' in her chambers, emerges twice into the garden, the first time to swear her love for Viola–Cesario, the next to be married to Sebastian. In *Much Ado*, both Beatrice and Benedick are gulled into hearing supposed tidings of the other's love, and each revelation takes place in the orchard. And with ironic appropriateness, the same orchard becomes the scene of Don John's revelation to Claudio of Hero's 'infidelity'.

Walled enclosures play an important role in *Measure for Measure*, from the cloisters of St Clare and the duke's adoptive monastery to the 'moated grange' which walls up Mariana, Angelo's jilted fiancée, and Angelo's own establishment, so tellingly described by Isabella:

> He hath a garden circummured with brick,
> Whose western side is with a vineyard backed;
> And to that vineyard is a planchèd gate,
> That makes his opening with this bigger key.
> This other doth command a little door
> Which from the vineyard to the garden leads.
> There have I made my promise
> Upon the heavy middle of the night
> To call upon him.   (IV. i. 28–36)

Just as Mariana's grange is the emblem of her enclosed virginity, so Angelo's garden is the counterpart of his. In a startling – but not inappropriate – reversal of roles, Isabella is entrusted with the phallic key; Angelo himself exhibits a double perversity, first by insisting on denying his sensual nature (more unusual and unnatural perhaps in a man than a woman), then by veiling his lust under the continued guise of the reluctant virgin. The entire dramatic action of the play becomes, at least in one sense, the freeing of the individual from the walled enclosure, no matter how defined or how enforced. Moreover, if we call to mind Freud's association of beheading with symbolic castration, we may observe that the severed head of the prisoner Ragozine, produced in counterfeit for that of the expectant father Claudio, once again suggests how close Viennese events have come to answering Pompey's blunt inquiry: 'Does your worship mean to geld and splay all the youth of the city?' (ii. i. 228–9).

But perhaps the best known of all walled garden encounters in Shakespeare is that dramatic moment in *Romeo and Juliet* more usually described as the 'balcony scene' (ii. ii). 'The orchard walls are high and hard to climb,' as Juliet points out (63), and Romeo, though he stands in the posture of a Petrarchan suitor gazing up at his unattainable lady, has already crossed the first barrier by entering the garden at all. The orchard as a dramatic locale appears three times more in the play, each time in direct connection with the courtship, marriage and consummation of the lovers. In ii. v. Juliet impatiently awaits the Nurse's message, announcing the time and place of the marriage. The Nurse, who has early expressed her eagerness to see Juliet 'married once' (i. iii. 61) – and perhaps more – hastens to fetch a ladder, 'by the which your love / Must climb a bird's nest soon when it is dark' (ii. v. 74–5). In iii. ii. Juliet appears alone on the balcony overlooking the orchard, and speaks her moving lines of sexual longing to the 'love-performing night':

> Come, civil night,
> Thou sober-suited matron all in black,
> And learn me how to lose a winning match,
> Played for a pair of stainless maidenhoods. . . .
> O, I have bought the mansion of a love,
> But not possessed it; and though I am sold,
> Not yet enjoyed.   (10–13, 26–8)

Significantly, there are *two* maidenhoods to be lost; in her view Romeo is as virginal as she. The image of the 'mansion' provides yet another interior space which must be entered and 'possessed'. The implicit reversal of Freudian categories – Juliet is the possessor, Romeo associated with the mansion – emphasizes their interchangeability, and calls attention to Juliet's remarkable forthrightness and self-knowledgeability in sexual desire.[36] The final orchard scene (iii. v.) shows us Romeo 'aloft' on the balcony with Juliet. The sundering of the sexual barrier between the lovers finds its counterpart in the conquest of the physical barriers which have kept them apart.

Both balcony and orchard now disappear as dramatic loci, and are replaced by another kind of enclosure, the tomb. The womb–tomb symbolism of the play, articulated by Friar Lawrence but present throughout, is too well known to need further documentation. Capulet's lament, 'Death is my son-in-law, Death is my heir; / My daughter he hath wedded' (IV. v. 38–9) particularizes and personifies the image, as does Romeo's more elegant and lyrical version of the same fantasy:

> Shall I believe
> That unsubstantial Death is amorous,
> And that the lean abhorrèd monster keeps
> Thee here in dark to be his paramour?   (v. iii. 102–5)

We have noticed other instances of this figure, in which death replaces or displaces marriage, but the situation in *Romeo and Juliet* is in some respects unique, suggesting yet another dimension of Shakespeare's treatment of sexual rites of passage. To understand why this is so, it will be helpful to return to the balcony scene (II. ii.) and in particular to Romeo's explanation of his presence in the garden.

When Juliet expresses surprise at his presence, he replies that 'with love's light wings' he was able to mount the wall, for 'what love can do, that dares love attempt.' This is not the first time in the play that Romeo has been directly linked with the persona of 'love'. It is he who proposes a prologue to the intended masque at the Capulet ball, only to be told by Benvolio that such a practice is out of date: 'We'll have no Cupid hoodwinked with a scarf, / Bearing a Tartar's painted bow of lath' (I. iv. 4–5). He declines to dance in the mask, saying that his 'soul of lead' keeps him to the ground. 'You are a lover,' Mercutio replies. 'Borrow Cupid's wings / And soar with them above a common bound.' (I. iv. 17–18). As so often happens in this play, a verbal cliché applied to Rosaline becomes a vivid and literal metaphor when Romeo meets Juliet.

The association of Romeo with 'love', Cupid or Eros, the god of desire, is augmented by other details of the balcony scene. Repeatedly we are reminded that the scene is played in darkness and that Juliet cannot see the man who stands below her window. Her very appearance and her unguarded words poured out to the receptive night suggest that she is sure she is alone. The speech is both soliloquy and apostrophe, summoning in fancy one who must in reality be far away.

> Romeo, doff thy name;
> And for thy name, which is no part of thee,
> Take all myself.

Suddenly, shockingly, out of the darkness comes a reply:

> I take thee at thy word.
> Call me but love, and I'll be new baptized;
> Henceforth I never will be Romeo.   (II. ii. 47–51)

Juliet's response is telling: 'What man art thou, that, thus be-screened in night, / So stumblest on my counsel?' (52–3). He has just said his name – and offered to replace it with the name of 'love'. But Juliet, stunned and taken aback, can register at first only an alien presence in the darkness. Recognition, when it comes, occurs by stages and emphasizes not his hidden figure but his revealed voice. 'I know the sound. / Art thou not Romeo, and a Montague?' (59–60). Her surprise is natural and persuasive; in effect her incantation has come true. Yet repeatedly the scene draws attention to the darkness. Twice she warns that if her kinsmen 'do see thee, they will murder thee', and he rejoins that 'I have night's cloak to hide me from their eyes' (75). Love, the blind, has led him there. 'He lent me counsel, and I lent him eyes' (81). Can she see him? Or does 'night's cloak' hide him from her sight as well? The language she uses is suggestively ambiguous. 'Thou knowst the mask of night is on my face' – 'knowst', not 'seest'. And the business transacted between the lovers in this scene is entirely aural and verbal: Juliet's reverie, and Romeo's interruption of it; his attempt to swear by 'yonder' moon (which both of them can see); her suggestion that he swear by himself, 'Which is the god of my idolatry' (114); the ex-change of vows; her repeated summonings, and his replies: 'Romeo! – My sweet?' (168), and, again, 'Hist! Romeo, hist! O for a falc'ner's voice / To lure this tassel gentle back again!' (159–60). Moreover, Romeo's reply to this last call is itself significant, in line with the Cupid figures we have already noticed.

> It is my soul that calls upon my name.
> How silver-sweet sound lovers' tongues by night,
> Like softest music to attending ears!   (165–7)

Once again we may notice the emphasis upon hearing and speaking, rather than beholding, the beloved. But the identification of Juliet with 'my soul' not only recalls the contrasting 'soul of lead' produced by love for Rosaline, but also brings to mind a myth which seems structurally related to this scene and to the play as a whole: the myth of Cupid and Psyche.

The myth is briefly recounted: Psyche, the youngest of three daughters, was so beautiful that she was compared to Venus herself, arousing Venus' jealousy and enmity. She therefore instructs Cupid, or Eros, to cause Psyche to fall in love with the ugliest of men. Psyche is led to a cliff top, following the instructions of an oracle, which predicts that she will be taken by a snake-like monster. The procession which leads her to the peak thus resembles that of a funeral. But she is rescued by the West Wind and taken to a palace by Cupid, who, against his mother's orders, has fallen in love with her. He takes Psyche for his wife, but will not let her look at him, coming to her only at night and in darkness. Persuaded by her two jealous sisters (who have been permitted to visit her), Psyche fears that her husband may be a monster, and one night when he is sleeping she lifts a lamp to look at him. She sees, of course, a remarkably beautiful youth. But a drop of oil falls on his shoulder, waking him, and he leaves her in anger. The rest of the tale involves the three seemingly impossible tasks set her by Venus, the last of which is to visit Hades and bring back a casket of beauty from Persephone. She achieves this last task, but (again prompted by curiosity toward the forbidden) she opens the casket, which contains not beauty but a deathly sleep. Now Cupid, convinced of her sincere repentance, persuades Jupiter to make her immortal, and she reawakens and is married to him.

The story of Cupid and Psyche is told by Apuleius in *The Golden Ass*, which had been published in London in 1566 in the English translation of William Adlington. Shakespeare would therefore have had access to it in his own language, as well as – probably – in the Latin original. Apuleius, a neo-Platonist, may indeed have been offering an allegory of what his modern translator, Robert Graves, calls 'the progress of the rational soul toward intellectual love',[37] but psychologists have found other aspects of the myth equally fascinating and suggestive. Freud points out that Psyche is a kind of love- and death-goddess: 'Her wedding is celebrated like a funeral, she has to descend into the underworld, and afterwards sinks into a death-like sleep.'[38] A Jungian interpretation offered by Erich Neumann sees the myth as essentially 'a rite of initiation'[39] in which Psyche is awakened from 'the darkness of unconscious and the harshness of her matriarchal captivity and, in individual encounter with the masculine, loves, that is recognizes, Eros'.[40] According to Neumann the casket of beauty that Psyche must steal is 'the beauty of the glass coffin, to which Psyche is expected to regress, the barren frigidity of mere maidenhood, without love for a man (as exacted by the matriarchate)';[41] in just this way Friar Lawrence offers to 'dispose of' Juliet 'among a sisterhood of holy nuns'. The happy ending of the story Neumann describes as

> The feminine mystery of rebirth through love. In no goddess can Eros experience and know the miracle that befalls him through the human Psyche, the phenomenon of a love which is conscious, which, stronger than death, anointed with divine beauty, is willing to die, to receive the beloved as the bridegroom of death.[42]

Here again there are congruences with *Romeo and Juliet*, in the semi-divine Rosaline, the conscious love stronger than death, the image of love as a bridegroom.

Bruno Bettelheim, associating the story with what he called the 'animal–groom' cycle of fairy tales, sees the funeral procession as an emblem of the death of maidenhood, and Psyche's curiosity about her mysterious husband as a reaching out toward mature knowledge, putting aside mere narcissistic pleasure. He singles out for special attention the fact that 'the groom is absent during the day and present only in the darkness of night . . . in short, he keeps his day and night experiences separate from one another.'[43] In Bettelheim's view, the myth describes a movement toward maturity on the part of Cupid as well as Psyche. The objective, which each must come to accept, is 'to wed the aspects of sex, love, and life into a unity'.[44] He remarks, as well, on the 'timely' message of the tale: 'Notwithstanding all the hardships woman has to suffer to be reborn in full consciousness and humanity . . . this is what she must do.'[45] Psyche, as the mortal partner and the one forced to undergo privation and hardship, is properly viewed as the protagonist, with whose thoughts and feelings the reader will associate his own.

I would like to suggest that when viewed in this context the resemblances between *Romeo and Juliet* and the myth of Cupid and Psyche are both striking and fundamental. In both there are an unseen lover and a love relationship which is possible only in darkness. Both describe the passage of a woman from paternal domination to sensual submission and thence to individuation through pain and sacrifice. Both offer a vivid image of the marriage with Death, and in each the entire pattern is capable of being viewed as one of initiation for the woman. I do not – and would not – contend that Shakespeare consciously borrowed from the legend, either from Apuleius or through folkloric sources. But what I do suggest is that certain congruences are arresting and persuasive, that the myth of Cupid and Psyche represents a basic, underlying pattern of human maturation and, specifically, of sexual growth, and that, however derived, this pattern is clearly present and significant in many of Shakespeare's plays.

NOTES

1 Keith Thomas, 'The changing family', *The Times Literary Supplement* (21 October 1977), 1226–7.
2 Gellert Spencer Alleman, *Matrimonial Law and the Materials of Restoration Comedy* (Philadelphia: University of Pennsylvania Press, 1942), pp. 1–12.
3 Lawrence Stone, *The Family, Sex and Marriage in England 1500–1800* (London: Weidenfeld & Nicolson, 1977), pp. 40, 519.
4 James Boswell, *Life of Samuel Johnson, LLD* (London: Everyman, 1906), I, p. 627.
5 Stone, p. 180.
6 Stone, p. 87.
7 Stone, pp. 282–7.
8 Stone, pp. 99–100.
9 Stone, pp. 108, 376–7.
10 Some nuns did in fact bring dowries to their religious houses, in defiance of Church law but at the behest of the convents. Nonetheless, the expenses would not have compared to those of an important marriage. Cf. Eileen Power, *Medieval English Nunneries* (Cambridge: Cambridge University Press, 1922), pp. 14–24.

WOMEN'S RITES   171

11 Power, pp. 42–95.
12 Lytton Strachey, *Elizabeth and Essex* (London: Chatto & Windus, 1928), p. 141.
13 J. Oliphant (ed.), *Educational Writings of Richard Mulcaster* (Glasgow, 1903) pp. 51, 52.
14 *Certain Sermons or Homilies appointed to be read in Churches* (Oxford, 1844), pp. 46–58. Stone, p. 198.
15 Stone, p. 196.
16 Thomas Sargrove, quoted in Lacey Baldwin Smith, *Elizabeth Tudor, Portrait of a Queen* (Boston: Little, Brown, 1922), p. 119.
17 Smith, p. 120.
18 J. E. Neale, *Queen Elizabeth: A Biography* (London: Jonathan Cape, 1934; rpt. Doubleday, 1957), p. 142; Smith, pp. 118–33.
19 Erasmus, *The Comparation of a Virgin and a Martyr*, Thomas Paynell (trans.), 1537; facsimile rpt. of Berthelet edition, intro. William James Hirten (Gainesville, Florida: Scholars' Facsimiles and Reprints, 1970), p. 50.
20 Stone, p. 135.
21 William Perkins, 'Of Christian oeconomie, or household government', in *Works* (London, 1626), III, p. 689.
22 John Halkett, *Milton and the Idea of Matrimony* (New Haven: Yale University Press, 1970), pp. 50–5. Stone, pp. 137–8.
23 Sigmund Freud, 'On the sexual theories of children' (1908) in James Strachey (ed. and trans.), *The Standard Edition of the Complete Psychological Works of Sigmund Freud*, IX (London: Hogarth Press and the Institute of Psycho-Analysis, 1959, rpt. 1962), p. 215.
24 W. W. Greg (ed.), *Lodge's 'Rosalynde', Being the Original of Shakespeare's 'As You Like It'*, (New York: Duffield & Company; London: Chatto & Windus, 1907), pp. 93–7.
25 For example, *Measure for Measure* III. ii. 82–4; *King Lear* IV. vi. 199; *Antony and Cleopatra* IV. xiv. 99–101.
26 T. J. B. Spencer (ed.), *Shakespeare's Plutarch: The Lives of Julius Caesar, Brutus, Marcus Antonius and Coriolanus in the Translation of Sir Thomas North* (Middlesex, England, and Baltimore, Maryland: Penguin Books, 1964; rpt. 1968), pp. 82–3.
27 For example, John Gower, *Confessio Amantis*, II, 334: 'O Pallas noble quene . . . Help that I lose nought my flour.'
28 *Paradise Lost*, IV, ll. 269–72, in *John Milton, Complete Poems and Major Prose*, Merritt Y. Hughes (ed.) (New York: Odyssey Press, 1957).
29 Geoffrey Grigson, *The Englishman's Flora* (London: Phoenix House, 1955). Ophelia's 'long purples' have been identified as the marsh plant, purple loosestrife (*Lythrum salicaria* L.), but Grigson

argues persuasively that 'Shakespeare meant the bawdier plant, *Orchis mascula*', the early purple orchid (p. 194). Because of its appearance, this plant has been regarded as an aphrodisiac since classical times. Grigson's description makes the reason clear: 'Dig up an Early Purple Orchid and you find two root-tubers in which food is stored, a new, firm one, which is filling up for next year's growth, an old slack one, which is emptying and supplying the present needs. The symbolism of the kinds of *Orchis* with undivided tubers could hardly be overlooked' (p. 425). Like the purple loosestrife, the early purple orchid is popularly known as 'long purples', and also as 'dead man's finger', the name Gertrude says is used by 'our cold maids' (*Ham.* IV. vii. 169–71). It is also called 'cuckoo cock', 'dog stones' and 'priest's pintel', any of which might be the 'grosser name' employed by 'liberal shepherds'. As Grigson remarks, 'in *Hamlet* Shakespeare knew exactly what he was about' when he included this flower among Ophelia's garlands (p. 427). This identification has been accepted by most modern Shakespeare editors, including W. J. Craig, 1930; J. Dover Wilson, 1936; Hardin Craig, 1951; I. Ribner and G. L. Kittredge, 1971; G. Blakemore Evans, 1974. For another view, identifying the 'long purples' as *Arum maculatum*, the Wild Arum or Cuckoo-Pint, see Karl P. Wentersdorf, '*Hamlet*: Ophelia's long purples', *Shakespeare Quarterly*, XXIX, 3 (Summer 1978), 413–17.

30 Juliet, too, makes 'the prettiest sententious of [Romeo] and rosemary' before her marriage (*R&J* II. iv. 215–16), and the friar will then propose that her corpse be strewed with rosemary after her supposed death, proclaiming that 'she's best married that dies married young' (IV. 5. 78).

31 Sigmund Freud, *The Interpretation of Dreams*, in James Strachey (ed. and trans.), *The Standard Edition of the Complete Psychological Works of Sigmund Freud*, V (London: Hogarth Press and the Institute of Psycho-Analysis, 1953, rpt. 1958, 1962), p. 354.

32 See Marjorie Garber, '*Cymbeline* and the languages of myth', *Mosaic*, X, 3 (Spring 1977), 104–15.

33 Money is frequently described by Freud as a symbol of feces, and Shylock's retentiveness in this respect seems intimated by such remarks as his animadversion on bagpipes (IV. i. 49–50) and his command to Launcelot 'Shut up my house's ears – I mean my casements' (II. v. 34), where 'ears' and 'arse' would arguably have been pronounced the same. The connection of feces and sexuality is suggested in Freud's essay 'On the sexual theories of children' (1908) and elsewhere. A tentative theory about Shylock's 'immaturity' in psychological terms might perhaps be advanced, based upon his 'infantile' conflation of daughter and ducats throughout

the play. On the other hand, Shylock also significantly bewails the loss of his 'two stones, two rich and precious stones' (II. viii. 20), which have been taken away by Jessica. In Shakespeare's time 'stones' was a common term for testicles (cf. the comic use of the pun in the 'Pyramus and Thisbe' play, *MND* v. i. 190). Symbolically, Jessica thus gelds Shylock twice by removing his daughter and his ducats, leaving him both without child and without money to 'breed' with (I. iii. 93).

34 Cf. E. A. M. Colman, *The Dramatic Use of Bawdy in Shakespeare* (London: Longman, 1974), p. 77: 'jokes equating a ring with the female pudendum are fairly numerous in Renaissance literature'. Colman cites as one example an anecdote from Rabelais, *Gargantua and Pantagruel*, J. M. Cohen (trans.) (New York: Penguin Books, 1955), p. 368. We might also compare here the symbolic act of DeFlores in *The Changeling*, who severs the ring-bearing finger of Alonzo de Piracquo, Beatrice's murdered suitor, and produces both ring and finger in evidence of his deed. In the same play Alibius, counseling wariness against cuckolding, advises old Lollio, 'I would wear my ring on my own finger' (I. ii. 27).

35 T. Nichols, *Lapidary*, cited by Steevens in his edition of Shakespeare (1773). See the Arden edition of *The Merchant of Venice*, John Russell Brown (ed.) (London: Methuen, 1955; rpt. 1969), p. 75.

36 Imogen will speak of 'The innocent mansion of my love, the heart' (*Cymb.* II. iv. 68).

37 Apuleius, *The Transformations of Lucius, Otherwise Known as The Golden Ass*, Robert Graves (trans.) (New York: Farrar, Straus & Giroux, 1951), translator's introduction, p. xix.

38 Sigmund Freud, 'The theme of the three caskets' (1913) in James Strachey (ed. and trans.), *The Standard Edition of the Complete Psychological Works of Sigmund Freud*, XII (London: Hogarth Press and the Institute of Psycho-Analysis, 1958, rpt. 1962), p. 300n. The footnote attributes this observation to Otto Rank.

39 Erich Neumann, *Amor and Psyche: The Psychic Development of the Feminine, A Commentary on the Tale by Apuleius* (New York: Bollingen Series, Princeton University Press, 1956), p. 112.

40 Neumann, p. 78.

41 Neumann, p. 118.

42 Neumann, p. 125.

43 Bruno Bettelheim, *The Uses of Enchantment: The Meaning and Importance of Fairy Tales* (New York: Alfred A. Knopf, 1976), p. 294.

44 Bettelheim, p. 294.

45 Bettelheim, p. 295.

6

COMPARISON
AND DISTINCTION

'COUNTERFEIT PRESENTMENT'

❧❦

That 'comparisons are odious' is an opinion that has been both oft thought and oft expressed in English letters. As early as the fifteenth century Henry VI's Chief Justice, Sir John Fortescue, used the phrase in his treatise on English constitutional law (1471). John Donne concluded his Petrarchan / anti-Petrarchan elegy 'The Comparison' by declaring that 'She, and comparisons are odious', and writers as various as Lydgate, Burton, Swift and Hazlitt found room in their works for versions of the same sentiment. On the continent, Berni in Italy and Cervantes in Spain also cited the proverb with approval. The spectacle of Dogberry memorably mangling it into 'comparisons are odorous' suggests that in Shakespeare's time the original was widely known, for otherwise there would be no joke.

But despite the popularity of the maxim, comparisons were no more odious to the poets and playwrights of Elizabethan and Jacobean England than to succeeding generations. In their more elegant guise as similes, metaphors and conceits they were, indeed, such stuff as poetry was made on. For this very reason, they were considered potentially dangerous. Puttenham, discussing figures of speech in *The Arte of English Poesie*, calls them 'guilefull and abusing', and 'occupied of purpose to deceive the ear and also the mind' – 'for what else is your *Metaphor* but an inversion of sense by transport, your *allegorie* but a duplicitie of meaning or dissimulation under covert and darke intendments', and so forth.[1] Such abuses were much on the mind of

Spenser, whose villains often use language to entrap and delude; even the names of the necromancers Archimago and Busirane suggest image-making, conceit and abuse.

Puttenham goes on to distinguish between poets and judges; the poet is not a judge but a 'pleader', and since 'all his abuses tend but to dispose his hearers to mirth and sollace by pleasant conveyance and efficacy of speach, they are not in truth to be accompted vices but for vertues in the poetical science'.[2] Even if absolved of an intention to distort or deceive, however, comparisons could be odious for reasons which were aesthetic rather than moral or ethical. The vogue of Petrarchism had encouraged such forms as the blazon and the catalogue, and extravagant but predictable analogies were the rule rather than the exception in mediocre verse. At the same time the development of what came to be popularly known as 'Euphuism' encouraged a profusion of elaborate similes and antitheses in prose.[3] Shakespeare is very sensible of this assault from within the literary ranks, and finds numerous occasions to mock it in his plays. Thus Demetrius, bewitched by Puck's magic love-juice, wakes to declare his passion for Helena in elaborate terms:

> O Helen, goddess, nymph, perfect, divine!
> To what, my love, shall I compare thine eyne?
> Crystal is muddy. O, how ripe in show
> Thy lips, those kissing cherries, tempting grow!
> (*MND* III. ii. 137–40)

And so on and on. The jangling internal rhyme in 'thine eyne' shows quite clearly what the playwright thinks of this derivative mode of versifying. Likewise in *Love's Labor's Lost* Rosaline observes drily that in Berowne's love letter 'I am compared to twenty thousand fairs' (v. ii. 37), while in the same play Don Armado's letter to Jaquenetta draws the stock analogy between his situation and that of King Cophetua:

> I am the king, for so stands the comparison, thou the beggar, for so witnesseth thy lowliness. (IV. i. 80–1)

Whenever this mode of facile and hyperbolic comparison appears in the plays, it carries with it an implicit criticism of the speaker's self-knowledge, and of the quality of the relationship being described. Shakespeare sums up the matter neatly in the final couplet of sonnet 130, 'My mistress' eyes are nothing like the sun':

> And yet by heaven, I think my love as rare
> As any she belied with false compare.

The concept of 'false compare', as exemplified in the sonnet's mock-Petrarchan catalogue, reflects not only upon the lady but upon the poet who makes the comparison. Perhaps the furthest extension of this dangerous mode can be found in *Troilus and Cressida*, where the lovers attempt to metamorphose themselves into the very standard of 'true compare', and in so doing signal to the audience the extreme fragility of their position:

> *Troilus*   True swains in love shall in the world to come
>   Approve their truth by Troilus. When their rhymes,
>   Full of protest, of oath and big compare,
>   Wants similes, truth tired with iteration,
>   'As true as steel, as plantage to the moon,
>   As sun to day, as turtle to her mate,
>   As iron to adamant, as earth to the center,'
>   Yet, after all comparisons of truth,
>   As truth's authentic author to be cited,
>   'As true as Troilus' shall crown up the verse
>   And sanctify the numbers.   (III. ii. 171–81)

Troilus' proposal to replace the tired iteration and 'big compare' of love poets with his own example of truth is replete with ironies, since by Shakespeare's time Troilus had himself become one of the biggest clichés of all. No figure is more frequently cited by Shakespearean lovers than Troilus. Lorenzo includes him in his catalogue of sighing lovers on summer nights (*Merch.* v. i. 4), Rosalind cites him as 'one of the patterns of love' (*AYLI* IV. i. 94), and Benedick explicitly associates him with the conventions of love poetry: 'Leander the good swimmer, Troilus the first employer of panders, and a whole book full of these quondam carpetmongers, whose names yet run smoothly in the even road of a blank verse' (*Ado* v. ii. 30–4). Even Petruchio has a spaniel named Troilus, who is presumably so called because of his fidelity.[4] Moreover, Shakespeare from the first presents Troilus as infatuated with the same language he will later disparage: in Act I scene i, for example, we hear him describe

Cressida's 'hand / In whose comparison all whites are ink, / Writing their own reproach' (57–9). His celebrated characterization of the 'monstruosity in love', when 'we vow to weep seas, live in fire, eat rocks, tame tigers', pretends to more anti-Petrarchism than it embodies, since he immediately follows it by yet another claim to perfect love: 'what truth can speak truest [shall be] not truer than Troilus' (iii. ii. 76–82, 96–7).

Manifestly, there are qualitative distinctions to be made among the kinds of self-delusion shown by Troilus, Berowne and Demetrius, but their kinship seems clear: whether infatuated by love, sex, or the mere idea of being in love, each chooses a language of comparison which comes perilously close to 'false compare'. Such language is 'abusing', to use Puttenham's term, because it falsifies both the beloved and the sentiment – and it does so in precisely the same way as do the conventional poets criticized in sonnet 130: it denies humanity and particularity to the subject, and thus reveals the shallowness of the speaker.

We know that in the sixteenth century sonnets and satirical epigrams were considered to be versions of the same type of verse, Scaliger's *mel* and *fel*, which became in English terms sugar and salt, or honey and gall, or naive and pointed.[5] We should not be surprised, therefore, to discover a second kind of 'abusing' comparison in Shakespeare's plays – that offered by skeptics, satirists, scoffers and persons in positions of detached observation. The word 'comparative' itself becomes a substantive noun to denote such persons; thus King Henry IV describes the public conduct of his predecessor Richard II as such that he 'Had his great name profanèd with their scorns / And gave his countenance, against his name, / To laugh at gibing boys and stand the push / Of every beardless vain comparative' (1HIV iii. ii. 64–7). Rosaline, provisionally rejecting Berowne's suit in *Love's Labor's Lost*, offers him this frank assessment of his character:

> the world's large tongue
> Proclaims you for a man replete with mocks,
> Full of comparisons and wounding flouts,
> Which you on all estates will execute
> That lie within the mercy of your wit.   (v. ii. 840–4)

In *Troilus and Cressida* Nestor characterizes Thersites as a slave 'whose gall coins slanders like a mint', who strives 'To match us in comparisons with dirt' (*T&C* I. iii. 193–4). And in *King Henry IV Part I* Falstaff and Prince Hal, both quick with an epithet, trade inventive insults at the same time that they reproach each other with the practice. 'Thou hast the most unsavory similes, and art indeed the most comparative, rascalliest, sweet young prince' (*1HIV* I. ii. 80–2), Falstaff complains, while after the Gad's Hill caper Hal successfully engages his companion in a flouting match:

> *Prince* I'll be no longer guilty of this sin; this sanguine
>   coward, this bed-presser, this horseback-breaker, this
>   huge hill of flesh –
> *Falstaff* 'Sblood, you starveling, you eelskin, you dried
>   neat's-tongue, you bull's pizzle, you stockfish – O for
>   breath to utter what is like thee! – you tailor's yard,
>   you sheath, you bowcase, you vile standing tuck!
> *Prince* Well, breathe awhile, and then to it again; and when
>   thou hast tired thyself in base comparisons, hear me
>   speak but this.   (II. iv. 243–53)

Falstaff's 'base comparisons', like the 'false compare' of conventional sonneteers and doting lovers, obstruct communication and truth, in this case by endlessly delaying the true story of the Gad's Hill robbery; as Hal goes on to observe, 'Mark now how a plain tale shall put you down' (256–7). And just as 'false compare' signifies a failure in self-knowledge and communication on the part of the comparer, so 'base comparisons' are usually self-protective ploys, employed to distance the speaker from the events or persons he is describing. Thus Berowne is found lacking in compassion, Thersites in idealism and heroism, and Falstaff in courage by those who address or characterize them.

But such deliberately negative characterizations of the comparer are in fact the exception rather than the rule in Shakespearean drama. Indeed, it is for that reason that they have been worth our notice. For the most part, however, the capacity to compare, contrast and discriminate is highly valued in the plays, and becomes a further rite of passage for the Shakespearean protagonist. Far from being odious, the act of comparing takes on the status of a trial or test, which marks the initiate as successful – or not – in his relationships with himself, with other persons, and with history. We found in sonnet 130 an object lesson of 'false compare', and we may perhaps look to the sonnets once again for a model of more judicious comparison.

Sonnet 18 sets forth just such a pattern in its opening lines: 'Shall I compare thee to a summer's day? / Thou art more lovely and more temperate.' The speaker's objective here is not a facile identification of lips with cherries and cheeks with rosebuds, but neither is it a programmatic repudiation of such figures. Instead, by setting up the terms of the comparison – you are like a summer's day – and then immediately qualifying them, he preserves both comparison and distinction. The beloved is enough like the summer's day – lovely, temperate, and fair – that the juxtaposition provides a starting point for finding out what he is really like. The sonnet has other purposes and other directions: what we ultimately discover is a truth about the poet–speaker, rather than about the beloved. But the general pattern of analogy conjoined with differentiation is one which Shakespeare puts to valuable use in the plays.

An example from the romances will provide a useful demonstration of how this pattern can be transferred to a dramatic context. In *The Winter's Tale* Paulina instructs a repentant Leontes never to marry, 'Unless another, / As like Hermione as is her picture, / Affront his eye' (v. i. 73–5). Leontes agrees, citing the impossibility of finding a suitable successor: 'No more such wives, therefore no wife' (56). Paulina, however, has an ulterior motive. She is planning to exhibit the 'statue' of the supposedly dead queen – a work of art which the clown significantly describes, in an unconscious echo of Paulina's own language, as 'the queen's picture' (v. ii. 177–8). Leontes is struck, as he must be, by the resemblance, but the key moment of the recognition scene is his perception of a difference: 'Hermione was not so much wrinkled, nothing so agèd as this seems' (v. iii. 28–9). This sounds like a complaint, but Paulina deftly turns it into an instructive compliment: 'So much the more our carver's excellence' (30). The 'carver' now assumes for the audience the several alternative identities of Time, Nature, God and the playwright Shakespeare himself. As Leontes continues to gaze, he discovers further contrasts. The statue seems to breathe, its veins to bear blood: 'What fine chisel / Could ever yet cut breath?' (78–9). He leans forward to kiss it, and Paulina once more intervenes, but her point is already made: in recognizing the marks of time and the signs of life in the 'statue' of his wife, Leontes has undergone a crucial transition. As he progresses through a sequence of comparisons and contrasts, his faith is awakened.

We shall see shortly how such works of art as the statue and the picture are used to facilitate comparison and contrast on Shakespeare's stage. In a sense, however, these aesthetic objects are variants – though distinct variants – of an even more common metaphor used in literary comparisons: that of the glass or mirror.

The popularity of the mirror metaphor in western literature goes back to classical and even biblical times. Plato uses it disparagingly in the *Republic*, alleging that the artist is only a reflector of things,[6] and a Sophist commentator praises the *Odyssey* by calling it 'a beautiful mirror of life'. Terence and Cicero both use *speculum* to describe works of art – to Cicero comedy was *imitatio vitae, speculum consuetudinis, imago veritatis* [7] – a characterization which bears a striking similarity to Hamlet's advice to the players. The 'glass, darkly' of 1 Corinthians alludes presumably not only to man's fallen condition, but also to the ways he tries to come to terms with his earthly state. Cassiodorus compares the human mind to a mirror.[8] As time went on, both 'mirror' and its Latin equivalent *speculum* came to denote first a mode of instruction, and then a pattern or model. Gower's *Speculum Meditantis* or *Mirour de l'Omme* describes a contest for man's soul between vices and virtues, and concludes that all men are corrupt, needing the intercession of the Virgin. Nigel Wireker's *Speculum Stultorum*, or *Mirror of Fools*, was a well-known satire on monks, and the extensive medieval encyclopedia of Vincent of Beauvais was titled *Speculum naturale, historiale, doctrinale*. In 1559 there appeared in England the *Mirror for Magistrates*, collected by Ferrers and Baldwin with a preface by Thomas Sackville, which presented accounts of the rise and fall of famous men, patterned after Lydgate's translation of Boccaccio's *Falls of Princes* and Chaucer's *Monk's Tale*. Thus by Shakespeare's time 'mirror' as a metaphor had acquired the primary meaning of 'example' or 'model', and it is frequently used in this way in his plays. Talbot calls Salisbury the 'mirror of all martial men' (*1HVI* i. iv. 74), Oxford speaks of 'Henry the Fourth / Whose wisdom was a mirror to the wisest' (*3HVI* iii. iii. 83–4), Buckingham in *Henry VIII* is described as 'the mirror of all courtesy' (ii. i. 53), and Henry V is celebrated by the Prologue as 'the mirror of all Christian kings' (*HV* ii. Prol. 6). A more dramatically startling and innovative use of the mirror figure occurs in the great apparition scene in *Macbeth*, where the witches conjure up '*A show of eight* Kings *and* Banquo, *last* [King] *with a glass in his hand*' (iv. i. SD). The Arden editor, Kenneth Muir, comments that this glass is 'not an ordinary mirror in which King James would see himself but a prospective, or magic, glass'.[9] Yet the two kinds of glass do not seem incompatible. As Banquo was supposedly King James' ancestor, and the present line presumed to derive from him, the use of an actual mirror to reflect the king's face or form would reinforce, rather than war with, the idea of lineality, while at the same time renewing the audience's awareness of the play's pertinence. In any case, the 'glass' is here once again associated with ideal deportment and kingship, offering yet another model of conduct.

We may notice that all of these exemplary figures are aristocrats, either royal or noble. The concept of the individual as a mirror appears, at least in Shakespeare's history plays, to reflect a kind of *noblesse oblige*, a social responsibility to set an example for one's soldiers, servants, or subjects. Perhaps as a result, the description of such a 'mirror' became something of a topos, an encyclopedic catalogue of noble virtues. This may in part account for the curious similarity between two lengthier 'mirror' passages – the lament of Lady Percy for her slain husband, Hotspur, and Ophelia's equally grief-stricken report of the madness of Hamlet. Lady Percy begins and ends her eulogy with the image of the 'glass':

> He was indeed the glass
> Wherein the noble youth did dress themselves.
> He had no legs that practiced not his gait;
> And speaking thick, which nature made his blemish,
> Became the accents of the valiant,
> For those that could speak low and tardily

> Would turn their own perfection to abuse,
> To seem like him. So that in speech, in gait,
> In diet, in affections of delight,
> In military rules, humors of blood,
> He was the mark and glass, copy and book,
> That fashioned others.   (2HIV II. iii. 21–32)

Ophelia's account, though it describes a living man, likewise verges on the elegiac:

> O what a noble mind is here o'erthrown!
> The courtier's, soldier's, scholar's, eye, tongue, sword,
> Th' expectancy and rose of the fair state,
> The glass of fashion, and the mold of form,
> Th' observed of all observers, quite, quite down!
>   (Ham. III. i. 151–5)

We are accustomed to think of Hotspur primarily as a blunt soldier, Hamlet as a thoughtful and articulate scholar. Yet in these speeches the two men sound oddly alike. Their grieving ladies have made use of the mirror topos to generalize a model. In a very similar way Castiglione urged upon the erring 'princes of [his] day', an emulation of the ancients,

> who, even though they erred in some things, yet did not flee
> from the promptings and teachings of anyone who seemed to
> them able to correct those errors; nay, they made every effort
> to order their lives on the model of excellent men.[10]

With this convention in mind, we can appreciate the consternation of the elderly Duchess of York as she perceives in her son Gloucester a warped or distorted mirror, unlike his father or his dead brothers: 'I have bewept', she says, 'a worthy husband's death, / And lived with looking on his images':

> But now two mirrors of his princely semblance
> Are cracked in pieces by malignant death,
> And I for comfort have but one false glass
> That grieves me when I see my shame in him.
>   (RIII II. ii. 49–54)

Like the 'noble youth' who follow Hotspur, the duchess peers into the mirror, not to see her own image, but in quest of the 'model' of her husband and sons. Characteristically, however, Richard uses the mirror, not to improve but purely to reflect himself. Despite his playful denials, he is aware of and occasionally obsessed by mirrors from the moment he takes the stage in *Richard III*. In the opening soliloquy he alleges that he is 'not shaped for sportive tricks / Nor made to court an amorous looking glass' (I. i. 14–15). Yet the wooing of Anne brings out an ironic reappraisal of his charms:

> I'll be at charges for a looking glass
> And entertain a score or two of tailors
> To study fashions to adorn my body. . . .
> Shine out, fair sun; till I have bought a glass
> That I may see my shadow as I pass.   (I. ii. 255–63)

In Olivier's remarkable film version of the play, the shadow plays a recurrent and important role. The initial confrontation between Gloucester and King Edward is presented entirely as a meeting of shadows, until we are finally afforded a glimpse of Edward's white and terrified face. After the scene with Anne, Richard's dark shadow looms in her bedroom, this time again counterbalanced by a fragile glimpse of white in Anne's dress as she turns toward him. During Clarence's soliloquy, the malignant shadow of his brother looms yet again larger than life over the spy-hole of his prison cell.[11] In cinematic terms, the dark shadow, grotesquely misshapen, has replaced the clear image in the looking glass – as Richard had foretold, and as his mother implied in her metaphor of the 'false glass'.

When we turn to another Richard, and another looking glass, we see a different variation on this same theme. Richard II requests a mirror in the deposition scene 'That it may show me what a face I have, / Since it is bankrout of his majesty' (IV. i. 265–6). When the glass is brought, the king is astonished to see no change: 'O flatt'ring glass! / Like to my followers in prosperity, / Thou dost beguile me' (278–80). Hurling it theatrically to the ground, he turns to address the impassive Bolingbroke:

> Mark, silent king, the moral of this sport:
> How soon my sorrow has destroyed my face.
>
>   (289–90)

But Bolingbroke's reply makes clear that he has understood both symbol and self-deception: 'The shadow of your sorrow hath destroyed / The shadow of your face' (291–2). In one sense Richard's tragedy is summed up in his failure to distinguish, even albeit rhetorically, between the shadow of his face and that face itself. The changes are within, as is the case – to compare small things with great – with the picture of Dorian Gray. The literal looking glass has not altered, but 'the glass wherein the noble youth did dress themselves', the model and ideal of kingship, had been shattered long before, by Richard's own venal conduct and by his self-absorption – of which his penchant for ritual is only a part. We have already mentioned Bolingbroke's later comment about Richard's behavior in office, when he had to 'stand the push / Of every beardless vain comparative' (1HIV III. ii. 66–7). In the deposition scene, as throughout the play, Richard is not enough of a comparative. He does not distinguish the shadow from the substance, the human face of kingship from its authority and merit. When finally in Pomfret Castle he comes to study 'how I may compare / This prison where I live unto the world' (v. v. 1–2) he is already imprisoned, not only by Bolingbroke, but also by solipsism and soliloquy. Had he hammered out his analogy much earlier, both kingdom and kingship would have benefited.

In a rather roundabout way, then, we have come to the central pitfall of the mirror metaphor, which is, most simply stated, that of narcissism. If the image given back by the mirror is principally for the delectation of the self, then judgment, discrimination, and comparison are all denied. Venus cautions Adonis, with some justification, against such a fate:

> Is thine own heart to thine own face affected?
> Can thy right hand seize love upon thy left?
> Then woo thyself, be of thyself rejected;
> Steal thine own freedom, and complain on theft.
>   Narcissus so himself himself forsook,
>   And died to kiss his shadow in the brook.
>   (Ven. 157–62)

Both Richards in their different ways are thus infatuated and themselves themselves forsake. But this is hardly an exclusive prerogative of the history plays; indeed, it is in the comedies that we see it most often, with results which are appropriately less dire. In As You Like It, for example, the Ovidian story of

Narcissus, suitably cited in Shakespeare's Ovidian poem, undergoes a Circean transformation to become the folkloric story of
the fool in the brook.

> *Jaques*   By my troth, I was seeking for a fool when I found
> you.
> *Orlando*   He is drowned in the brook. Look but in and you
> shall see him.
> *Jaques*   There I shall see mine own figure.
> *Orlando*   Which I take to be either a fool or a cipher.
>
> (III. ii. 285–91)

Not a particularly subtle or edifying exchange, but one which
reveals something of a home truth about Jaques. Elsewhere in
the play we have seen him compare himself to an injured stag,
and 'moralize this spectacle . . . into a thousand similes' (II. i.
44–5). Shortly thereafter he will encounter a fool in the forest,
and delightedly report on how he 'moral[s] on the time' (II. vii. 29).
Yet as David Young has observed, not only the fool Touchstone
but the forest of Arden and much that it contains are in fact
reflectors, showing to the visitors from the city either ironic
portraits of themselves or subjective reflections of their own
preconceived ideas.[12] That Jaques elects to stay in the forest at
the play's end is a further commentary on his character. He is
more at home within the mirror than outside it.

Other versions of the fool in the brook, equally 'low' and
folkloric in origin, appear in *Twelfth Night* and *The Merchant of
Venice*. In *Twelfth Night* Feste alludes drily to the 'picture of We
Three', a picture of two asses so titled, in which the spectator was
invited to recognize himself as the third. The implication,
genially accepted by Sir Toby, is that those who address Feste as
'fool' may well deserve the label themselves. The *Merchant of
Venice* offers a graphic example of such a fool in the Prince of
Aragon. Aragon elects to open the silver (mirror-like?) casket,
emblazoned with the motto 'Who chooseth me shall get as much
as he deserves' (II. ix. 35), and finds inside 'the portrait of a
blinking idiot / Presenting me a schedule' (53–4). It is possible to
imagine a production in which the point would be underscored
by changing the portrait literally into a mirror, but the
'schedule', or enclosed scroll, and the response of Aragon himself make the identification sufficiently plain. 'Take what wife

you will to bed, / I will ever be your head,' proclaims the scroll (69–70), and Aragon supplies a further gloss:

> Still more fool I shall appear
> By the time I linger here.
> With one fool's head I came to woo,
> But I go away with two.   (72–5)

Not only pictures of fools, but the fools themselves, often serve this mirroring function. We have noted Touchstone's parody of Jaques as a fool in the forest. We might also cite the behavior of Feste toward Olivia, and that of Lear's Fool toward both the king and Kent. In each case the incident has a comparative structure: the Fool, addressed or labelled as such by his employer or another person ostensibly his 'better', contrives in reply a witty comparison which neatly turns the tables (and the labels). Olivia bids her servants to take away the fool; Feste retorts by demonstrating that it is she who is the fool, since she continues to mourn for her brother, although he is safely in heaven (*TN* I. v. 38–72). Lear observes that his companion is a 'bitter fool', and is answered with a rhyming riddle:

> That lord that counseled thee
>   To give away thy land,
> Come place him here by me,
>   Do thou for him stand.
> The sweet and bitter fool
>   Will presently appear;
> The one in motley here,
>   The other found out there.   (*Lr* I. iv. 142–9)

Kent, shamed and shackled at Cornwall's order, is offered similarly pithy advice when he receives a visit from the Fool, and asks him a question which deserves – and gets – a neat reply:

> *Kent*   Where learned you this, Fool?
> *Fool*   Not i' th' stocks, Fool.   (II. iv. 84–5)

All three of these incidents suggest a basic truth about the characters who take part in them. Olivia is indeed in bondage to her brother's memory, and uses it as an excuse to turn away from life. Lear is only beginning to realize the depths of his own folly. As for Kent, he has been put in the stocks for his conduct toward Goneril's servant, Oswald; he follows Lear out of loyalty and love, but also out of a sense of hierarchy and natural authority. For a moment, in the Fool's not-unsympathetic jest, he is offered a more complex view of social and class distinctions and their relationship to individual merit.

The method of comparison used by the Fool in these confrontations is what was known to the Renaissance – and to the Augustan age – as 'wit', the perception of similarities between things which at first appear unlike. A lively discourse on the shifting meaning of 'wit' took place throughout the period, with 'wit' being allied to such terms as 'fancy' and 'imagination', and identified with the essential element of poetry. From Aristotle's *Rhetoric* on, however, wit denoted the ability to make apt comparisons. Wimsatt and Brooks define it as 'the faculty of seeing difficult resemblances between largely unlike objects', and 'in practice . . . the enforcement of such resemblances by all the verbal resources available'.[13] Such a concept of wit gave rise, in turn, to the definition of its opposite – the capacity, not to find similarities, but to discern differences, or what Wimsatt and Brookes call 'an emphasis on analysis rather than synthesis'. This faculty, rather more scientific and philosophic than the very literary (and oratorical) 'wit', came to be known as 'judgment'.[14]

Seventeenth-century theorists were quick to point out the synecdochic relationship between wit and such figures of speech as metaphor, which performed the same activity (finding similarities in things unlike) on the verbal as wit did on the intellectual plane.[15] Extending the analogy one further step, we may find it useful to see in the relationship of wit to judgment a model of the pattern we have already observed in the growth of a dramatic character: a progression from the perceiving of similarities between oneself and another to the discerning of significant differences. Dryden compared wit without judgment to the movement of a 'high-ranging spaniel', which 'must have clogs tied to it, lest it outrun the judgment'.[16] In our investigations thus far, we have begun to discern a similar pattern, whereby distinction, or judgment, is a necessary qualification for comparison, or wit. For the men and women of Shakespeare's plays, the ability to use these faculties and to discipline them is a crucial aspect of maturation. The progress from ignorance to wit to judgment is a sign of increased self-knowledge. However, even wit must be well used to be effective. When witty comparisons come too close to identification or tautology there is danger of misperception.

Once again, the mirror metaphor will provide a useful example of how this comes about, for those Shakespearean characters who are not licensed fools frequently discover that to make oneself a mirror, or to perceive another in that guise, is potentially both dangerous and misleading. This is demonstrably the case with twins, who bring the 'mirror' metaphor to life on the stage. At the close of *The Comedy of Errors*, for instance, we hear one Dromio remark to another, 'methinks you are my glass, and not my brother' (v. i. 418). The physical similarity between the two servants and the parallel likeness of their masters have been the source of comic confusion throughout, but it is the fact that they are *not* interchangeable that causes the difficulty. When Dromio of Syracuse is claimed by Nell the kitchen maid, or his master by Adriana, the necessity for differentiation becomes clear. The plot, in fact, depends both on wit and on judgment; the scrambling of the brothers leads initially to revelation and fruitful reordering, but a restoration of individual identities is necessary to provide a harmonious social resolution. A similar situation obtains in *Twelfth Night* when Viola, dressed in the clothing of a brother she believes to be dead, contemplates her image in a mirror and exclaims, 'I my brother know / Yet living in my glass' (iii. iv. 383–4). As was the case with *Errors*, confusing the twins is essential to the working out of the play, and mistaking the one for the other makes possible the growth and change of those around them. Yet as Viola herself is shortly to learn, differentiation is again as important as similarity, contrast as crucial as comparison, if she, Olivia and Orsino are each to be matched with a suitable partner.

Twins constitute what might be described as 'natural' or 'physical' mirrors. When one twin reflects the other in Shakespearean drama the distortion involved is usually unintentional, and remains for most of the play undetected by any of the play's characters. Much more complex and disturbing is the situation in which one character deliberately sets himself up to be a mirror for another, for all too often in these cases there enters a certain resemblance to the Duchess of Gloucester's 'false glass'. This is the accusation Rosalind levels at the doting

shepherd Silvius in *As You Like It*. His lovesick pursuit of Phebe
has made her proud and disdainful, with little justification:

> 'Tis not her glass, but you, that flatters her,
> And out of you she sees herself more proper
> Than any of her lineaments can show her.
> But mistress, know yourself. (III. v. 54–7)

The injunction to 'know yourself', as always a Shakespearean
invitation to maturity, is here expressed by Rosalind in the most
straightforward way. Phebe will ignore this excellent advice, as
will Silvius, but the play's comic structure makes possible an
eleventh-hour solution. To the last, however, Phebe appears
infatuated with the fool in the brook: her acceptance of Silvius is
based upon the same false glass of his devotion, suddenly con-
verted to an asset: 'Thy faith my fancy to thee doth combine'
(v. iv. 150).

A more ominous version of the friend-as-glass can be found in
the famous exchange between Brutus and Cassius, in which the
seduction is both more calculating and more difficult.

> *Cassius* Tell me, good Brutus, can you see your face?
> *Brutus* No, Cassius; for the eye sees not itself
> But by reflection, by some other things.
> *Cassius* 'Tis just:
> And it is very much lamented, Brutus,
> That you have no such mirrors as will turn
> Your hidden worthiness into your eye,
> That you might see your shadow. I have heard
> Where many of the best respect in Rome
> (Except immortal Caesar), speaking of Brutus,
> And groaning underneath this age's yoke,
> Have wished that noble Brutus had his eyes.
> *Brutus* Into what dangers would you lead me, Cassius,
> That you would have me seek into myself
> For that which is not in me?
> *Cassius* Therefore, good Brutus, be prepared to hear;
> And since you know you cannot see yourself
> So well as by reflection, I, your glass,
> Will modestly discover to yourself
> That of yourself which you yet know not of.
> (*JC* i. ii. 51–70)

'I, your glass' – the phrase is sufficient warning to the audience familiar with Shakespeare's way with mirrors. What Cassius shows Brutus is not a lie, but it is a colored truth. The real danger lies, not in Brutus' credulity, but in Cassius' pretense that he is a disinterested observer, reflecting nothing but fact. The obligation placed upon the listener, or spectator, is to determine the point at which resemblance ceases between himself and the portrait drawn of him.

The problem is complicated further by the necessity Brutus acknowledges in his first reply to Cassius. Without some mode of reflection, the eye cannot see itself, the individual cannot know or recognize himself.[17] But for that very reason the uncautious gazer is vulnerable to deception by his 'glass', as Cassius himself is quick to acknowledge, once alone:

> Well, Brutus, thou art noble; yet I see
> Thy honorable mettle may be wrought
> From that it is disposed; therefore it is meet
> That noble minds keep ever with their likes;
> For who so firm that cannot be seduced?
>
> (I. ii. 306–10)

The seduction of Brutus follows the same forked path we have been observing: he is first persuaded of a likeness, and then of a difference, between himself and Caesar. 'Brutus and Caesar,' argues Cassius, / 'What should be in that "Caesar"? / Why should that name be sounded more than yours? / Write them together, yours is as fair a name; / Sound them, it does become the mouth as well' (142–5). In the same way, although without the same calculation, the plebians will hail Brutus after the murder: 'Let him be Caesar.' 'Caesar's better parts / Shall be crowned in Brutus' (III. ii. 51–2). Shakespeare seems to urge this parallel upon us: in Act II scene i Portia kneels to Brutus, imploring him to unburden his soul; in the scene that follows, with Portia's action still vivid in the audience's mind, Calphurnia will kneel to Caesar, and plead with him not to go to the Capitol. Yet ultimately it is a distinction, as much as a resemblance, that works on Brutus. Cassius has cleverly invoked the name of that other Brutus, Lucius Junius, 'that would have brooked / Th' eternal devil to keep his state in Rome / As easily as a king' (I. ii. 159–61). And throughout the play Brutus is convinced that he is

acting with a disinterestedness and a loyalty to the state which
no longer characterize Caesar. The rhetoric of eyesight which
begins the mirror passage is suggestive of his dilemma within
the play as a whole. 'Brutus, I do observe you now of late,'
Cassius remarks, 'I have not from your eyes that gentleness / And
show of love as I was wont to have' (I. ii. 32–4) – and Brutus
replies, 'If I have veiled my look, / I turn the trouble of my
countenance / Merely upon myself' (37–9). For neither the
self-absorption of these early moments nor the resolution imparted to him by his 'glass' shows Brutus the truth as history will
show it, until he reasserts the resemblance, and slays himself as
he slew Caesar.

Such is the situation when Hamlet confronts his mother in
her closet, determined to persuade her of her errors. 'You shall
not budge,' he tells her,

> You go not till I set you up a glass
> Where you may see the inmost part of you!
>
> (III. iv. 19–21)

Hamlet, with his 'antic disposition' and his feigned – or real –
madness, is another version of the fool, with the fool's capacity
and predisposition to make himself a glass. The mirror he holds
up to Gertrude's nature is not only verbal but visual, a distant
cousin to the portrait of the blinking idiot and the picture of We
Three: 'Look here upon this picture, and on this, / The counterfeit presentment of two brothers' (54–5). 'Counterfeit' is a
telling word here; the portraits are only artists' renderings,
hence to some degree false, yet one of the brothers is doubly
counterfeit, having presented himself to her in a dissembling
guise. What Hamlet argues is that his mother has unaccountably failed to distinguish between the godlike Old Hamlet and
the despicable Claudius (65). She has invented a likeness where
none exists; she has failed to exercise judgment. 'Have you
eyes?' he twice demands of her (66, 68), and again, 'What devil
was't / That thus hath cozened you at hoodman-blind?' (77–8).
We may perhaps expect there to be some family resemblance of a
physical kind between the two men; it is moral discrimination
within that superficial similarity which is chiefly called for – and
apparently wholly absent. Gertrude for her part not only accepts
Hamlet as her mirror, but borrows his metaphor: 'Thou turn'st

mine eyes into my very soul' (90). Yet the appearance of the Ghost, immediately following this exchange, adds an ironic dimension to the scene: once more Hamlet sees what Gertrude does not; once more she is convinced that 'all that is I see' (133). Is the Ghost, too, a 'counterfeit presentment'? The question vexes Hamlet from the first. Is he himself only a 'counterfeit presentment' of his father? But for Hamlet, a reflective reflector, his mother's failure to make a simple discrimination is a reminder of his own constant necessity to tell a hawk from a handsaw, a weasel from a whale, in a world of shifting perceptions and shadowy truths.

To compare and contrast – to exercise both wit and judgment. The 'mirrors' represented by historical collections and anthologies of the fall of princes have their counterpart in a more generalized use of history as a module. In *Richard II*, York's nostalgic praise of the Black Prince – his brother and Richard's father – bears a stylistic resemblance to the encomia for Hotspur and Hamlet. Instead of holding the Black Prince up as a generalized model, however, York chooses to compare him directly with his son. Richard looks like his father,

> But when he frowned it was against the French,
> And not against his friends; his noble hand
> Did win what he did spend, and spent not that
> Which his triumphant father's hand had won;
> His hands were guilty of no kindred blood,
> But bloody with the enemies of his kin.

The elegant and apposite use of chiasmus in the last four lines shows clearly how York is balancing the one man against the other, and also gives an indication of his rising emotion. At this point in the speech he himself becomes aware of the force of his own rhetoric, and hastily interrupts the flow of words:

> O, Richard, York is too far gone with grief,
> Or else he never would compare between –
>
> (II. i. 178–85)

But Richard has not really been listening, and the apology (like the analogy) is both unnecessary and unheeded.

Shakespeare uses the inverse of this comparative structure to comic purpose in *Henry V* when he has Fluellen attempt to develop the parallels between King Henry and Alexander the Great. Here we, like the skeptical Captain Gower, should expect a certain degree of contrast – but Fluellen is implacable. Macadon and Monmouth, after all, are both located on rivers – and if Henry did not exactly kill his best friend, as did Alexander, he did turn away Sir John Falstaff. As Fluellen explains, 'I speak but in the figures and comparisons of it' – 'If you mark Alexander's life well, Harry of Monmouth's life is come after it indifferent well, for there is figures in all things' (IV. vi. 43, 31–3). Like so many of Fluellen's remarks, this one rings true. In effect, his analogy is a 'low' counterpart for the Prologue's earlier identification of Henry V as 'the mirror of all Christian kings'. At the same time it is an unconscious but apt application of Castiglione's advice, to find classical models for virtuous conduct. Moreover, the total seriousness of Fluellen's tone presents this 'witty' comparison in an effectively naive light. To Gower he may appear to be talking nonsense, but the audience, in the midst of its laughter, will recognize a time-honored and appropriate use of comparison to interpret contemporary history.

When the comparison is offered by one of the parties compared, this device takes on a new vitality, becoming at once a mode of learning and an aspect of self-knowledge. In the much discussed third scene of the fourth act of *Macbeth*, Malcolm makes use of just such a method to test out the loyalty of a befuddled Macduff. 'I am not treacherous,' Macduff asserts, and Malcolm replies pointedly, 'But Macbeth is. / A good and virtuous nature may recoil / In an imperial charge' (18–20). His father, Duncan, had made a fatal mistake in finding the mind's construction in the face; moreover, he had done it twice, and been betrayed by two successive Thanes of Cawdor. Malcolm will take another path, one which assumes a disjunction between appearance and fact. Thus, seeming to accept Macduff's protestation, he embarks upon the lengthy description of a man who threatens Scotland more even than its present king. 'What shall he be?' asks Macduff, and Malcolm replies

> It is myself I mean, in whom I know
> All the particulars of vice so grafted
> That, when they shall be opened, black Macbeth

Will seem as pure as snow, and the poor state
Esteem him as a lamb, being compared
With my confineless harms.   (50–5)

Malcolm goes on, then, to detail his iniquities: there is 'no
bottom . . . in [his] voluptuousness' (60–1), he is afflicted with
'stanchless avarice' (78), he lacks all 'king-becoming graces, / As
justice, verity, temp'rance, stableness, / Bounty, perseverance,
mercy, lowliness, / Devotion, patience, courage, fortitude'
(91–4). As he has hoped, Macduff is scandalized and horrified;
the test has succeeded, and he now may 'unspeak [his] own
detraction' (123), abjuring all the faults he has claimed. Here
comparison has become a doubly valuable tool for the revelation
of character. By employing the false formula, 'I am like Macbeth, only worse,' Malcolm can gauge the truth of Macduff's
disinterested patriotism. More subtly, by the very act of making
this fictive comparison, he also establishes for the audience a
crucial distinction between himself and his father, Duncan. He is
not, as he pretends, like Macbeth; he *is* like Duncan, in that he is
upright and virtuous. But he is also unlike him in a vital way,
unwilling to trust the untested appearance of fidelity on the part
of his subjects. It is this combination of likeness and unlikeness
that makes Malcolm a fit ruler for the new Scotland which is
emerging, and which safeguards both the land and the play from
the dangers of a merely cyclical repetition.

    The overt act of transformation Malcolm accomplishes in his
final speech, when he commands that Scottish thanes shall 'henceforth be earls' (v. viii. 63), is an outward sign of this essential
distinction. The conferring of a new name, and a name which
links Scotland more closely with England, corresponds directly
to the growth and change in Malcolm himself – a change itself
made manifest in his assertion of his father's title and power,
without his father's fatal flaw. This fundamental pattern, which
progresses from a perceived dissimilarity, to an acknowledgment of resemblance, and then to a distinction within that
resemblance, is the dominant pattern of analogy as it applies to
the individual in Shakespeare's plays. The pattern closely
parallels, and indeed is a crucial element in, the hero's
growth to self-knowledge – a growth we have identified with
'maturity'.

Malcolm's brief pretense of venality calls to mind the larger
and more complicated situation of Prince Hal, whose youthful
associations with thieves, topers and prostitutes are of such
urgent concern to his father, the king. Despite the famous 'I
know you all' speech (1HIV I. ii. 192–214), with its assertion of a
calculated plan for 'redeeming time', Hal's taste for 'small beer',
the friendship of Ned Poins and his fellows, is genuine, and his
rejection of Falstaff is not the less painful for its prediction as
early as II. iv. of *Part I* (*Falstaff*: 'banish plump Jack, and banish
all the world!' *Prince*: 'I do, I will' – (485–6). This extraordinarily
well-balanced and finely structured play offers a series of complex interrelationships, in which its several characters are deliberately placed in juxtaposition to one another. The king and
Hotspur are both rebels and potential usurpers, but the king
comes to stand for authority, Hotspur for rebellion. The king
and Falstaff are each in their way subversive, and each is an
example and a mentor to Prince Hal, but they also demarcate the
opposite poles of rule and misrule. Hotspur and Falstaff both
exemplify rebellious anarchy, yet one is an idealist, one a cynical
realist, one a young athlete only at home on a horse, the other an
old reprobate forever on foot, though he longs for a charge of
horse. Falstaff and Hal are companions and fellow scoffers at the
righteousness of court life, but one is young and shrewd, the
other old and inclined to folly, Hal ever conscious of time,
Falstaff heedless of it. Hotspur and Hal bear the same name, and
are alike in youth and valor, though they are very different in
their reputations, and in their attitudes toward history, the
common people and – once again – time. The king and his son
are opposed and allied at once, Henry certain from the closing
moments of *Richard II* that Hal is a wastrel yet discerning in him
even then 'some sparks of better hope' (v. iii. 21), both men
essentially pragmatists, astute politicians, apt dissemblers,
Plantagenets.

The three stages of development we have posited are present
in Hal's story in a highly visible way. The king, Hotspur and the
tavern world itself all regard him as behaving in a manner
essentially the converse of what is suitable for the heir apparent. Early in *Part I* the king, hearing of Hotspur's latest
exploit, envies Northumberland his son, and expresses the
wish

That some night-tripping fairy had exchanged
In cradle clothes our children where they lay,
And called mine Percy, his Plantagenet!
Then would I have his Harry, and he mine.   (i. i. 86–9)

As has often been noted, Shakespeare's alteration of historical
fact, in making the two Harrys parallel in age, reinforces the
inevitable comparison, which is again pointed by Hal's assurance
to the king in iii. ii. ('the time will come / That I shall make this
northern youth exchange / His glorious deeds for my indigni-
ties' – 144–6), and by Hotspur's typically fiery rhetoric ('Harry
to Harry shall, hot horse to horse, / Meet, and ne'er part till one
drop down a corse' – iv. i. 121–2). The one who does drop down a
corse is Hotspur himself, who appears as much astonished as
chagrined by this development, and who seems indeed to cede to
Hal his 'glorious deeds', and even his rhetoric itself, as Hal
completes the sentence spoken by his dying rival. As was the
case with Priamond, Diamond and Triamond, the three brothers
in Spenser's Book of Friendship, the life seems to flow out of one
Harry and into the other, making Hal a 'double man' (v. iv. 136)
in yet another way.

Much the same can be said of Hal's actions at his father's
deathbed in *Part II*. The king's interpretation of his taking the
crown – that the son wishes his father dead – provides an
opportunity for both a comparison and a contrast between the
two men. Hal does seize the crown, symbolically repeating his
father's act of usurpation, but there is no doubt that he considers
himself a 'true inheritor' (iv. v. 168), legitimately succeeding to
the throne, and this, as much as his cultivation of the common
people, marks a vital distinction between father and son. In
confronting first another Harry, and then another Henry, Hal
engrosses up good deeds and plain titles to which, as Henry V, he
will give a distinctive color of his own. We have noted elsewhere
that Falstaff errs fatally in thinking that the new monarch is
'King Hal'; unlike Hal himself, Falstaff is unable to perceive the
distinctions within similarities which set the young king apart,
both from his riotous past and from his father's burden of
usurpation and guilt.

In *Henry V* the same pattern is repeated in a condensed form.
The Dauphin, a fellow prince and age-mate of the king, taunts

him with the gift of tennis balls, as ocular proof that one 'cannot revel into dukedoms' in France (I. ii. 253). Henry's reply disposes eloquently of the charge of revelry, but within the play the comparison goes further than the Dauphin's insult; subsequent scenes show clearly that it is the Dauphin, and not the King of England, who is a reveller, a braggart and a rake. The king's descent to the battlefield disguised in the cloak of Sir Thomas Erpingham makes him for a moment the anonymous equal of the common soldiers Bates, Court and Williams. He himself seeks the analogy, and speaks with meanings which are likewise cloaked: 'I think the king is but a man, as I am; the violet smells to him, as it doth to me. . . . His ceremonies laid by, in his nakedness he appears but a man' (IV. i. 100–5). But when the soldiers leave the stage, Henry V's apostrophe to ceremony firmly outlines those responsibilities which fall to a king alone. He is a mortal man, subject to the fear of battle and of death, like his subjects – yet he is also, of necessity, different from them. The joke he plays on the soldier Williams accentuates this dual identity, as Williams ably defends himself from the charge of planning to strike the king:

> Your majesty came not like yourself: you appeared to me but as a common man; witness the night, your garments, your lowliness. And what your highness suffered under that shape, I beseech you take it for your own fault, and not mine; for had you been as I took you for, I made no offense.
>
> (IV. viii. 50–5)

Had the king been a common man, Williams would indeed have made no offense. Because he is not, he offers Williams a reward for his honesty and bravery – a reward which is paid in 'crowns'. From the aloofness of Richard II, and even of Henry IV, King Henry V has deliberately moved toward an acknowledgment of what he holds in common with his subjects. Yet once this is established, it remains for him to acknowledge and assert, as well, his inescapable and crucial differences from them, his unique identity as their king.

The progress of Prince Hal from riotous adolescent to mature man and king may be thought of as an example of successful integration. Hal borrows freely from the personalities of others, acquiring and reflecting Falstaff's appetitiveness, Hotspur's aggression and honor, King Henry's sense of duty. He forces upon his two audiences – the populace of England and the spectators in the theater – the realization that he is not only the 'mirror of all Christian kings', but the mirror of all England, from tavern to court. Those he seems at first to resemble, he will later reject; those whom he seems most unlike he will confront, and bear away from that confrontation their crucial strengths.

In *Hamlet* Shakespeare again approaches this question of integration, and its relationship to a character's dynamic use of comparison and contrast as a vehicle for self-knowledge. For *Hamlet* is a play in which the principal character spends four of the five acts noting and exploring disjunctions between himself and the models of behavior he sees about him. All around him Hamlet finds contrasting figures who emphasize his own isolation. He is not like Old Hamlet, or Laertes, or Fortinbras, or the First Player, or the Gravedigger; nor is he like Claudius, or his 'schoolfellows', Rosencrantz and Guildenstern. Two of the major soliloquies bear directly upon this sense of disjunction: The 'rogue and peasant slave' speech (II. ii. 555–612) elaborately contrasts the First Player's response to fictive grief with Hamlet's failure to respond to reality; 'How all occasions do inform against me' (IV. iv. 32–66) similarly contrasts Fortinbras' martial defense with Hamlet's inactivity. And dramatic events within the play seem to support his feeling of contrast with those he should resemble. Hamlet, coming upon Claudius kneeling in prayer, will not kill him; Laertes, asked what he would undertake against Hamlet 'To show yourself in deed your father's son / More than in words', replies shortly, 'To cut his throat i' th' church!' (IV. vii. 125–6). Hamlet will not claim his rights to 'Th' election', the kingship; yet both Fortinbras (from without) and Laertes (from within) present themselves forcibly as candidates for the office. Laertes is successful in his suit to return to France; Hamlet is denied permission to go back to Wittenberg. Dutiful and avenging sons, deft courtiers, shrewd politicians, eloquent speakers, pithy truth-tellers – from all of these Hamlet feels himself set apart.

In his valuable study, *Psychoanalysis and Shakespeare*, Norman Holland remarks upon 'Hamlet's fondness for comparisons', and attributes it to a 'tendency to turn inner life into outward shows'. 'Hamlet', he says, 'either uses outer events to express inner ones, or he compares inner attitudes by means of "counterfeit" outer representations of them.'[18] Moreover, Hamlet's mode of personal reflection is not only frequently comparative, but usually comparative to his own detriment. Consider his account, in the first soliloquy, of his mother's hasty marriage. Only a month before, she had followed his father's body 'Like Niobe, all tears' (I. ii. 149). His father, 'so excellent a king', was to Claudius as 'Hyperion to a satyr' (139–40). But the allusions – and the contrast – do not stop there. Inexorably, Hamlet draws himself into the equation. Claudius is

> My father's brother, but no more like my father
> Than I to Hercules.   (152–3)

Why does he bring in Hercules, and the unflattering reference to himself? His point has already been made by the two previous mythological references, both of which turn inward, pointing through the parent to the child. Niobe wept not at the death of her husband, but at the deaths of her children, who died through her vanity. She had boasted that she was superior to Leto because she had seven sons and seven daughters, while Leto had only two children, Apollo and Artemis. Hearing of the boast and the insult to their mother, Apollo slew Niobe's sons, and Artemis her daughters. Renaissance mythographers allegorized this story into a justification of the Second Commandment, which speaks of visiting the sins of the fathers upon the children.

> Niobe sinned, but her children are killed; by this we see that it is no injustice in God to visit the iniquity of the parents upon the children, seeing they are a part of their parents, and in their punishment the parents suffer oftentimes more than in their own.[19]

So Gertrude's sins are visited upon the son, and she will be made to suffer by his suffering. Hyperion the sun-god was the father of Phaethon, whose mother was a mortal woman. The son, taunted with having no father, obtained permission to drive the chariot of the sun through the sky, but lacking his father's strength, fell to his death and scorched the earth beneath him. Hamlet, as the Phaethon-figure, feels likewise unworthy to take his father's place – and feels, as well, that he appears fatherless, by reason both of his father's murder and of his own unheroic posture. But why Hercules? The allusion seems again a reference to Old Hamlet, who smote the sledded Polacks (or pole-ax) on the ice and slew Old Fortinbras in single combat. To this titanic figure young Hamlet, the Wittenberg scholar, an indifferent rapier duellist, and at age thirty 'fat and scant of breath', bears small resemblance. Is he, then, associating himself with Claudius, as a diminished or corrupted version of the dead king? When we bear in mind the numerous critics who, following Freud and Jones, have argued for Hamlet's oedipal impulses, and thus for his subliminal identification with the man who has married his mother, the link seems a possible one. Certainly, as Ernst Kris, among others, has shown, Hamlet appears to have a 'dangerously submissive attachment to his idealized father'.[20] But the deprecatory self-reference is, as we have seen, characteristic. Moreover, as shrewd as Hamlet is in applying mythological archetypes, there is an aspect of the Hercules story which does fit him: not the Hercules of the twelve labors, but the allegorical Hercules of the famous choice between pleasure and virtue. Hamlet, too, stands at a crossroads, and ultimately will commit himself to the harsh path of action, rather than the seductive path of introspection and 'words, words, words'.

Whatever complexities and nuances lie beneath his rhetorical flourish, Hamlet as we encounter him at the beginning of the play is, as we have said, pre-eminently concerned with his own isolation, his difference from other people. The degree of personal integration he achieves by the time he returns from England is manifested by a discovery, on his part, of analogies between himself and others. On the eve of that journey, he is still preoccupied with differences:

> Examples gross as earth exhort me.
> Witness this army of such mass and charge,
> Led by a delicate and tender prince
>
> *   *   *   *   *
>
> How stand I then,
> That have a father killed, a mother stained,
> Excitements of my reason and my blood,
> And let all sleep   (IV. iv. 46–8, 56–9)

But by Act V he has turned the tables on Rosencrantz and Guildenstern, in effect making a mirror exchange between their fates and his. It is at this point that he is ready to come to terms with the terrible leveling process of the graveyard, where the skulls of unknown lawyers, courtiers and politicians mingle indifferently with that of the king's beloved jester, and the specter of Alexander's 'noble dust' stopping a bunghole gives way to the spectacle of Ophelia's maimèd rites. In death all differences are resolved in sameness: 'let her paint an inch thick, to this favor she must come' (v. i. 193–4). But for Hamlet this is more than an existential truth. He now seeks and finds analogies not only with the dead but with the living; in effect he has acknowledged his own identity as a player, a trier-on of roles, and taken his own advice, to hold the mirror up to nature.

> I am very sorry, good Horatio,
> That to Laertes I forgot myself,
> For by the image of my cause I see
> The portraiture of his.   (v. ii. 75–8)

The final duel pits two avenging sons against one another, and the exchange of rapiers underscores their resemblance. As Horatio observes, 'they bleed on both sides' (306). Moreover, the arrival of Fortinbras adds another dimension to the analogy: one 'delicate and tender prince' confers his dying voice upon another as successor to the kingdom for which their fathers fought. And on his part, Fortinbras ordains for Hamlet a soldier's funeral, and a king's:

> Let four captains
> Bear Hamlet like a soldier to the stage,
> For he was likely, had he been put on,
> To have proved most royal; and for his passage
> The soldiers' music and the rite of war
> Speak loudly for him.   (v. ii. 397–402)

These are the terms in which Hamlet has spoken of Fortinbras; now they are used of him. The audience, like Hamlet himself, has gradually come to realize the degree to which he is like those around him. Like Laertes he can be gallant and impetuous; like Horatio, prudent and studious; like Fortinbras, princely and courageous; like the First Player, expressive and emphatic; like Old Hamlet, resolute and royal; even, like Claudius, unscrupulous and sly.

Many critics have remarked upon the technique of character

splitting in the play: the three father-figures (Old Hamlet, Claudius, Polonius), the five young age-mates, sons and school-fellows (Horatio, Laertes, Fortinbras, Rosencrantz and Guilden-stern). Each of these stands in a special relationship to Hamlet, and many reflect aspects of his persona. Even non-psycho-analytic critics, as Holland observes, agree that in Hamlet 'inner impulses are given outer expression', and Holland himself goes on to rephrase this insight in psychoanalytic terms: 'the de-fensive maneuver that permeates the language, events, and characters of the play is *projection*.'[21] By 'defensive maneuvers', Holland (and Freud) mean the ways in which the mind protects itself against unwelcome knowledge, by such devices as con-densation and displacement.[22] In condensation two or more persons, images, words or events are combined into one; the most readily discerned example in *Hamlet* is his penchant for wordplay, including both ambiguity and punning or wit. Dis-placement, on the other hand, involves a diffusion or spreading out of characteristics. It may entail projection, as Holland sug-gests (Hamlet's oedipal desire for his mother is transformed into Claudius' marriage with her), splitting (also called decom-position), reversal, or symbolization.

All four of these modes of displacement are present in the structure of *Hamlet*, and all, interestingly, bear directly or indirectly on the matter of comparison and contrast. We have already noticed splitting as a major technique of the plot. Rever-sal is evidenced by the figure of Fortinbras, who is the son of Old Fortinbras as Hamlet is the son of Old Hamlet, but who is as well a successful, martial, active crown prince. But in Hamlet's eyes, as we have seen, his other age-mates also appear to be reversals, or opposites, of his own character: this is the preliminary stage of development with which the hero begins his journey toward maturity and self-knowledge, and Freud's word 'defensive' is useful as a way of reminding us that such mental disguises must be penetrated for the self to be known and accepted. Finally, the kind of displacement called symbolization involves the transfer of an association from one thing to another based upon a re-semblance, whether physical or psychic, between the two. The manner of Old Hamlet's death, by poison poured into the ear, is perhaps the most notable of many such devices in the play. Hamlet, told of this event by the Ghost, accepts it as a literal fact (and remembers a similar scene in *The Mousetrap*), but he also begins to speak of 'cleav[ing] the general ear with horrid speech' (II. ii. 568), of a knavish speech sleeping in a foolish ear (IV. ii. 24), of Claudius as a 'mildewed ear [of corn] / Blasting his wholesome brother' (III. iv. 65–6), and of words, words, words. Moreover, not only Hamlet, but Horatio, the First Player and even Claudius all refer repeatedly to knowing ears, ears that infect, or ears that will make the listener dumb. The 'mildewed ear' is one kind of symbol, seemingly provoked by an unconscious pun (condensation) – Claudius *has* blasted his brother through the ear; the repeated mention of ears by characters other than Hamlet combines symbolization with splitting. In Freudian terms, then, Hamlet's progress from disjunction to comparison represents in a fictional way something like the progress made by a patient in analysis, recognizing by slow degrees certain crucial latent patterns in his life.

It may be argued, and persuasively so, that such a conclusion is unsound because it treats Hamlet as a real person, rather than as a literary character. But to this objection it may be replied that this would be the case only if we confined our scrutiny to what Hamlet learns, rather than what the audience learns – or the playwright invents. Many of the congruences to be found in *Hamlet* are congruences of which Hamlet himself remains unaware. Fortinbras' final speech about his soldiery, for example, is spoken after Hamlet's death, and many of the 'ear' speeches occur out of his own hearing. The discerning of such congruences, in fact, is very close to the most traditional kinds of literary criticism, which, like psychology and psychoanalysis, speak of patterns of imagery, and of symbolism, as providing a fundamental unity to the text. Whether Hamlet the character achieves such a unity – as I have argued for Prince Hal – is a more vexed question, and one directly related to the final stage of the rite of passage we have been describing: discrimination within analogy, a sense of healthful and vital difference.

Erik Erikson, in a 'psychosocial' examination of Hamlet, describes him as essentially a delayed adolescent, experiencing belatedly in his thirtieth year the fundamental crisis of youth, which Erikson takes to be a search for fidelity – something to believe in and be loyal to. Because of the rottenness in Denmark, he argues, Hamlet is unable to benefit from the example of his age-mates, who are 'all sure (or even overdefined) in their identities as dutiful sons, courtiers, and future leaders'.[23] But since all of them are 'drawn into the moral swamp of infidelity', Hamlet suffers an 'identity confusion', which leads to the establishment of a 'negative identity', the assumption of those impulses and character traits which he has so long tried to avoid: the mad revenger, the warlike soldier–prince. Erikson thus concludes that Hamlet's failure to find a model of fidelity prevents his achievement of a positive, integrated personality; in fact, he generalizes this conclusion to apply to all heroes of tragedy: 'Thus do inner reality and historical actuality conspire to deny tragic man the positive identity for which he seems exquisitely chosen.'[24] In other words, Erikson sees Hamlet's development as culminating in capitulation.

A somewhat similar argument by K. R. Eissler, subtitled 'A Psychoanalytic Inquiry', contends that the central issue in the play is Hamlet's initial childishness.[25] Eissler takes a dynamic or developmental view of Hamlet's character, discerning a pattern of growth in the soliloquies, from excessive adulation of his father (and an equation of incest with sexuality) toward a criticism and even rejection of his father in the fourth soliloquy, and a final union with Gertrude in death, thus fulfilling the oedipal wish in a symbolic act of 'dying together'. Essentially, Eissler finds that Hamlet grows up in the course of the play, and replaces a childish and ineffectual way of dealing with his problems with a mature and functional one. He does integrate his personality and accomplish his objectives – but he does so at the cost of his own life, and is symbolically 'reborn' in the person of Fortinbras, who is both his mirror opposite and his twin. Like Erikson's, Eissler's is an argument which examines Hamlet as a real person, not a fictional construct. On the other hand, in suggesting a developmental pattern, both of these psychological approaches touch squarely upon a problem which does fall within the province of the literary critic: the degree to which Hamlet understands himself, and the events in which he is the central actor. And in order to suggest a plausible solution to this fundamental problem, we must, fittingly, return to the text.

A close examination of Hamlet's remark about Laertes, 'by the image of my cause I see / The portraiture of his,' suggests one additional factor of importance. For the analogy in effect reverses Hamlet's earlier injunction to Gertrude, 'Look here upon this picture, and on this, / The counterfeit presentment of two brothers.' In both cases, the verbal figure is of two paintings or simulacra, the first pair (Claudius and Old Hamlet) in violent contrast to one another, the second (Laertes and Hamlet) very similar. But it is useful to notice the obliquity of the second comparison. Hamlet does not merely say, as he might, 'By my cause I see [i.e. understand] his.' The crucial words 'image' and 'portraiture' remind us of the play's thematic emphasis on painting and disguise, but they also emphasize the fictive, created nature of comparison itself. Once again we are dealing with simile, not metaphor. Notice the rhetorical stress on the closely linked pronouns 'my' and 'his' surrounding the inquiring and analyzing 'I'. Hamlet's cause is not the same as Laertes', though they have something in common; nor is Hamlet himself Laertes, any more than he is Fortinbras, or Horatio, or any of the other men on whom he models his own conduct. As was the case with *Macbeth*, and indeed with *Richard II* and the *Henry IV* plays, the possibility of identity (and therefore of repetition) is first suggested, and then adroitly avoided. Hamlet learns in the course of the play that he cannot be his father; this is what Eissler calls his achievement of independence. But Hamlet – along with his audience – also learns that he is different from those around him, not in the absolute, negative ways he has feared, but instead in the uniqueness of his individual persona. Polonius' tired advice, 'to thine own self be true', finds a new and vital referent in the need for individuation. Mythologically, Hamlet may be 'reborn' in Fortinbras, but in more strictly literary terms he will gain new life through the retelling of his 'story' – which is the play itself. At the close, the audience is brought to a realization of Hamlet's place in the world of *Hamlet*, a realization achieved through the judicious detection of comparisons and contrasts within the context of the play.

Comparison is a particularly useful criterion by which to judge Hal and Hamlet because of their social roles as sons, heirs and successors. For them, as for such other developing figures as the two Richards, there exists a generation of 'fathers' and a generation of age-mates, against which the protagonist can – and must – measure his own progress. It is not surprising, therefore, that we are able to find a similar pattern of likeness and differentiation in the career of yet another successor, Octavius Caesar. Like Hal and Hamlet, the young Caesar of *Antony and Cleopatra* appears at first to be the direct opposite of his symbolic 'fathers', in this case the martial triad of Julius Caesar, Gneius Pompey, and in particular Antony himself. Caesar is an administrator and a politician; the generation of the fathers was heroic in war, striving with one another in single combat (III. vii. 31–2) – like Old Hamlet and Old Fortinbras, or Bolingbroke and Mowbray. Moreover, they were also heroic in love. Apollodorus Sicilian carried Cleopatra to Caesar in a mattress; she is Antony's mistress, but she has also been as 'a morsel cold upon / Dead Caesar's trencher', and 'a fragment of Gneius Pompey's' (III. xiii. 116–18). Caesar is described by Cleopatra as 'scarce-bearded' (I. i. 21), an epithet which she intends as a commentary on his youth, but also an oblique reflection on his manhood; Antony by contrast has a 'goodly thick beard', according to Plutarch[26] and Enobarbus (II. ii. 7). In addition to Cleopatra, Antony has two wives; Caesar appears to have none, and lavishes his affection instead upon his sister and virtual name-sake, Octavia. When, as he believes, Antony treats her shabbily, he is roused to an unaccustomed fury, almost as if he himself has been spurned. According to his rival, Antony 'fishes, drinks, and wastes / The lamps of night in revel' (I. iv. 4–5), preoccupying himself with 'lascivious wassails' (56); Caesar is abstemious, even puritanical. For political purposes, he consents to drink at the banquet, but deplores both the excess and the tipsy result, declaring with a characteristic excess of his own that he would 'rather fast from all, four days, / Than drink so much in one' (II. vii. 103–4). It is not clear whether or not he participates in Enobarbus' version of the 'Egyptian bacchanals' (105), in which the drinkers dance hand in hand, but it is perfectly clear that he is uncomfortable throughout the proceedings: 'our graver busi-ness / Frowns at this levity' (121–2). In short, in almost every way Octavius is the opposite of Antony, and also of his other heroic forebears.

The presence in the plot of young Sextus Pompey, the son of Gneius, helps to emphasize this generational conflict and the sense of diminishment which is felt by the younger men and their lieutenants. Young Pompey has a legitimate grievance against Antony, who acquired his father's house and then refused to pay for it; nonetheless, he is willing to make peace, and to accept the loss. As Menas, one of his friends, points out in an aside, 'Thy father, Pompey, would ne'er have made this treaty' (II. vi. 82–3). The world of the fathers seems a lost world of warlike grandeur, very different from the manipulative Rome of the present.

In a way, it might be argued that *Antony and Cleopatra* is one of the most oedipal of Shakespeare's plays, full of complex emotions directed by the 'sons' (Octavius, Pompey) toward the 'fathers' (Caesar, Pompey, Antony) and the 'mother' (Cleopatra). Describing the public enthronement of Antony and Cleopatra in the Alexandrian marketplace, Caesar speaks bit-terly of the presence at their feet of 'Caesarion, whom they call my father's son' (III. vi. 6). He himself is only an adopted son, born the nephew of Julius Caesar. His disgust at 'all the unlawful issue that their lust / Since then hath made between them' (7–8) reflects his prudishness, but seems at the same time particular and personal. Caesarion and the sons of Antony, Egyptian princes all, appear to displace the youthful Caesar of Rome.

But Octavius' jealousy is directed as much at the father as at the sons. Antony's continual references to his rival as 'the young man' (III. xi. 62) 'the young Roman boy' (IV. xii. 48), and 'the boy Caesar' (III. xiii. 17) obviously nettle him. 'He calls me boy, and chides as he had power / To beat me out of Egypt. My messenger / He hath whipped with rods' (IV. i. 1–3). Whipping with rods was a punishment for wayward children, and the word 'chides', too, suggests condescension to a youthful inferior. Though the two men are in many ways sharply different, Octavius in this may remind us of Coriolanus, who is also shamed by the label of 'boy' – a man in thrall to a powerful mother. For Octavius, it would appear, Cleopatra is a figure at once sexual and maternal, his father's mistress and his rival's. In his conciliatory message to her, as delivered by Thidias, there is, again, a personal note, as well as a political ploy: Caesar 'partly begs / To be desired to give'. He wishes to be 'a staff / To lean upon' for her. In particular, says Thidias, 'it would warm his spirits / To hear from me you had left Antony, / And put yourself under his shroud' (III. xiii. 66–71). A shroud is a shel-ter, but it is also a garment. Caesar's offer is to become her protector, and in so doing, to take the place of Antony. Cleopatra, for her part, is not unaware of this ambiguity. After Antony's death, she kneels in mock submissiveness to Caesar, and twice in their short audience she addresses him as 'my master and my lord' (v. ii. 116, 190). But in her own suicide (which is itself both sexual and maternal in its symbolism), she eludes him at last, and is laid at his command by Antony's side.

This brief excursion into the play's psychological undercurrents has not taken us far from our main point, which is that Octavius Caesar, like Hal and Hamlet, undergoes a process of growth and change, from the perception of unlikeness to others, to the recognition of similarities, and thence to differentiation – and that a parallel series of changes in perception is offered to the audience. Opposite to Antony in so many ways, Caesar oddly resembles him in others, and the resemblance is reinforced by the dramatic action. We have seen that, whatever his motivations, he himself becomes one of Cleopatra's suitors, hoping to possess and rule her. He thus follows the path of the heroic forebears from whom he has seemed to set himself apart. We also learn in the course of the play that Antony wept at the deaths of Julius Caesar and Brutus, his political predecessors (III. ii. 55–7). Addressing his servitors after the loss at Actium, he speaks so movingly that Enobarbus suggests he means 'To make his followers weep' (IV. ii. 24), and another follower, Eros, later does weep at his words (IV. xiv. 21). When the death of Antony is announced to Caesar, we see him weep too, and hear him declare that 'it is tidings / To wash the eyes of kings'(v. i. 27–8). He has become one of Antony's 'followers', both a servant and a successor.

Significantly Maecenas, observing him weep, employs a familiar metaphor: 'When such a spacious mirror's set before him, / He needs must see himself' (34–5). The 'spacious mirror' that is Antony inevitably reflects, and refracts, Caesar's own identity. Even in what seems to be a minor incident in the play's last act, Caesar unwittingly follows Antony's path. With characteristic generosity Antony, having heard of Enobarbus' defection, gave orders for all his treasure to be sent after him to Caesar's camp. In v. ii. Caesar, learning from Cleopatra's treasurer that she has falsified her account of money, plate, and jewels, acts with a similar (apparent) magnanimity: 'Not what you have reserved, nor what acknowledged, / Put we i' th' roll of

conquest: still be 't yours' (v. ii. 180–1). Both of these incidents
are mentioned by Plutarch, so that the resemblance between
them in *Antony and Cleopatra* might be thought to be due to the
source rather than the playwright. But North's Plutarch calls
Domitius' (i. e. Enobarbus') goods 'his carriage, train, and men',
and Cleopatra's, 'ready money and treasure'.[27] In this form,
there seems small parallel between them. By slightly changing
the terms, Shakespeare makes possible the analogy, as Antony
returns a 'treasure' to Enobarbus (iv. v. 12), anticipating
Cleopatra's echoing call for her 'treasurer' (v. ii. 142).

The final stage of differentiation for Caesar is appropriately
brief, for the similarities between him and Antony have not been
so pronounced that their difference ever entirely fades from our
awareness – or from his. In his eulogy over the dead Cleopatra,
Caesar himself draws the crucial distinction, when he speaks of
'their story' as 'No less in pity, than his glory which / Brought
them to be lamented' (v. ii. 361–2). The 'story' of Antony and
Cleopatra is 'pity', a tragedy; that of Caesar is 'glory', a history
and a chronicle. Antony's desperate attempt to encompass
simultaneously the spheres of love and politics has come, inevitably, to a tragic end, while Caesar's much diminished – and
fleeting – gesture at courtship is likewise crowned by failure.
Rome demands a politician, and in Octavius Caesar it has one.
But in his coming of age Caesar at last takes note – as he must –
of the qualities as well as the defects of his predecessor. The
process by which he recognizes and to some degree absorbs
aspects of Antony's persona is not as definitive as it was for Hal,
who could speak of Hotspur as his 'factor', laboring 'To engross
up glorious deeds on my behalf' (*1HIV* iii. ii. 147–8). Yet the
struggle between these mighty opposites is far more interesting
than it would have been were it entirely one of opposition. The
complex character of each man and the complexity of their
relationship challenge the discrimination of the audience, and
offer to us, as well as to them, an intriguing opportunity for the
exercise of wit and judgment.

NOTES

1 George Puttenham, *The Arte of English Poesie*, Bk. iii, Ch. vii,
   p. 166, in *English Reprints*, iv (New York: AMS Press, 1966).

2 Puttenham, p. 167.

3 'Euphuism' derives its name, of course, from John Lyly's prose romance, of which the first part, *Euphues the Anatomy of Wit*, was published in 1578, and the second part, *Euphues and his England*, in 1580. The name 'Euphues', which means to produce or to grow, was suggested by a passage in Ascham's *Scholemaster* (1570) in which he asserts that ''Ευφυη'ς is he that is apte by goodness of witte, and appliable by readines of will, to learning, hauing all other qualities of the minde and partes of the bodie that must another day serue learning.' The *Oxford English Dictionary* defines the chief features of 'euphuism' as

> the continual recurrence of antithetic clauses in which the anthithesis is emphasized by means of alliteration; the frequent introduction of a long string of similes all relating to the same subject, often drawn from the fabulous qualities ascribed to plants, minerals, and animals and the constant endeavour after subtle refinement of expression.

4 *Shr.* IV. i. 139. Cf. *MND* II. i. 203–7:

> I am your spaniel; and Demetrius,
> The more you beat me, I will fawn on you.
> Use me but as your spaniel, spurn me, strike me,
> Neglect me, lose me; only give me leave,
> Unworthy as I am, to follow you.

5 J. C. Scaliger, *Poetices Libri Septem* (Lyons, 1561), p. 171, Appendix pro Epigrammate; also cf. Ben Jonson, *Epigrams* (1616), 2, 49; John Peter, *Complaint and Satire in Early English Literature* (Oxford, 1956), p. 297; and Geoffrey Hartman, *Beyond Formalism: Literary Essays 1958–1970* (New Haven: Yale University Press, 1970) pp. 45–7.

6 *Republic*, l. 596 D-E., cited in E. R. Curtius, *European Literature and the Latin Middle Ages*, Willard R. Trask (trans.) (New York: Bollingen Foundation, 1953; rpt. New York: Harper & Row, 1963), p. 336.

7 Aelius Donatus, *Commentum Terenti*, Paul Wessner (ed.) (Leipzig, 1902–08), I, 22.

8 Jacques Paul Migne, *Patrologiae cursus completus: Series latina* (1844–55), LIX, 502C.

9 *Macbeth*, Kenneth Muir (ed.), Arden edition (London: Methuen, 1951; rpt. 1972), p. 114n.

10 Baldessare Castiglione, *The Book of the Courtier*, Charles S. Singleton (trans.) (Garden City, N. J.: Doubleday, 1959), pp. 292–3 (IV, 8).

11 Roger Manvell, *Shakespeare and the Film* (New York: Prager Publishers, 1971), pp. 48–50.

12 David Young, *The Heart's Forest: A Study of Shakespeare's Pastoral Plays* (New Haven: Yale University Press, 1972), pp. 50–8.

13 William K. Wimsatt and Cleanth Brooks, *Literary Criticism: A Short History* (New York: Vintage Books, 1957), p. 229.

14 ibid.

15 As Wimsatt and Brooks point out, Francis Bacon in the *Novum Organum (i, 55)* describes these 'two powers – that of perceiving resemblances and that of perceiving differences . . . without recourse to either of the terms "wit" or "judgment"' (*Literary Criticism*, p. 229). For the widespread acceptance of wit and judgment as linked opposites, see, for example, Emanuele Tesauro, *The Aristotelian Prospective Glass* (1654), Richard Flecknoe, *A Short Discourse on the English Stage* (1664), John Dryden, *An Essay on Dramatic Poesy* (1668), Alexander Pope, *Essay on Criticism* (1711), Samuel Johnson, *Life of Cowley, Life of Pope* (1779–81).

16 'To the Right Honorable Roger, Earl of Orrery', Epistle dedicatory of *The Rival Ladies* (1664), in W. P. Ker (ed.), *Essays of John Dryden* (Oxford: Clarendon Press, 1900), i, 8.

17 This is a point of view upon which Achilles elaborates in *Troilus and Cressida*, in his discussion with Ulysses on the subject of time and fame:

> The beauty that is borne here in the face
> The bearer knows not, but commends itself
> To others' eyes; nor doth the eye itself,
> That most pure spirit of sense, behold itself,
> Not going from itself; but eye to eye opposed
> Salutes each other with each other's form;
> For speculation turns not to itself
> Till it hath traveled and is married there
> Where it may see itself.   (III. iii. 103–11)

G. B. Evans in *The Riverside Shakespeare* chooses the reading 'is mirrored there' for line 110, following the Singer and Collier manuscripts ('married' is given in both the Quarto and the First Folio). It is an attractive choice, both for the imagistic consistency of the speech and because of the marked similarity between this passage and that quoted above from *Julius Caesar*.

18 Norman N. Holland, *Psychoanalysis and Shakespeare* (New York: McGraw-Hill, 1964; rpt. Octagon Books, 1976), pp. 203–4.

19 Alexander Ross, *Mystogogus Poeticus* (London, 1647), p. 317.

20 Ernst Kris, *Psychoanalytic Explorations in Art* (New York: Inter-

national Universities Press, 1952), pp. 17–18. See also Ernest
Jones, 'The death of Hamlet's father', *The International Journal of
Psycho-Analysis and Bulletin of the International Psycho-
Analytical Association* (London), xxix (1948), 174–6.
21 Holland, p. 203.
22 Sigmund Freud, *The Interpretation of Dreams*, in James Strachey
(ed. and trans.), *The Standard Edition of the Complete Psychological Works of Sigmund Freud*, v (London: Hogarth Press and
the Institute of Psycho-Analysis, 1953, rpt. 1958, 1962), pp. 279–
309; Holland, pp. 14–15, 29–30.
23 Erik Erikson, *Identity: Youth and Crisis* (New York: W. W.
Norton, 1968), p. 238.
24 Erikson, p. 241.
25 K. R. Eissler, *Discourse on Hamlet and Hamlet: A Psychoanalytic
Inquiry* (New York: International Universities Press 1971).
26 T. J. B. Spencer (ed.), *Shakespeare's Plutarch: The Lives of Julius
Caesar, Brutus, Marcus Antonius and Coriolanus in the Translation of Sir Thomas North* (Middlesex, England, and Baltimore,
Maryland: Penguin Books, 1964; rpt. 1968), p. 177.
27 Spencer, pp. 253, 287.

7

DEATH AND DYING

'THIS THING OF DARKNESS I ACKNOWLEDGE MINE'

As the most mysterious and most traumatic of the life crises, death has traditionally been accorded society's most extensive ritual attention, and ceremonies connected with death and dying are among the most complex and elaborate of rites of passage. Manifestly, death differs from most other such crises in that it can only be seen from one side. We are all novices to dying; except for spiritualists, or those who have medically 'died' and returned to life, none of us can claim to have conversed with the initiates, who by the very fact of their initiation are silent. This is perhaps one reason for the recurring interest evinced by many cultures in the phenomenon of those who claim to have come back from the dead, through intervention either medical or divine. These journeys to the 'other side', and the experiences and sensations encountered there, are of perpetual fascination not only to doctors of thanatology or to the popular press, but to many ordinary persons as well.[1] The underworld journeys of Odysseus and Aeneas and the experiences of the soldier Er in Book X of Plato's *Republic* – however complex and symbolic they are as literary events – are on one level at least classical explorations of this kind, and they speak to an enduring human curiosity.

When we bear in mind the universality of this preoccupation with death and dying, we should not be surprised to find rites of passage concerned with death among the other maturation patterns in Shakespeare's plays. Yet once again the uniqueness of the event sets it apart. In our previous examinations of rites of passage in the plays, it became clear that Shakespeare was interested in these rites as they affected both the individual and his society before and after, as well as during, the period of transition itself. And this is just what we cannot know about dying. The playwright's dilemma is thus closely analogous to that of every human being: how to envisage and describe experiences of which neither he nor his audience can have any real knowledge. As we shall see, Shakespeare evolved a number of dramatic strategies to cope with this problem. In doing so he was responding to the profound and pandemic need to imagine the unimaginable: to come face to face with the fact that each of us will die. But at the same time, by the very nature of the dramatic solutions he proposes, he does more. As in the sonnets, he suggests ways in which art – the act of writing and playing – can confront and transcend the limits of mortality. He explores and makes use of the common myths of return handed down in western culture: myths of ghosts and spirits, of death and rebirth. Most importantly, however, he crosses the boundary between the actor and the spectator, the Globe Theater and the great globe itself, to create for the audience in the theater a role peculiarly its own, as the repository of memory and the instrument of transmission and transcendence.

*

It is a curious fact that whether in highly developed or less sophisticated societies, eastern or western, primitive or modern, the rites of separation for the dead, which we should expect to be pre-eminent among funerary rites of passage, are usually of a simple and fairly brief nature: the closing of the coffin or tomb, the disposal of implements (and sometimes persons and animals) involved in the interment, the ritual expulsion of spirits. More central, and much more extensive, are the rites of transition and incorporation.

Traditionally, transition rites include a journey by the deceased to the land of the dead, whether visualized as a Christian heaven or a country of shades. The ancient Greek rite of the 'coin for Charon' to pay the ferryman for passage to the underworld has its counterpart in many religions. In a literary variant of this rite, Aeneas takes the golden bough into the land of the dead, as a talisman assuring him the right to return to earth; and Hamlet might be said to make a similar use of his father's signet ring, which protects him from the death intended for him in England and allows him to return safely to Denmark. Typically, persons who have failed to undergo other rites of passage may be doomed to a lengthy or even eternal period of wandering, rather than permitted incorporation with the dead. Catholic doctrine holds that infants who have not been baptized are destined to wander in a transitional zone or limbo, and in a number of tribal societies this is also the fate of those who have not been named, initiated or accorded funeral rites. In Shakespeare's time unquiet spirits, those that had been murdered (like Old Hamlet) or 'damnèd spirits . . . That in crossways and floods have burial' (*MND* III. ii. 382–3), were believed to be unable to rest, condemned instead to roam the nights aimlessly in search of vengeance, expiation or suitable obsequies. The Catholic concept of purgatory, an intermediary state in which the souls of those who have died in a condition of grace must expiate their sins, is another familiar type of transition rite that has its counterpart among many primitive groups.[2]

Rites of incorporation for the dead are often thought of as congruent with hospitality rites among the living: the new arrival is supposedly offered food or other gifts by those who have gone before him, or by the divine inhabitants of the other world.[3] Such rites are by their nature taboo for the living if they wish to return to earth after their sojourn among the dead. Thus Proserpina, eating the seeds of a pomegranate, unwittingly accepted Pluto's hospitality and was incorporated for six months a year into his kingdom. To be welcomed by St Peter at the gates of heaven, or into Abraham's bosom, is to undergo a similar incorporation in Christian terms. (Falstaff, we may notice, is welcomed not into Abraham's bosom but into Arthur's – or at least so Mistress Quickly tells us. His is a specifically English heaven, tailor-made for his quintessentially English spirit.)

For the survivors a separate series of rituals is ordained. The period of mourning signals a cessation of normal activities, marked by such external signs as changes in clothing or appearance (e.g. Hamlet's 'inky cloak', Pericles' unshorn hair, or Olivia's veil – all of which have counterparts in popular practice). The length and intensity of the mourning period usually varies with the importance of the deceased, and the death of a reigning monarch, for example, will often be observed by a public restriction on all social activities. The coronation of his successor puts an end to the period of mourning, and may be marked by public festivals, fireworks or other celebrations.

In his first soliloquy Hamlet dwells bitterly on the violation of this mourning period, interrupted by his mother's untimely marriage. Four times in sixteen lines he specifically mentions the brief space that has intervened between the two events: 'But two months dead, nay, not so much, not two' (I. ii. 138); 'and yet within a month – / Let me not think on't; Frailty, thy name is woman – / A little month, or ere those shoes were old / With which she followed my poor father's body' (145–8); 'Within a month . . . She married' (153–6). The 'maimèd rites' (v. i. 219) that accompany the interment of Ophelia at the play's close form a pendant to this truncated observance, as Laertes asks repeatedly, 'What ceremony else?' (v. i. 223, 225), and 'Must there no more be done?' (235). In both cases, although for different reasons, the mourners are deprived of comfort, and there is no unifying rite of incorporation.

Among such unifying rites, one of the most characteristic and universal is the shared meal, which may take place immediately after the funeral, on commemorative occasions or at the time of the lifting of mourning. Such practices as the traditional Irish wake and the custom in many faiths of bringing food to the house of mourning are contemporary versions of this rite. Once again, Hamlet records such a ceremony in broken form: 'The funeral baked meats / Did coldly furnish forth the marriage tables' of his mother and uncle (I. ii. 180–1).

The emphasis upon the survivor as one who needs to undergo rites of passage as much as do the dead is, I think, central to Shakespeare's dramatic approach to death and dying. In fact, rites of passage concerned with death in the plays are almost always related to a change in perception of those who survive, whether the survivor be an individual, a city or a state. We do not follow Hamlet or Othello or Cordelia beyond the grave, but we are vouchsafed a glimpse of how their deaths affect others, as well as an insight into the ways ceremonies and rites of mourning may work therapeutically, to restore equilibrium to the society. As van Gennep remarks about such rites of incorporation,

> their purpose is to reunite all the surviving members of the group with each other, and sometimes also with the deceased, in the same way that a chain which has been broken by the disappearance of one of its links must be rejoined.[4]

In the simplest terms, this is one way by which the playwright can transcend the limitations of knowledge implicit in his subject; by showing the effect of a death upon the living, he can in some measure compensate for the impossibility of showing the 'other side'. In effect, both the onstage and the offstage audience are constituted as a society of mourners, who must be reunited with one another, and reintegrated into the world of normal activities – which for the offstage audience means the world beyond the theater. We might go so far as to imagine that in the act of walking out of the playhouse – crossing its threshold – the audience experiences the lifting of the rites of mourning. No more than for the members of a group of literal mourners, however, does this mean that they forget.

When we look more closely at several scenes from the plays, we will see that over and over again the emphasis falls upon the survivors, the mourners, the spectators. Furthermore, we will see that Shakespeare continuously creates an interplay between rites ordinarily associated with death and those we have already seen in life's earlier stages: marriage, sexual maturity, naming, self-knowledge. And, as we have seen in our examination of other rites, the central figures responding to these events are measured by the degree to which they learn and mature through their experiences.

*

There is one device used in the plays that does purport to show something of the 'other side', the world beyond the grave, and that is the appearance of a ghost, whether Old Hamlet, Banquo, Julius Caesar or the several victims of Richard III. True to the revenge tradition from which they derive, these spectral figures come to admonish, accuse and affright, and we may notice that in most cases those to whom they appear will shortly die. These

ghosts are profoundly disturbing not only to their chosen spectators or auditors on the stage, but also to the audience in the
theater. As harbingers of death, they elicit a moment of particular self-knowledge for their murderers (Macbeth, Brutus,
Richard) or avengers (Hamlet, Richmond). In a more generalized sense, however, they are harbingers of death for the larger
audience as well. By their very presence the audience is invited
to learn what Hamlet learns: that 'If it be now, 'tis not to come;
if it be not to come, it will be now; if it be not now, yet it will
come' (v. ii. 222–4). Like the skull of Yorick, the Ghost is a
memento mori, and the 'readiness' for death that Hamlet
achieves in the last act remains a challenge for those who survive
him.

A particularly effective version of the harbinger of death is
provided by a figure who is not a ghost at all: the messenger
Marcade who enters in the final scene of *Love's Labor's Lost*.
Marcade's news, that the princess's father – the King of France –
is dead, metaphorically casts a pall over the entire previous
action of the play, and effects a transition between the wooing
games of the previous acts and the ladies' banishment of their
suitors for a twelvemonth of mourning. Berowne, commanded
by Rosaline to 'visit the speechless sick' and entertain them with
his wit, replies in terms which indicate a lesson abruptly learned:
'To move wild laughter in the throat of death? / It cannot be; it is
impossible; / Mirth cannot move a soul in agony' (v. ii. 853–5).
Here in a comic context where ghostly figures of revenge would
be incongruous, a black-garbed figure from another world again
intrudes, instructs and falls silent, his message delivered. Marcade is a pivotal presence, although he is hardly developed as a
character at all; he speaks only three lines, and the princess
guesses his message before he can give it. But his unexpected
appearance –no doubt made more startling on the stage by the
contrast of his black mourning clothes with the gay raiments of
the lovers and the costumes of the 'Worthies' – is a *memento
mori* of the most direct kind: an intimation of mortality.

Significantly, Shakespeare very rarely depicts a funeral ceremony, or even a funerary procession, despite the opportunity
for pageantry such spectacles might have afforded. The body of
Henry VI is borne onstage in the opening moments of *Richard
III*, and the 'maimèd rites' of the self-slain Ophelia are observed

in the closing moments of *Hamlet*. In the midst of a storm at sea Pericles must cast the body of his queen Thaisa 'scarcely coffined, in the ooze' (*Per*. III. i. 61), and the young boys in *Cymbeline* hold a touching funeral ceremony, with songs and traditional floral strewings, over the body of their beloved 'Fidele', who is Imogen in disguise.

These last two instances, however, have unusual sequels, for in neither case is the mourned one really dead. Both Thaisa and Imogen will awaken from their death-like sleeps, ultimately to participate in a literal reunion with their families that replaces (at the same time that it acknowledges and depends upon) the symbolic reunion of the funeral rite. Several versions of this reawakening or rebirth occur in Shakespeare's plays, and unlike actual funeral ceremonies they offer an opportunity for both the one who has 'died' and the onlookers to examine the experience and its meaning in retrospect. Thus, for example, Friar Lawrence administers to Juliet a sleeping potion that he says will produce the 'borrowed likeness of shrunk death' (*R&J* IV. i. 104) for a period of forty-two hours, after which she will 'awake as from a pleasant sleep' (106). To an alert audience this plan will seem dangerously close to sacrilege: a resurrection designed and brought about by the agency of man. The biblical paradigm is that of Jairus' daughter, as described in the Gospels according to Matthew, Mark, and Luke:

> And when Jesus came into the ruler's house, and saw the minstrels and the people making a noise, He said unto them, Give place: for the maid is not dead, but sleepeth. And they laughed him to scorn. But when the people were put forth he went in, and took her by the hand, and the maid arose.[5]
>
> (Matt. 9 : 23–5)

This is the part the friar has chosen for himself. We should not be surprised, therefore, when his plan miscarries. At the same time it is worth noting that Juliet has imaginatively experienced her own death in IV. iii., as she prepares to take the potion. She speculates first that the friar may 'Subtly hath minist'red to have [her] dead' (25) to conceal the fact that he performed the secret marriage, and then, rejecting this idea, she goes on to dwell in highly realistic terms upon the smells, sounds and bones within the tomb.

Juliet's resolve to conquer these fears marks a turning point in her growth to personal maturity; from this point she will no leading need. Her brave toast, 'Romeo, Romeo, Romeo, I drink to thee' (58), is answered in the tomb itself by Romeo as he drinks the poison: 'Here's to my love!' (v. iii. 119). By dying in imagination before she does so in fact, Juliet not only comes to terms with her own mortality, but in effect reverses the very conditions of life and death. She kisses Romeo's lips, hoping to find there 'some poison [that] yet doth hang on them / To make me die with a restorative' (165–6). Restoration now is union with Romeo; 'cordial and not poison', in Romeo's words (v. i. 85). The flawed and hubristic rebirth stage-managed by the Friar is thus superseded by a 'restoration' of another kind, made possible by the power of love.

Some happier restorations from apparent death, each similarly supervised by a person of spiritual authority, take place in the comedies and romances. In *Measure for Measure* the Duke of Vienna, disguised as a friar, undertakes to conceal and restore Claudio, who has been condemned to death for the crime of impregnating his fiancée. Like Juliet, Claudio experiences an imaginative confrontation with death, pleading with his sister Isabella to ransom him at the cost of her virginity. In fact, the process of education and self-discovery Claudio undergoes in the course of Act III scene i is strikingly similar to that which Elisabeth Kübler-Ross has observed in her studies of terminally ill patients.[6] Such patients (like Claudio) must come to terms with the unimaginable fact of their own death, and according to Kübler-Ross they pass through five stages of response: denial and isolation, anger, bargaining, depression and finally acceptance. All patients may not complete the full progression, but this is a characteristic pattern – and it compares very closely to the conflicting emotions felt by Claudio. Advised by 'Friar Lodowick' to 'be absolute for death' (5) in much the same way that a patient learns the seriousness of his condition from a doctor, Claudio responds at first by hoping for a 'pardon from Lord Angelo' (1) – a denial of the reality of his sentence. He is imprisoned, and thus physically as well as emotionally isolated, visited only by the 'friar' and the Provost – again, close counterparts of the visiting teams of doctor and chaplain in Kübler-Ross's study. From denial Claudio passes to anger at Angelo (the

person who sentenced him) and then to bargaining – if not with
Angelo or with God, then with Isabella: 'Sweet sister, let me
live' (132). His ruminations on the physical deprivations of
death – 'ay, but to die, and go we know not where, / To lie in cold
obstruction and to rot, / This sensible warm motion to become /
A kneaded clod' (117–20) – give voice to what is clinically known
as depression: what Kübler-Ross describes as 'taking into
account impending losses'.[7] 'Tis too horrible!' he exclaims, 'The
weariest and most loathèd worldly life / That age, ache, penury,
and imprisonment / Can lay on nature is a paradise / To what we
fear of death' (127–31). At last the 'friar' intervenes once more,
to dispel all hope: 'Tomorrow you must die' (168), and at this
point Claudio indicates what Kübler-Ross calls acceptance: 'Let
me ask my sister pardon. I am so out of love with life that I will
sue to be rid of it' (170–1). Significantly, these are the last words
we hear him speak; in a sense he *does* die to the world of the
play, reappearing only once more, in the final scene, when the
duke unmuffles him and restores him to life. And even in that
scene he remains mute, more an emblem than a dramatic
character, a liminal figure suspended between life and death.

There are two elements of this final scene that merit our
particular attention. First we should notice that although the
audience is aware of the ruse to save his life, Isabella is not. The
duke has been accused of cruelty and callousness for this
omission, despite his explanation that 'I will keep her ignorant
of her good, / To make her heavenly comforts of despair / When
it is least expected' (iv. iii. 110–12). But in fact Isabella is
being tested as Claudio had been tested. Her self-righteous
obstinacy – 'more than our brother is our chastity' (ii. iv. 184)
– will itself undergo a transformation, as she participates
in the 'friar's' plot, and falsely claims that she has been violated by Angelo. Claudio's 'death' becomes the instrument of
Isabella's conversion from justice to mercy, as she now pleads for
Angelo's life: 'My brother had but justice, / In that he did the
thing for which he died. / For Angelo, / His act did not o'ertake his
bad intent' (v. i. 450–3). It is at this point that Claudio is revealed.

Tellingly, it is to his sister and not to his fiancée that the Duke
restores him. The rite of passage Claudio has undergone has
made possible a parallel transformation for the 'survivor',
Isabella. She, too, has passed from a kind of emotional 'death' to

a new life, in which earthly love has its place, and the selfishness of 'Isabel, live chaste, and brother, die' (II. iv. 183) is replaced by a wish for the married happiness of Mariana and Angelo despite her own (supposed) bereavement. As Claudio had observed earlier, in the characteristically riddling language which is so often associated with rebirth in Shakespeare's plays, 'To sue to live, I find I seek to die, / And seeking death, find life' (III. i. 42–3). In a metaphorical sense this is true of Isabella as well, and represents a truth she has had to learn.

The second element of particular significance in the last scene of *Measure for Measure* is Claudio's appearance. 'What muffled fellow's that?' asks the duke (v. i. 488), and from his question we can infer that Claudio is concealed from the audience by a blanket, shawl or scarf that hides his features. In other words, his costume closely resembles a shroud. Viewing this spectacle, an audience familiar with the more popular Bible stories might well think of the story of Lazarus, whom Christ restored to life at the behest of his sisters, Mary and Martha. When the sisters declared their faith in Him, Jesus led them to the tomb, where he called out the name of Lazarus: 'And he that was dead came forth, bound hand and foot with graveclothes: and his face was bound about with a napkin. Jesus saith unto them, Loose him, and let him go' (John 11 : 44). Not only the shrouded man and the faithful sisters, but also the motifs of loosing and binding, restraint and liberty, link this episode closely to Shakespeare's play.

From another perspective, it is useful to recall that in initiatory rituals pertaining to puberty and sexual coming of age the novice is often covered with a blanket or rug, and that this act of covering is a symbol of death, as the later uncovering signifies rebirth. The connection between the two customs – shrouding the dead and initiating the adolescent – is a suggestive one here, since Claudio has experienced a double transition. He has 'died' and been reborn, but he has also 'died' sexually, consummating his marriage and begetting a child. By extension we might even say that some similar changes have occurred for Isabella, who in turning away from the nunnery and actively participating in the marital reconciliations of others has begun to recognize and acknowledge her own sexual nature. Whether or not we expect her to accept the duke's proposal, the possibility of such a match is surely greater at the close of the play than it was in its opening scenes.

The two symbolic attributes that link Claudio with death – muffling and silence – are explicitly described early in the play as part of the condition of religious sisterhood. Once she has taken her vows, a nun reminds Isabella, she may only speak to men in the presence of the prioress, and even then, 'if you speak, you must not show your face, / Or, if you show your face, you must not speak' (I. iv. 12–13). Instead of taking the veil, however, Isabella learns a new way of speaking and a new way of revealing herself – as she explains to Mariana:

> To speak so indirectly I am loath:
> I would say the truth; but to accuse him so,
> That is your part. Yet I am advised to do it,
> He says, to veil full purpose.   (IV. vi. 1–4)

One kind of veiling replaces another, as the desire to sequester oneself away from the world is replaced by an accommodation to the needs and vicissitudes of that world. In the next scene we will hear Isabella's public appeal to the duke, which contains what is for the audience a striking homophonic echo. 'Speak loud,' urges Friar Peter, and Isabella complies: 'Justice, O royal duke!' she calls out. '*Vail* your regard / Upon a wronged – I would fain have said, a maid' (v. i. 20–1). Oddly, in a play so much concerned with veiling, these are the only instances of either word to occur, and they do so within thirty lines of one another. Although the two words – 'veil' and 'vail' – are not etymologically related, they play against one another in an interesting way. A veil is a covering that conceals, but the friar's instruction, 'to veil full purpose', is a stratagem that is designed to reveal a hidden truth. 'Vail' as a verb means to lower, doff, cast down or throw down, all emblematic acts of submission, but the duke is asked to vail his regard in order to bring himself down to the level of his subjects, to condescend to them. Each kind of veiling (or vailing) thus produces an effect directly opposite to its most evident meaning, and contributes to the sense of paradox that infuses the entire last scene of the play. Moreover, to 'vail' one's regard is in this context the opposite of 'veiling' or concealing it, making it inaccessible. The audience hears both words in one, and a further paradox is achieved.

224   COMING OF AGE IN SHAKESPEARE

Isabella's petition to the duke and her complicity in the
'friar's' plot demonstrate an important change in her behavior;
now she is willing to temporize with the letter of the law, in
order to pursue its spirit. This distinction between letter and
spirit, so crucial to Angelo's governance and indeed to all of
Measure for Measure, is, interestingly enough, propounded by
St Paul in a chapter of 2 Corinthians that is also much concerned
with veils and veiling. Paul reminds his listeners that Moses
covered his face when he brought down the tablets of the law,
and alleges that the children of Israel have since been symbolically veiled, prevented from seeing the truth of Christ. Chris-
tians, he says, 'use great plainness of speech' (3 : 12), 'with open
face beholding as in a glass the glory of the Lord' (18); when the
heart of Israel is turned to Christ, 'the veil shall be taken away'
(16).

The gesture of taking away the veil is repeated several times,
literally as well as metaphorically, in the climactic scene of
Measure for Measure. Mariana is veiled, and will not show her
face 'until my husband bid me' (v. i. 170); Lucio challenges the
disguised duke to 'show your knave's visage . . . your sheep-
biting face' (355–6) and himself pulls off the friar's hood;
Claudio is unmuffled, Angelo is exposed, and Isabella will (perhaps) not take the veil. The appearance of the muffled Claudio
thus functions not only as a visual emblem of the rite of passage
he has undergone, but also as an iconic representation of the
transformations undergone by others. In a sense, he concretizes
the more metaphorical kinds of dying and restoration with
which the play has dealt. His presence is very like that of
Marcade, a living *memento mori* who speaks (by his silence) to
onstage and offstage audience alike.

As we have begun to see, shrouds, veils and masks are almost
always part of the ritual of symbolic death and rebirth in
Shakespeare's plays, and this is perhaps to be expected, since the
veil in many cultures is a traditional symbol of separation from
one world and entrance into another. By religious law, Moslem
women once they come of age must always be veiled in public,
and when in public must be separated from men; much the same
is true among the women of certain Orthodox Jewish groups.
Not only in the Catholic Church, but also among those who
practiced the ancient Greek mysteries, the ceremony of 'taking

the veil' was part of the process of initiation. And the widow's veil, in western culture usually a temporary sign of mourning, is in some others worn permanently after bereavement.[8]

The veil worn by Olivia in *Twelfth Night* seems to combine a number of these functions, since it is a sign at once of mourning for another and of the death-like condition of the wearer. Obsessively grieving for her dead brother (or, in Valentine's suggestive phrase, for 'a brother's dead love' – 1. i. 32), Olivia paces her chamber 'like a cloistress . . . veilèd' (29) until she falls in love with Viola–Cesario and consents to unveil herself. Unveiling for her is a rite of transition marking the passage from self-love to love for another, which in this play, as elsewhere in Shakespeare, is also a passage from spiritual death to life. (In this it is akin to Isabella's *not* taking the veil of the votarists of St Clare.) The metaphor Olivia chooses to describe her emergence from behind the veil is an interesting one: 'We will draw the curtain and show you the picture' (1. v. 231–2). Just as Elizabethan paintings were protected by curtains, so Olivia has protected herself from intercourse with the world. Her image here prefigures the more complex unveiling of the statue of Hermione in *The Winter's Tale*, another emergence from 'death' to life, from stasis to action. Equally significant, the eventual marriage between Olivia and Sebastian takes place in a 'chantry' located in, or near, Olivia's garden. The outdoor setting of the wedding is in sharp contrast to the closed chamber of her earlier grief, a chamber that was in many ways the equivalent of a living tomb. Moreover, a chantry is a chapel (or part of a church) specifically endowed for the maintenance of priests to sing daily mass for the souls of the founders. The daily ritual of mourning with which the play began now sustains its final transformation, as the chantry becomes a place of beginning as well as of ending, of marriage as well as memorial.

Olivia's veil and the muffling of Claudio have their counterparts in the mask of Hero in *Much Ado about Nothing*, another comedy with undertones of tragic possibility. The pattern of 'death' and 'rebirth' in *Much Ado* is in fact quite similar to that in *Measure for Measure*. Hero is accused of infidelity by her fiancé, Count Claudio; she swoons and is thought dead. Friar Francis – yet another of these transforming friars – who was to perform the marriage between them, now suggests that her family and friends 'Publish it that she is dead indeed; / Maintain a mourning ostentation . . . and do all rites / That appertain unto a burial' (IV. i. 203–7). The friar's hope is that Claudio will come to realize his mistake; if not, he intends to place Hero 'in some reclusive and religious life' (241) out of the sight and hearing of society. Like Friar Lawrence, then, Friar Francis threatens to 'dispose of' the bride 'among a sisterhood of holy nuns' (R&J v. iii. 156–7). His words as he leads her off are significant, and may serve as the apothegm for this entire dramatic trope: 'Come, lady,' he invites her, 'die to live' (IV. i. 252). To die to live is to die into life, to counterfeit death as a transitional rite which will lead to a new incorporation with a husband and a society – once again the opposite of the nunnery, which is 'out of all eyes, tongues, minds' (IV. i. 242).

Some time after Hero's departure Claudio learns the truth – that she has been impersonated and slandered – and we might imagine that his subsequent repentance would be sufficient to restore her to him at once. Instead there is a delay analogous to that in *Measure for Measure*, when Isabella was not told that her brother was alive. Hero's father Leonato tells him that he 'cannot bid you bid my daughter live; / That were impossible' (v. i. 278), but instructs him to do obsequies at her tomb, and offers him the hand of her 'cousin' – who will turn out to be Hero herself. Although the 'cousin' is declared to be joint heiress to Leonato's fortune and his brother's, Claudio apparently undertakes the marriage at least in part as a form of penance and an act of faith. We see him performing funeral rites at the monument, and hear him swear that 'Yearly will I do this rite' (v. iii. 23); we then hear Don Pedro, his companion in both the accusation and the act of repentance, urge him to 'put on other weeds' (30) – exchange his mourning clothes for a wedding suit – and proceed to Leonato's for the ceremony. When Claudio arrives, Leonato asks if he is still determined to marry the unknown 'cousin', and he replies, 'I'll hold my mind, were she an Ethiope' (v. iv. 38). The acceptance of a bride sight unseen reverses the dangerous and misleading demand for ocular proof ('If I *see* anything tonight why I should not marry her tomorrow, in the congregation where I should wed, there will I shame her' – III. ii. 118–20), and Claudio, although tempted ('Sweet, let me see your face' – 55) adheres to his vow and takes the masked lady by the hand. The incident suggests a submerged analogy with the story of Orpheus and Eurydice, another situation in which the dead bride can be retrieved from the underworld only by her husband's faith. Orpheus in looking back lost Eurydice forever, Claudio by not looking gains back the bride he lost. When Hero unmasks herself the play's language becomes, for a moment, translated into redemptive terms:

> *Hero*   And when I lived I was your other wife; [*unmasking*]
>   And when you lived you were my other husband.
> *Claudio*   Another Hero!
> *Hero*   Nothing certainer.
>   One Hero died defiled; but I do live,
>   And surely as I live, I am a maid.
> *Don Pedro*   The former Hero! Hero that is dead!
> *Leonato*   She died, my lord, but whiles her slander lived.
> *Friar*   All this amazement can I qualify,
>   When, after that the holy rites are ended,
>   I'll tell you largely of fair Hero's death.
>   (v. iv. 60–9)

What is of special interest here is the rhetorical insistence on the actuality of Hero's death. She is not called 'Hero that *was thought* dead', but 'Hero that *is* dead'. More than a mere pretense or masquerade has taken place.

We noted earlier in this study that a pattern of death and resurrection was part of all pubertal initiation ceremonies among primitive peoples, as well as among some sects and tribes of ancient Greece, and even in the Europe of the medieval period.[9] But in this case, as in the case of many similar rites in Shakespeare, the initiatory experience is indirect or transferred: a change takes place in Claudio as well as – and more centrally than – in Hero. This is part of the reason for the length of time Claudio remains unenlightened. The stages of ritual through which he passes – the mourning at Hero's tomb, the promise to renew the rite yearly, the change of clothing, and finally the marriage – are clearly analogous to the basic pattern of separation, transition and incorporation. At the same time there remains an evident reminder of the Pauline doctrine 'that Christ died for our sins . . . that he was buried, and that he rose again the third day' (1 Cor. 15 : 3–4). Hero is no Christ, but she is an innocent victim of others' perfidy, and her symbolic death is the instrument of Claudio's own rebirth.

We have already seen certain instances in which Claudio clearly needs to change, to come to terms with his own sexual nature and with the nature of love. In Act II scene i, the dance at Leonato's house, it is Claudio who is masked, as are the other men. (In v. iv. the pattern will be reversed, and the masks will be worn by the women.) He is persuaded by Don John that Don Pedro is wooing Hero on his own account, not, as he has promised, as Claudio's proxy. In a bitter soliloquy Claudio bids goodbye to her with a rhetorical flourish: 'Farewell therefore Hero!' (II. i. 176). His eyes have deceived him; he has misinterpreted the scene. Notice that this is precisely the same mistake he will make, with more serious consequences, in the church scene, again deceived by the troublemaker Don John, again too quickly and mistakenly rejecting Hero, only to be once more reunited with her and promised her hand in marriage. Even his language is the same – 'fare thee well, most foul, most fair, farewell' (IV.i.102) – so that the audience is given an aural clue to the congruence between the two scenes. Hero does 'die' for Claudio's errors here – indeed she does so twice. Her apparent death and resurrection provide the initiatory experience which enables him to come to know himself.

A close parallel to the Hero–Claudio situation occurs in *The Winter's Tale*, where Hermione is suspected of infidelity, Leontes accuses her, and she is concealed by Paulina. In this case the 'yearly rite' promised by Claudio becomes a penance performed by Leontes 'once a day' (III. ii. 236) for a period of sixteen years. Like Leonato, who took charge of Claudio's marital prospects and matched him with Hero's 'cousin', Pauline extracts a promise from Leontes that he will be guided by her in a future marriage choice – and then in riddling terms adds, 'That / Shall be when your first queen's again in breath; / Never till then' (v. i. 82–4). After this act of faith comes another, in the chapel, and the unmasking of Hero is transmuted into the more elaborate and more richly resonant 'awakening' of the supposed statue of Hermione. A curtain replaces the mask, but the language of rebirth is fully as strong. Where the two situations differ is in the degree of previous knowledge given the audience; we knew that Hero was still alive, but Paulina conceals from us, as from Leontes, the truth about Hermione. Her invitation, 'It is required / You do awake your faith' (v. iii. 94–5), is extended to those off the stage as well as to those upon it, and the wonder of the moment of awakening – or rebirth – is shared by every spectator.

As we have seen, this fundamental pattern of 'death' and 'rebirth' can have a strong effect upon the survivors – or the audience – as well as upon those who undergo the literal experience of transition. Indeed it might well be argued that the transferred effect is far stronger – that Leontes and Claudio are more psychologically and emotionally altered by the 'deaths' and restorations of their ladies than are the ladies themselves. Like tragedy itself, which happens *for* us on the stage so that it need not have to happen *to* us in our lives, these apparent losses and reversals are cathartic events that transform those who observe them. This is perhaps most vividly the case when the restoration or rebirth is fleeting, as it is for Desdemona, or even wholly illusory, as with Cordelia.

Desdemona anticipates the possibility of her death in iv. iii., and requests that Emilia shroud her in her wedding sheets. The audience, which has already seen ample evidence of Othello's obsession, receives explicit notice of his intention to kill her as v. ii. opens, and hears her plead with him in vain. We thus expect her death, and our expectations are apparently confirmed by Othello's own words after he smothers her: 'She's dead' (91), and '[she's] Still as the grave' (94). At this point he performs a gesture which is both a natural attempt at concealment and a familiar symbolic indication of death: he closes the curtains around the bed. The bed curtains are in this case a kind of veil or shroud, but they are also analogous to the curtains of a theater; the play appears to be over. Thus, when the voice of Desdemona speaks through the curtains, the audience is likely to be as startled as Othello. There is nothing supernatural about Desdemona's 'rebirth', any more than in the other instances we have seen. Othello's certainty that she is dead is yet another error of perception and judgment on his part. But the dramatic effect here is so shocking that we seem almost to be hearing a voice from another world.

J. L. Styan appropriately notes the resemblance of this scene to that of a church: 'The taper makes of her death-bed a sacrificial altar, one upon which man's love of life and hope of heaven are annihilated.'[10] Yet there is no language of Christian mystery here. Instead of the riddling phrases of *Much Ado* and *The Winter's Tale* we have a riddle posed in purely human terms: the riddle of a woman's self-destructive goodness. Desdemona's reply to the question, 'who hath done this deed?' – the magnificently generous 'Nobody – I myself. Farewell' (124) – may offer us, in its very generosity, something of tragic truth.

In terms of staging, the difference between Desdemona's first 'death' and her second is the presence of Emilia. She, like the audience in the theater, hears those final poignant lines of disclaimer and forgiveness, and her anger and grief are forerunners and counterparts of our own. Emilia is a consummately ordinary woman, whose ordinariness is repeatedly contrasted with the extraordinary qualities of Desdemona. In her mediocrity, her moral frailty and her instinct for survival the audience may find a reflection of its own quotidian self. But in the almost literally disembodied voice of Desdemona we hear, as well, the language of grace and human possibility, of that which lives on after death.

With the death of Cordelia the transference of effect from victim to survivor becomes even more direct. The stage direction, '*Enter* Lear, *with* Cordelia *in his arms*', describes a posture that has been compared to that of a Pietà. Yet Lear refuses to believe that she is dead, asking for a looking glass to mist with her breath, holding a feather before her and fancying that it stirs. His dying words repeat this wish, replacing the agonizing realism of 'Thou'lt come no more, / Never, never, never, never, never' (v. iii. 309–10) with a last burst of hope: 'Look on her. Look, her lips, / Look there, look there' (312–13). What does he see? In all but remotest possibility, nothing. Her revival, the rebirth that would in his phrase 'redeem all sorrows / That ever I have felt' (268–9) occurs only in his mind, while around him the young men, Edgar and Albany, strive to reassert the world of government, to lift the burden of mourning and begin the act of reintegration with society. It is left to Kent to point out not only Lear's wish for death but his own; reintegration for them will happen only once they have departed 'this tough world' (316). 'I have a journey, sir, shortly to go; / My master calls me, I must not say no' (323–4).

Twice before in the play we have encountered the dramatic metaphor of resurrection, once staged by Edgar, a second time imagined by Lear. Edgar persuades the blinded Gloucester that he has fallen from an immense height, and tells him that 'Thy life's a miracle' (IV. vi. 55). The 'child-changèd' Lear awakes from sleep and madness to find himself dressed in fresh garments, soothed with music, and welcomed by a Cordelia whom he identifies as 'a soul in bliss' (IV. vii. 46). 'You are a spirit, I know,' he tells her, 'Where did you die?' (49). In both scenes the fathers are 'child-changed', changed not only into children but by their children, and brought to a new understanding of patience, love and the radical condition of humanity. As the doctor says of Lear, 'the great rage, / You see, is killed in him' (78–9).

It may be useful here to recall the observations of Elisabeth Kübler-Ross on the dying patient's progression from denial and isolation to anger, bargaining, depression and finally acceptance of death. For Lear, although he will not acknowledge it, is a dying man. His denial, isolation and anger are all too visible in the first three acts. As Freud points out, the silence of Cordelia may be seen as a reminder of the silence of death, the thing Lear refuses to see that he has to choose – and of which his division of the kingdom is an unmistakable sign.[11] Denying her, he passes through rage to bargaining, first with his elder daughters about the size of his retinue, then, turning to matters more desperate and fundamental, with the heavens and his neglected subjects: 'O, I have ta'en / Too little care of this! Take physic, pomp; / Expose thyself to feel what wretches feel' (III. iv. 32–4). The scheme he proposes to Cordelia as they are taken prisoner is yet another version of the bargain for life: 'Come, let's away to prison; / We two alone will sing like birds i' th' cage . . . and we'll wear out, / In a walled prison, packs and sects of great ones / That ebb and flow by th' moon' (V. iii. 8–9, 17–19). but it is with the death of Cordelia that there comes upon him the final stages of preparatory depression and ultimate acceptance. Freud's comment on the stage direction I have already mentioned is worth citing here, because it bears directly on this subject of acceptance:

Let us now recall that most moving last scene, one of the culminating points reached in modern tragic drama: 'Enter

Lear with Cordelia dead in his arms.' Cordelia is death. Reverse the situation and it becomes intelligible and familiar to us – the Death-goddess bearing away the dead hero from the place of battle, like the Valkyr in German mythology. Eternal wisdom, in the garb of the primitive myth, bids the old man renounce love, choose death, and make friends with the necessity of dying. [12]

Cordelia becomes, if not his Valkryie, then his psychopomp, his guide of souls, who leads him willingly from one world to the next. Kent's compassionate injunction explicitly touches on this theme of acceptance: 'Vex not his ghost: O let him pass! He hates him / That would upon the rack of this tough world / Stretch him out longer' (v. iii. 315–17). Edgar earlier touched upon the same theme as he led the blind Gloucester from the field of battle, and cautioned him that 'Men must endure their going hence, even as their coming hither: / Ripeness is all' (v. ii. 9–11).

Cordelia's death is unlike the previous 'deaths' we have considered, because her restoration is entirely illusory. She is 'dead as earth' (v. iii. 263); she will 'come no more' (309). And yet it is hardly accurate to say that Cordelia's death is 'real'. It is real within the confines of the play – it is real to Lear – but for the audience of Shakespeare's plays, necessarily, there is more than one kind of 'reality'.

In his short poem 'On the Life of Man', Walter Ralegh develops an elaborate conceit comparing theater and life, to conclude with a crucial distinction: 'Only we die in earnest, that's no jest.' A literal-minded observer might wish to point out the same kind of truth about Cordelia's death that Bottom is so eager to declare about Pyramus': 'That Pyramus is not killed indeed' (*MND* iii. i. 18). 'The most lamentable comedy, and most cruel death of Pyramus and Thisby' is no sooner over, and the stage littered with corpses, than Bottom and the others leap to their feet to offer the duke his choice of an epilogue or a Bergomask dance. So too with the players in Shakespeare's company, or any company: the play over, its actors do not die in earnest, but rather return the next day to perform it again. And in this common fact of theatrical life we find the central truth about death as a rite of passage in Shakespearean drama.

We have seen the ways in which Shakespeare uses a fictive experience of 'death' to bring about a change in the survivors, the mourning spectators on the stage, as well as in the person who 'dies' and is 'reborn'. But there are, after all, many major characters who face the final crisis and do not come back. Most obviously this is true of the protagonists of tragedy, for whom, as for Lear, the experience of the play is also the experience of learning to die. By expanding our perspective we can see that these deaths, too, bring about a change, a new access of understanding. But in the tragedies the final act of transition and incorporation is performed, not by the players, but by the audience. To solve the dilemma of finitude and mortality, the silence of the grave, Shakespeare has created for his audience a crucial role that transcends the limitations imposed by the death of the hero – as well as the limitations implicit in 'the two hours' traffic of our stage'. It is therefore to the tragedies that we should turn, to find the most inclusive of all rites of passage concerned with death and dying: the injunction to retell the tale, or to replay the play. This is the task, and the role, that the playwright assigns to the survivors: at once an act of mourning and a first step toward social reintegration.

The general pattern of this rite is set forth very clearly in a passage that is not in fact from a tragedy, but does concern itself with a potentially tragic subject: the fear of death in battle. The passage is the great 'Saint Crispin's Day' speech in *Henry V*, in which the king attempts to rally his forces and to enable them to face the possibility of their own deaths. The scene is the English camp, and the onstage audience includes not only the nobles specifically named but also Sir Thomas Erpingham 'with all his host'.

> This day is called the Feast of Crispian:
> He that outlives this day, and comes safe home,
> Will stand a-tiptoe when this day is named,
> And rouse him at the name of Crispian.
> He that shall see this day, and live old age,
> Will yearly on the vigil feast his neighbors
> And say, 'Tomorrow is Saint Crispian.'
> Then will he strip his sleeve and show his scars,
> And say, 'These wounds I had on Crispin's day.'

Old men forget; yet all shall be forgot,
But he'll remember, with advantages,
What feats he did that day. Then shall our names,
Familiar in his mouth as household words –
Harry the King, Bedford and Exeter,
Warwick and Talbot, Salisbury and Gloucester –
Be in their flowing cups freshly rememb'red.
This story shall the good man teach his son;
And Crispin Crispian shall ne'er go by,
From this day to the ending of the world,
But we in it shall be rememberèd.   (IV. iii. 40–59)

This is a description of what we today call 'oral history', a process
of education through retelling that is a familiar tradition in
many cultures, but especially in those that do not employ the
written word. Whether it is historical, mythic or explicitly
fictive, an event is remembered and passed on from one generation to another by just such a process of transmission. But we
may notice that the king fully expects the old soldier to remember his own contributions 'with advantages' – embellishing
them in the course of the telling. If this is the case, what is the
true story of what happened on Saint Crispin's day? If the
soldier adds and changes, and his son does the same, how can we
remember 'to the ending of the world' the events and names
King Harry bids us celebrate? The answer implied here, and
made more explicit in the tragedies, is: by recalling and re-
enacting the play we have just seen. If the old soldier is a
spectator–participant, so too is the audience that watches and
endures. And, as we shall see, the audience in effect becomes
an actor, performing the rite begun by the injunction to
retell.

  Just as Henry V addresses himself to his troops and spectators,
so Hamlet as he lies mortally wounded addresses himself to
'You that look pale and tremble at this chance, / That are but
mutes or audience to this act' (v. ii. 336–7). His description
includes those both on the stage and off it, a community whose
human bond transcends the limitations of the stage itself. They
are an audience – which is to say, they hear; but they are also
spectators, who see; and, as Hamlet tellingly points out, they are
also 'mutes', who cannot – or will not – speak. At once active – in

emotional response, in pity and terror, in sympathy or identification – and passive – in its entrapment in seats or boxes, and
its inability to intervene – the audience occupies a dichotomous
position which is both difficult to maintain, and essential to the
workings of the play.

But the muteness of the spectators is a temporary rather than
a permanent state. In his next words Hamlet enjoins Horatio,

> If thou didst ever hold me in thy heart,
> Absent thee from felicity awhile,
> And in this harsh world draw thy breath in pain,
> To tell my story.   (v. ii. 348–51)

Horatio's task – and by extension that of Hamlet's other
'audience' – is to make history into story, fact into fable – to
replay the play, and bring it back to life. Very much the same
thing happens at the end of *Othello*, when Othello enjoins the
Venetians,

> When you shall these unlucky deeds relate,
> Speak of me as I am. Nothing extenuate,
> Nor set down aught in malice. Then must you speak
> Of one that loved not wisely, but too well.
>   (v. ii. 340–43)

The play does not end with the closing of the bed curtains, but
rather with Lodovico's final words of resolve:

> Myself will straight aboard, and to the state
> This heavy act with heavy heart relate.   (369–70)

To 'relate' becomes, in fact, the crucial action afforded to the
spectator of tragedy, both on and off the stage. He is invited to
'relate' in two senses – to retell the tale, and in retelling it to
reconstitute the human bonds that have been severed, to remake
a community and a society by placing the hero and his downfall
in the instructive context of history, and by 'giv[ing] sorrow
words', as Malcolm urges the grieving Macduff (*Mac.* iv. iii.
209), in order to come to terms with loss. Lodovico will return to
Venice and 'relate' the story of Othello, which is to say, the
events of the play itself.

As we have seen in other contexts, it is the survivors who

often bear the responsibility for responding to the implications
of death and dying. Thus at the close of *Romeo and Juliet* the
Prince of Verona instructs his mourning subjects to 'Go hence,
to have more talk of these sad things' (v. iii. 208) – to 'relate' to
one another the play's tragic events and their own feelings of
guilt and loss. In similar terms Edgar, a survivor of the storm
and a friend and kinsman of its victims, addresses the remaining
English forces in *King Lear*:

> The weight of this sad time we must obey,
> Speak what we feel, not what we ought to say.
> The oldest hath borne most; we that are young
> Shall never see so much, nor live so long.
>
> (v. iii. 325–8)

Here, in accordance with the changed circumstances, explicit
retelling – 'Speak what we feel' – entails, as well, implicit
remembering and recording. 'We that are young' refers not only
to those of Edgar's own generation, but to those who will follow
– the newly young of each succeeding generation, audiences as
well as actors, who are asked to remember and to learn from the
tragic past.

Moreover, even those who have caused the deaths of tragic
heroes invite us, in fact command us, to remember them.
Aufidius says of Coriolanus, 'Yet he shall have a noble memory'
(v. vi. 152); Macduff says of Macbeth, 'live to be the show
and gaze o' th' time' (v. viii. 24); Octavius says of Antony and
Cleopatra, 'No grave upon the earth shall clip in it / A pair so
famous' (v. ii. 358–9). Thus, at the close of every tragedy, our
attention is drawn to the necessary act of retrospection without
which the tragic experience would be incomplete.

Yet in each of these cases the relationship of onstage to
offstage audience is carefully measured, to suggest not only a
conjunction but also a disjunction between them. Horatio is
asked 'to tell my story', and he complies immediately by re-
questing those who remain – among whom we may properly
number ourselves – to see 'that these bodies / High on a stage be
placèd to the view' (v. ii. 379–80). The stage from which they
are to be regarded, of course, is simultaneously playhouse and
platform. But then Horatio goes on, in effect, to summarize
his story to the 'yet unknowing world':

So shall you hear
Of carnal, bloody, and unnatural acts,
Of accidental judgments, casual slaughters,
Of deaths put on by cunning and forced cause,
And, in this upshot, purposes mistook
Fall'n on th'inventors' heads. All this can I
Truly deliver. (*Ham.* v. ii. 382–8)

He can 'truly deliver' so far as he comprehends what he has seen. But do we recognize *The Tragedy of Hamlet, Prince of Denmark*, in this catalogue of catastrophes? Horatio, who cautions against considering too curiously, is himself a curious figure for the role of amanuensis; there are parts of Hamlet – and therefore of *Hamlet* – which he has never understood. Most obviously, he has not heard the soliloquies, without which the play of *Hamlet* as we know it is unimaginable. It is therefore to us as well as to Horatio that Hamlet – and Shakespeare – speak, in the command to 'tell my story'. We, mutes'and audience, are the only ones who 'truly' know it.

These final speeches of summation have sometimes been accused of a certain patness – of attempting to make all right with the world, when in fact that world has been destroyed. But this patness, when it exists, seems to me to be a part of the play's central design, and of the design it has upon its audience. Lodovico is even less qualified than Horatio to 'relate' the tragedy of which he is a part. He does not arrive at Cyprus until the beginning of Act iv, and has therefore missed, not only Iago's soliloquies, but the whole story of Othello's downfall. His account, were he to give it, would begin with the striking of Desdemona, omitting the delicate psychological interplay which lies at the heart of the tragedy. Edgar, who speaks of 'we that are young', counts himself among them, though he has been part of the tragedy of Gloucester and Lear. But to say that we 'shall never see so much, nor live so long', is to overlook, for a moment, the radical role of the spectator, who has seen it all – and through whose eyes and ears the personae of *King Lear* continue to live long after the actors have left the stage. The Montagues and Capulets, though united by mutual tragedy, remain blindly competitive, each pledging to rear a more appropriate monument to the other's child; the golden statues they intend to raise are mockingly lifeless counterparts of the flesh and blood children they have lost, and bear no relation to the 'story of more woe . . . of Juliet and her Romeo' (v. ii. 310–11). As for Octavius, his belated generosity is, as always, mitigated by self-interest:

> No grave upon the earth shall clip in it
> A pair so famous. High events as these
> Strike those that make them; and their story is
> No less in pity, than his glory which
> Brought them to be lamented.   (*A&C* v. ii. 358–62)

The easy rhyme of 'story' and 'glory', which seems to balance two types of fame, in fact suggests a false analogy. The play is not evenly divided in its emphasis between the lovers and the aspiring emperor; its conclusion is not greeted by the audience impartially, with an auspicious and a dropping eye – our sympathies and commitment are reserved for the dead, though we may recognize the political sagacity of those who survive. Octavius, in fact, does not understand his play, and would almost surely have staged in Rome the 'squeaking', 'drunken' parody Cleopatra imagines. The limited vision of the final speaker once again emphasizes the radical disjunction between his view and that of the work of art. Only in his intuition that the play must be replayed does he anticipate the response of the offstage audience; for just as Cleopatra herself declares, 'I am again for Cydnus, / To meet Mark Antony' (v. ii. 228–9), so Octavius senses in her death a paradoxical sign of continuity:

> she looks like sleep,
> As she would catch another Antony
> In her strong toil of grace.   (v. ii. 345–7)

The dramatic character of Cleopatra inhabits a self-renewing world which will outlast any single spectator, and any single performance.

In short, Horatio might conceivably write a *Horatio*, and Octavius an *Octavius Caesar*, but neither would accord completely with the plays as we have experienced them. As participants in the tragic drama they can speak only what they know;

we, who know more, have, in exchange for that privilege, for-
feited our right to speak. And as we have already seen, in
Shakespeare's tragedies the abdication of speech, whether by
Iago, Cordelia, Coriolanus or Banquo's ghost, is fraught with
danger; the character who refuses speech is vulnerable to the
accusation that he is concurrently refusing the human bond.
Manifestly, for Cordelia and Coriolanus, this is not wholly the
case: 'love and be silent,' and *'Holds her by the hand, silent'*
demarcate two of the most moving instances of human interac-
tion in the Shakespearean canon. But as moving as they are,
these moments are also tragic. Not to speak is to make oneself a
victim, by dissociating oneself from the world of human communication. Iago does this explicitly at the close of *Othello*, but
essentially he has been in this condition throughout the play,
never speaking with an intent to communicate, but always to
deceive. The audience, by accepting, as it must, the role of
'mutes', accepts as well the danger and responsibility of this
failed communication – and also something more. Our hearing,
our seeing – that is, our identity as audience and spectators – has
been our suffering, our participating in the tragic experience.
This experience has been deepened, made more private and
perhaps more painful, by the very passivity forced upon us. We
cannot act to affect the play's outcome, any more than the tragic
hero can act to save himself. Such is the decorum of our stage
that we cannot even cry out and expect to be heard. We are thus
as surely victims of the play, as the play's protagonists are
victims of its actions.

But if we are its victims, we are also its survivors, and its
celebrants. Old Hamlet, having told his tale of murder, exits on a
line which seems addressed to the audience as well as to his son:
'Adieu, adieu, adieu. Remember me' (I. v. 91), and the words
linger in the air after their speaker has departed the stage.
Hamlet, mulling them as a text, seems likewise to speak for both
audiences, for all audiences, in his reply.

> Remember thee?
> Ay, thou poor ghost, whiles memory holds a seat
> In this distracted globe.   (95–7)

The triple pun on 'globe' – head, world, theater – is underscored
by the ambiguity of 'seat'. 'Sitting at a play', the audience of

tragedy is precisely what Hamlet says it is – the memory of the play's world, the record of its action. When Aufidius promises that Coriolanus 'shall have a noble memory', it is only the audience which can keep his promise, and the nobility of this role is insisted upon:

> Let us haste to hear it,
> And call the noblest to the audience.
>
> (*Ham.* v. ii. 388–9)

In the comedies, this recognition of reciprocity between the worlds on and off the stage is often accomplished through the use of an epilogue, a device which, like the soliloquy, allows for a direct confrontation between actor and audience. Thus Rosalind 'conjures' her hearers 'that the play may please', and requests them to bid her farewell with their applause.

Prospero, having drowned his book, declares himself power-less, and asks for the help of our 'good hands' and 'gentle breath' to release him and sail him back to Milan. Puck, likewise, seeks our 'hands', in friendship and applause. In each case the speaker of the epilogue acknowledges his own fictionality at the same time that he, like Puck, teases us with the dramatist's favorite conundrum, that perhaps only the fictive is true.

But in the world of Shakespearean tragedy there is no such moment, suspended between 'fiction' and 'reality', in which the protagonist may reveal himself, and the charm dissolve apace – nor, significantly, is there an explicit clarification and release, as manifested in the welcome activity of applause. Hamlet and Lear are dead, and in a more than literal sense their fame lies in our hands – and in our gentle breath. The injunction to replay the play, 'to tell my story', to bear the bodies to the stage, suggests the ultimate role of the audience, no longer mute, and the ultimate reconstitution of the society disrupted by the tragic action. For each member of the tragic audience is asked to see himself as a survivor. Denied the easier mode of participation offered by comedy – a revels moment of song, dance or solicited applause which assures the communal bond – the spectator of tragedy is at once isolated and chosen, privileged and obligated by what he has seen and heard. The play itself becomes a rite of mourning, at once the ultimate and the quintessential Shakespearean rite of passage.

NOTES

1 The enormous success of *Life After Life*, by Raymond A. Moody, Jr, M.D. (New York: Bantam Books, 1975) attests to a continuing interest in such questions. Dr Moody, a former professor of philosophy who is currently training to be a psychiatrist, takes a balanced and sensitive view of the question of the afterlife, based on interviews with some 150 persons who have reported such experiences.

2 For some specific practices of tribal groups see Arnold van Gennep, *The Rites of Passage*, Monika B. Vizedom and Gabrielle L. Caffee (trans.) (Chicago: University of Chicago Press, 1960) Chapter 5; and Edward Norbeck, *Religion in Primitive Society* (New York: Harper & Row, 1961), Chapters 9 and 10.

3 Moody writes that many persons who have 'died' and returned to life report being welcomed by relatives or friends on the 'other side' (pp. 55–8); one woman described the experience as a 'homecoming' (p. 97).

4 Van Gennep, pp. 164–5.

5 Cf. also Mark 5 : 38–42, Luke 8 : 51–4.

6 Elisabeth Kübler-Ross, M.D., *On Death and Dying* (New York: Macmillan, London: Tavistock, 1969).

7 Kübler-Ross, p. 86.

8 Van Gennep, p. 168.

9 Mircea Eliade, *Rites and Symbols of Initiation: The Mysteries of Death and Rebirth*, Willard R. Trask (trans.) (originally published as *Birth and Rebirth*) (New York: Harper & Brothers, 1958; rpt. Harper & Row, 1975) pp. xii ff.

10 J. L. Styan, *Shakespeare's Stagecraft* (Cambridge: Cambridge University Press, 1967; rpt. 1971), p. 33.

11 Sigmund Freud, 'The theme of the three caskets' (1913) in James Strachey (ed. and trans.), *The Standard Edition of the Complete Psychological Works of Sigmund Freud*, XII (London: Hogarth Press and the Institute of Psycho-Analysis, 1958, rpt. 1962), pp. 294–301.

12 Freud, p. 301.

L'ENVOY

❧❧ ❦❦

Come, thy l'envoy – begin.
LLL III. i. 71

This way to the egress.
P. T. BARNUM

As Rosalind tells us, it is not the fashion to see the lady the epilogue – but it is never a surprise to find Prospero in that position, and it seems fitting that he should have the last word here. For it is Prospero, Shakespeare's last great dramatic character, who most clearly and memorably gives ˙ ʋice to the acceptance of death. In the tragedies we have heard other claims of acceptance – Hamlet's quiet declaration that the readiness is all, Edgar's caution that men must endure their going hence even as their coming hither – but at the close of *The Tempest* we hear that claim put forth in a new key, without regret, fear or reluctance. When Prospero solicits our applause and praise in order to fill his sails, he is enlisting our help in his passage to death – a journey over water that will take him first to Naples to see the marriage of his daughter (and thus to see himself superseded), then to Milan, 'where / Every third thought shall be my grave' (v. i. 311–12).

But it may be possible to localize this acceptance of death in a more dramatic moment earlier in the final scene – when Caliban, Stephano and Trinculo are brought before the company, their plot exposed. 'Two of these fellows you / Must know and own,' Prospero then says to the assembled onlookers, 'this thing of darkness I / Acknowledge mine' (274–6). What is 'this thing of darkness'? Literally, of course, it is the bestial Caliban – and by extension the beast in man, the boar chained beneath the rock in Spenser's Garden of Adonis, the Minotaur confined in his maze. But may we not extend this meaning even further, to find in 'this thing of darkness' not only bestial man but mortal man, man doomed to darkness because of his fallen nature? Shakespeare frequently uses darkness as a metaphor for death, as in Claudio's brave (and temporary) pledge in *Measure for Measure*: 'If I must die, / I will encounter darkness as a bride, / And hug it in mine arms' (iii. i. 82–4). To acknowledge 'this thing of darkness' is to look death in the face, and to see that his face is our own. In this sense the acknowledgment of Caliban is an act analogous to the other gestures by which Prospero signifies his acceptance of death: the drowning of his book and the releasing of Ariel. Through these actions he reclaims his mortality.

Nothing in Prospero's life becomes him like the leaving of it, for in the act of leave-taking he transcends dramatic occasion. His farewell to his greatness becomes in its own way a reinterpretation of that greatness, an affirmation of the human limits as well as the godlike capabilities of man. The last words he speaks are at once a reminder of the Golden Rule and a version of the last rites of the Church, a request for absolution – but with one characteristically Shakespearean addition: the rites Prospero proposes are reciprocal, absolving speaker and audience in the same act. 'As you from crimes would pardoned be, / Let your indulgence set me free' (Epil. 19–20). Prospero the character is poised on the threshold between life and death, the actor who plays him is poised between fiction and reality – and the audience participates crucially in both moments of transition.

It is entirely appropriate that this moment of frame-breaking should occur in the epilogue, which in *The Tempest*, as in many of Shakespeare's plays, is the most liminal element in the dramatic structure. In essence, the epilogue confirms the role of the play itself in educating and altering its audience, by acting simultaneously as a rite of separation and a rite of incorporation. The speaker addresses his hearers in a way at once intimate and direct; his remarks are part of a threshold ceremony of divestiture, revealing himself as an actor, the events of the play as a fiction, or both. 'If I were a woman,' says Rosalind – and the Elizabethan audience knows that she is not. 'You have but slumber'd here, / While these visions did appear,' says Puck – and the audience perceives that he is ringing one more change on the metaphor of dream and reality. Feste sings his melancholy song about mortality – 'the rain it raineth every day' – and then abruptly alters the refrain to remind us that he is really a player, his song an artifice like the play that contains it. Pandarus addresses himself to his 'Brethren and sisters of the hold-door trade' – that is, to other panders – but the door he holds open is also the threshold between the world of the play and the other world beyond it.

Jaques observed that men and women are merely players, but Shakespeare continually reminds us of the converse: that players are merely men and women. His characters live for us above all in their humanity and their consciousness of the nature and finitude of the common human condition. That is why it is not only possible but instructive to speak of maturation patterns in the plays, of characters coming of age and undergoing rites of passage. That is also why Shakespeare's plays have been translated into so many languages, and are read with such pleasure and understanding by people of widely divergent societies and cultures around the globe.

INDEX